Tiling 1-2-3®

Meredith® BOOKS

Tiling 1-2-3®

Editor: Larry Johnston
Copy Chief: Terri Fredrickson
Publishing Operations Manager: Karen Schirm
Senior Editor, Asset and Information Manager: Phillip Morgan
Edit and Design Coordinator: Mary Lee Gavin
Editorial and Design Assistant: Renee E. McAtee
Book Production Managers: Pam Kvitne, Marjorie J. Schenkelberg,
    Rick von Holdt, Mark Weaver
Contributing Copy Editor: Michael Maine
Contributing Proofreaders: Sara Henderson, David Krause,
    Cheri Madison
Contributing Indexer: Donald Glassman

Additional Editorial and Design contributions from
Abramowitz Creative Studios

Publishing Director/Designer: Tim Abramowitz
Graphic Designers: Kelly Bailey, Joel Wires
Photography: Image Studios
    Account Executive: Lisa Egan
    Photographers: Bill Rein, John von Dorn
    Assistants: Rob Resnick, Scott Verber
    Technical Advisor: Rick Nadke
Additional Photography: Doug Hetherington
Illustration: Jim Swanson, Performance Marketing

Meredith® Books

Executive Director, Editorial: Gregory H. Kayko
Executive Director, Design: Matt Strelecki
Managing Editor: Amy Tincher-Durik
Executive Editor/Group Manager: Benjamin W. Allen
Senior Associate Design Director: Tom Wegner
Marketing Product Manager: Brent Wiersma
National Marketing Manager—Home Depot: Suzy Johnston

Publisher and Editor in Chief: James D. Blume
Editorial Director: Linda Raglan Cunningham
Executive Director, Marketing: Steve Malone
Executive Director, New Business Development: Todd M. Davis
Director, Sales—Home Depot: Robb Morris
Executive Director, Sales: Ken Zagor
Director, Operations: George A. Susral
Director, Production: Douglas M. Johnston
Director, Marketing: Amy Nichols
Business Director: Jim Leonard
Vice President and General Manager: Douglas J. Guendel

Meredith Publishing Group

President: Jack Griffin
Senior Vice President: Bob Mate

Meredith Corporation

Chairman and Chief Executive Officer: William T. Kerr
President and Chief Operating Officer: Stephen M. Lacy
In Memoriam: E.T. Meredith III (1933–2003)

The Home Depot®

Marketing Manager: Tom Sattler

Note to the Reader: Due to differing conditions, tools, and individual skills, Meredith Corporation and The Home Depot® assume no responsibility for any damages, injuries suffered, or losses incurred as a result of following the information published in this book. Before beginning any project, review the instructions carefully, and if any doubts or questions remain, consult local experts or authorities. Because codes and regulations vary greatly, you always should check with authorities to ensure that your project complies with all applicable local codes and regulations. Always read and observe all of the safety precautions provided by any tool or equipment manufacturer, and follow all accepted safety procedures.

We are dedicated to providing accurate and helpful do-it-yourself information. We welcome your comments about improving this book and ideas for other books we might offer to home improvement enthusiasts.
Contact us by any of these methods:
Leave a voice message at: 800/678-2093
Write to:
    Meredith Books, Home Depot Books
    1716 Locust St.
    Des Moines, IA 50309–3023
Send e-mail to: hi123@mdp.com.

How to use this book

If you've been contemplating a new tile project for your home—maybe a ceramic mosaic in the bath or vinyl tile in the rec room—but have hesitated to try something new, this is the book you've been waiting for.

Professional tilesetters and store associates from Home Depot stores across the country created *Tiling 1-2-3* to give homeowners a comprehensive and easy-to-follow guide to a wide variety of tiling applications. Their expertise and years of experience guarantee successful completion of every job, from simple craft projects to tiling a shower stall. Clear instructions and step-by-step photography make every project accessible and easy to understand.

TRUST THE WISDOM OF THE AISLES

Associates at The Home Depot have a genuine desire to help people say, "I can do that!" That's why these experts from around the country have contributed their years of on-the-job experience and wisdom of the aisles to *Tiling 1-2-3*. Their contributions have helped create a hardworking, accurate, and easy-to-follow guide for every aspect of tiling with all tiling materials, including design and planning, installation, maintenance, and repair.

THE ORGANIZING PRINCIPLE

Tiling 1-2-3 consists of eight sections that provide detailed coverage of design and planning; preparing for installation; tiling floors, walls, countertops, patios, and a host of creative decorative projects; and an overview of all the tools and materials you'll need for any job.

DOING THE JOB STEP-BY-STEP

All the projects include complete instructions along with detailed, step-by-step photography to make successful completion easy. You've got everything you need to do the job right the first time, following standards set by manufacturers and the trades—just like the pros.

TIPS, TRICKS, AND TIMESAVERS

Each page includes more than just instructions for completing the job. To help plan your project and to schedule your time, you'll find information about how difficult a job is and how long it might take you to complete.

Project Details fills you in on the skills you'll need, time involved, and variables that might complicate the job.

Stuff You'll Need provides a materials list along with commonly used tools.

Additional features on the pages are filled with specific information: *Buyer's Guide, Closer Look, Design Tip, Good Idea, Old vs. New, Real World, Safety Alert, Timesaver, Tool Tip,* and *Work Smarter* are small bonus sidebars designed to help you work efficiently and economically. Whenever a project involves something special—whether it's safety tips or getting the right tool—you'll be prepared for whatever comes up.

To make the best use of what's inside, read through each project carefully before you begin. Walk yourself through each step until you're comfortable with the process. Understanding the scope of the job will limit mistakes and prevent you from spending the money to redo a job.

Helping hands

Tips, insights, tricks, shortcuts, and even the benefit of 20/20 hindsight from the pros at The Home Depot help make any do-it-yourself project a snap. Years of experience translate into instant expertise for you. As you use this book look for these special icons, which signal detailed information on a specific topic.

 BUYER'S GUIDE

Helps you select the best materials for the right price.

 CLOSER LOOK

Provides you with detailed information about a task.

 OLD VS. NEW

Find out new ways to work with old stuff.

 WORK SMARTER

Gives you information about work practices that will save you time.

 DESIGN TIP

Shows you design options you might want to consider for your home.

 TIMESAVER

Small shortcuts used by the pros to make the job go faster or easier.

 TOOL TIP

Shows you how to use specialty tools to get the most out of them.

 GOOD IDEA

Tips and tricks that will get you the results you want.

 SAFETY ALERT

Read these for information that will help make you safe on the job.

Tiling 1-2-3®
Table of contents

Chapter 1
DESIGNING WITH TILE — 6

Chapter 2
PREP AND DEMOLITION — 52

Chapter 3
FLOORS — 88

Chapter 4
WALLS — 132

Chapter 5
COUNTERTOPS
154

Chapter 6
PATIOS
166

Chapter 7
CREATIVE TILING PROJECTS
180

Chapter 8
MAINTENANCE AND REPAIR
206

Designing with tile

Designing with tile is an opportunity to combine your sense of artistry and style with the practical needs of any kind of room. No matter what kind of tile you employ—ceramic, vinyl, laminate, parquet, stone, or carpet tile—it will bring all the elements of design—color, texture, pattern, and form——to any surface where you install it.

The word "tile" often conjures up a vision of a floor or wallcovering used principally in kitchens or bathrooms. That may have been true some years ago, but not now. Tile can be installed on any surface in any room of the house. It is as well suited to a home office, a recreation room, a family room, or a foyer as it is to the kitchen or bathroom. What's more, there's a tile for every budget. And it is durable; while each variety will have different maintenance requirements, any kind will give you years of service if you take care of it properly.

Quality is the key

As with any home improvement project, you should consider quality when you select tile for any application. Strength and durability are not as important when tile is serving a purely

Chapter 1 highlights

decorative function, such as in a wall mural, but they are all-important where the tile will be exposed to heavy traffic or freeze-thaw cycles.

Creating your design

Creating your design is the fun part, where you bring all the variables of size, shape, color, and texture into one unified composition. If you need a little design help, this book shows the possibilities for various tiles and provides principles to help you create a design you'll like. For example, you may have never considered the use of art tiles on a plain wall or floor, but they can look like gems in a jeweler's setting. If this is your first effort at tiling, or even if you're an old hand at it, Tiling 1-2-3 is a great book to spark your creative genius and show you how to create the perfect room—just as you imagined it.

Lighting an imaginative spark

 Some tile installations create extravagant patterns; others, like the one shown here, are less intricate and symmetrical. The floor is uncluttered with a grid layout of natural clay-color tiles. The blue accent tiles add interest. A blue area rug harmonizes with the tile floor and adds warmth to the sitting area.

▲ The Southwest style combines Spanish and Native American influences. To achieve this look, rely on a strong desert color palette. Some materials to consider include thick, naturally pigmented quarry tile, natural stone, primitive patterns, and mosaic inlays.

DESIGN TIP

CREATING YOUR STYLE

By deciding to decorate a room in a particular style, you take a step in determining the right kind of tile to use in that room. Because style can be difficult to define, it's sometimes helpful to start with the big picture and work toward specifics. Start with two generalized categories—formal and informal—to help define your style.

Formal styles tend toward symmetry, using repetitive patterns and precise geometric relationships to create a sense of logic and order. Examples of more formal styles are traditional, colonial, and Victorian.

Informal styles incorporate asymmetry and natural patterns, shapes, and elements. Their geometries are often less precise and ordered. Logic is derived from mixing and highlighting elements. Examples of informal styles include contemporary, Arts and Crafts, and country.

▲ **A combination of polished stone tiles with patterned tiles, borders, and mosaics in a formal layout gives this bathroom a rich, elegant look.**

Discovering your own style

If you're confused about which style best suits you, here's one method to find an answer. First study home decorating magazines, books, and catalogs and cut out photos of rooms that appeal to you. Never mind why they have an appeal, just cut them out and put them in a manila folder. Look around when you visit friends and neighbors. When you get home, jot down things in their homes you liked. Put the notes in the folder. Continue this process for a few weeks, and when you get ready to make your final decisions, dump everything out of the folder onto a table. Go through your ideas one at a time and toss out those that don't have an immediate appeal. Study the photos you have left and look for consistent elements in them. Jot these elements down—those are the ones you want in your room.

▲ Pattern and form work together to enhance this bathroom. The mosaic tile by itself might have ended up looking busy laid over the entire area. Setting the small tiles as an inlaid mosaic "rug" leads to a nice balance of pattern and scale.

Patterns

To give the tile design interest of its own, set it in a pattern instead of a grid.

CREATING PATTERNS

Patterns are created using one or more of the variables of shape, size, color, or texture. Modular tile of differing sizes may be set in any of dozens of repetitive patterns, and tile of identical size and shape but different color may be set in the same patterns with even more dramatic effect. Or you can frame a plain field of tiles with a decorative border.

EXPERIMENT WITH JOINT ALIGNMENT

Rectangular tiles set end-to-end create a linear pattern. Running the lines lengthwise adds depth to a room; running the lines crosswise makes a room seem shorter and wider. Using tiles of different color enhances both effects. Tiles run diagonally create a tension that can be contained by a border.

▲ A combination of patterns and forms strengthens the visual impact of this design. The line of the border echoes the perimeter of the rug, and the colorful geometric pattern sets this dining space apart from other areas in the home dynamically.

Comfort underfoot

Comfort is easily overlooked when shopping for floor tile, but you should keep it in mind. That's because, in general, flooring materials are either hard or soft. Ceramic tile is a hard flooring, along with wood, stone, and concrete. Softer floor tiles include carpet and resilient materials, such as vinyl and cork. Comfort is primarily about how a floor feels underfoot, but it also has an emotional component. A tile floor may be hard material, but in a kitchen it may evoke pleasant memories. When you consider comfort, think not only about the physical properties of a material but how it supports the ambience you want for the room.

Hard tile floors also make for a chilly reception on a winter morning, but technology can give you a warmer welcome. Consider installing radiant heating—almost any material can be warmed up with electric mats or a hydronic system installed under the floor tile.

▲ To keep your design in perspective and its scale proportionate to the size of the room, follow the principle that the larger the room, the larger the tile you can use. For large areas, tiles up to 24×24 inches are available, but 12×12 inches is the most common size.

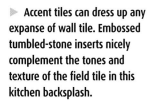 Parquet tile delivers the warmth of wood flooring with a geometric pattern. The parquet tiles, made of individual pieces of wood, also lend texture to the floor.

▶ Accent tiles can dress up any expanse of wall tile. Embossed tumbled-stone inserts nicely complement the tones and texture of the field tile in this kitchen backsplash.

▶ Mixing styles can create dramatic visual interest. This contemporary wall-hung sink goes well with a traditional-style bathroom wall—white tiles with subtle gray grout, ornamental cap tiles, and a molded ceramic baseboard. Designers often use color grout as a design element to make the individual tiles stand out.

 DESIGN TIP

USING COLOR WITH CARE

Color can affect your perception of space, alter your mood, hide a problem, or accentuate a feature. Using color effectively is a powerful design tool. Choosing color is perhaps the single most important design decision you'll make when designing a room. Color choices are important when you are deciding on finishes for the walls and ceilings, window treatments, and furnishings, but the color of the floor plays a significant role in the room design as well. Here are some guidelines you can rely upon.

■ Contemporary design allows ample freedom to mix and match colors. If you trust your instincts and give yourself time to test color choices before making a final decision, you will usually be pleased with the results. It helps to know the color basics, whether you choose to follow or ignore them.

■ In the natural world, darker colors tend to be at the bottom (earth) and lighter colors at the top (sky). You can reflect this natural scheme in your home. Darker flooring carries visual weight and anchors a room while lighter colors on the wall and ceiling give an airier feeling.

■ Plain and soothing schemes tend to have a single dominant color combined with complementary and accent colors.

■ Strong colors dominate. To add color without weight, break up the strong hues with an infusion of mosaic inlays or borders.

■ Colors usually have greater intensity in larger spaces, particularly where there's a lot of reflection and natural light.

■ Reds and oranges become focal points. Yellows and violets create a feeling of warmth. Greens and blues lend a sense of serenity and calm.

■ Deeper tones and shades lean toward formality.

■ Lighter tones and tints are more relaxed and informal.

■ Darker colors make rooms seem smaller while lighter colors increase the sense of spaciousness.

■ Glossy surfaces reflect light; flat finishes absorb light.

▲ Tiling a wall in one neutral color treats it as if it were an artist's canvas. In such an installation, like the one shown here, furnishings and accessories provide the color and accents. This kind of design scheme works well in rooms with a contemporary style.

◀ A fireplace always becomes the focal point of a room. You can blend it into the wall with a tile surround that harmonizes with the wall. Or you can accentuate its character with contrasting stone and embossed tiles, as shown here.

▲ Tile in random colors enlivens this backsplash. Even though it takes planning to work out a colorful design like this so it appears random, the effort results in a tile layout that avoids the ordinary checkerboard pattern.

▷ The subtle veining in marble tile creates a formal, flowing appearance on a wall in any room. All the elements of a tile material should work together to create the feeling you want.

◁ Borders, accents, and listellos—character tiles—can artfully break up a large expanse of tile. Here the lines of embossed tile add texture as well as pattern variation.

▲ Ceramic tile is a good choice for vanity tops. Here the tile provides a nice counterpoint to the stained birch cabinetry, creating a distinctive surface between the paired sinks.

 DESIGN TIP

PATTERN AND SCALE

Pattern and scale go hand in hand in enhancing the mood or feel of a room. "Pattern" refers primarily to how the individual tiles are arranged on a surface. The pattern can be achieved by varying the textures of the tiles, their color, or their size. Pattern concerns the relationships of individual pieces to each other and how they create a whole. "Scale" refers to the relationship of the size of the material (or the pattern itself) to the size of the room. Small rooms usually look better with smaller-scale tiles—mosaics in a small bathroom, for example. In larger rooms, you'll achieve a more comfortable relationship between floor and room with larger tiles. The same goes for wall tile. The size of the pattern, however, can also affect this relationship. If you arrange small tiles in a large pattern—a large mural, for example—the overall effect of the pattern might become more important than the size of the individual tiles. Such a pattern could overpower a small room. Here are some of the effects of pattern and scale:

▪ Using the same pattern throughout your home creates a connected, expansive feeling.

▪ A linear pattern laid parallel to the longest wall moves the eye forward, toward it, while horizontal layouts, parquet, or inlaid patterns retain the focus within their space.

▪ Shiny surfaces reflect light and feel more spacious while surfaces with little sheen, such as tumbled stone tile or carpet tile, absorb light and confine scale.

▪ Large tiles in a small room accentuate the sense of smallness while smaller tiles fit the scale.

▪ Isolated and irregular shapes in an otherwise symmetrical tile installation draw attention to themselves while a series of shapes inlaid in a uniform progression, such as a border around the edge of a hardwood floor, create a sense of motion. Mixing the two can produce a dramatic effect.

▪ Color is an essential part of the perception of scale. Darker floors draw attention, defining and confining space; lighter floors let other elements in the room become prominent, making the room feel larger.

▪ Avoid treating guidelines as rules. Experiment with different choices while you're making design decisions.

▶ Textures of different objects can work together to create a unified composition. The brushed nickel finish on the fixtures complements the texture of the tiled countertop. The same setting with a chrome faucet or glazed tiles would be quite different.

▼ Striking red glazed tiles and a bold backsplash pattern make what could be an ordinary kitchen dramatic. Light washing over the backsplash and red tiles adds spots of warmth.

▲ Natural-color tiles with a handmade look and wide grout joints create a country rustic
look for these countertops that goes well with the painted and stenciled cabinets.

▶ The countertops echo the
color and pattern of the floor
tiles in this contemporary
kitchen. An area rug adds a soft,
warm place to stand.

▲ Principles for designing a tiled patio or other outdoor surface are the same as those for an interior room. Think of the patio as the floor of an outdoor room. Good design and creativity are important outdoors too, so strive to create dramatic and inviting spaces by establishing interesting relationships of materials, textures, colors, patterns, and scale.

◀ Porcelain tile is durable and practically impervious to moisture, making it appropriate for outdoor locations like this patio. It is a versatile tile available in many styles and sizes.

▲ Perhaps nothing looks more at home outdoors than limestone. It imparts a natural look to any patio. Limestone comes with various surface textures. Choose a texture that will do the right job aesthetically, but not so deep it will pose a tripping hazard.

 DESIGN TIP

ADDING TEXTURE WITH TILE

Texture provides visual and physical elements to a floor design. It affects the comfort and look of a room and its maintenance requirements and safety. Texture is best understood in opposites—soft-hard, thick-thin, rough-smooth.

For example, textured natural stone tile looks rustic underfoot and is warm, friendly, and slip-resistant—perhaps an excellent visual choice for a backdoor mudroom or sunroom. In a mudroom, however, the rough texture would be more difficult to keep clean, which might offset its other design advantages. For a more formal look in stone (and one that's easier to clean), choose polished marble or machine-made pavers. Be careful of polished or glazed floor tile in a bathroom or other wet area. It's easy to clean but slippery when wet.

Textural juxtapositions add drama to a design while defining spaces. For example, a marble-tile foyer opening into a wood living room floor imparts a strong visual contrast while physically and visually separating the two areas. A flagstone floor on its own might be unsuitable for a family room but combined with a plush area rug, it could be the perfect marriage of practicality and design. Use texture to help define a room's style and to define its purpose as well.

BOLD OR SUBTLE STATEMENTS?

The more complex the pattern, the bolder the statement. Subtle patterns tend to meld into the overall concept of the room. Bigger and broader patterns become design statements in and of themselves. Bold choices, such as richly colored geometric tile patterns, make the surface the focal point of the room.

Practical planning

I t's quick and easy to change a room's looks with a new coat of paint or some wallpaper. Those materials are relatively affordable, and they easily accomplish a major facelift. Besides, you can come to the right design decisions with a few color chips or paper samples. A tiled floor or wall, however, represents a large expense and significant installation work. Be sure of your design decisions for tile work before the job begins. Once the tile is stuck down, you can't easily pick it up and start over.

Making good design decisions requires spending time researching possibilities and examining your taste and personal style as well as consulting with professionals as necessary. At the same time, you should decide how much of the installation you want to do yourself.

Basic questions

Your planning goal is to choose the kind of tile (including color, texture, and pattern) that will contribute aesthetically and practically to the overall scheme, and do it affordably. To start, act like a designer by answering the questions a designer would ask you when beginning a project.

Where will the tile go? It sounds like an obvious question, but the answer is important because the flooring you choose must be appropriate for its location. Parquet is not a good choice in a basement where moisture can be a problem. Vinyl tile might be perfect, however, especially if the area is wide open and makes for easy installation.

How will the room be used? Entryways see hard use and plenty of foot traffic. An entry floor has to be tough—ceramic tile or stone will be long wearing and attractive. Carpet tile might wear out quickly and stain. A floor in a bathroom will often get wet, especially if you have children. Kitchen floors might get dirty more quickly than any other floor—vinyl tile cleans easily and wears well. Make a family list of the uses of the room—let your lifestyle help define your flooring.

Is your tile project part of a complete makeover or is it the only change you're making? If you're only tiling a floor or wall and the rest of the furnishings will stay the same, take into account the existing color scheme, window treatments, and furnishing style. If you're starting from scratch, you can pick the floor first and decorate the room around it.

What is the style of the room? The answer to this can be elusive, but your goal is to create an integrated environment that makes a unified statement of style. If you're not sure what your personal style is or what style ideas you'd like to explore, pages 8–21 will help you find some direction.

If your tiling project includes the floor of a room, how will the new flooring relate to the rest of the house? No room exists in isolation. The kitchen floor moves into the dining room and that into the living room or family room. And although the flooring in each room should relate to the individual purpose and design of that room, it will also create a visual relationship with adjacent rooms. That visual (and physical) transition should be seamless and complementary.

Phase into planning stages

Planning a tiled installation is easier if you break the process into phases. It may seem obvious, but it's important that you complete your thinking about design before you move forward with installation plans. Problems, sometimes expensive ones, can arise if you start spending time and money before you're sure about what you want. It's easy to change your mind on paper or while poring over samples in the store. It's much harder when you're halfway through an installation and are unhappy with what you're seeing.

Need design help?

At some point you may want some design advice from a professional. Home centers usually have a staff of consultants who can advise and guide you through the process. Many also offer the same design and installation packages offered at interior decorating firms.

The planning and installation process from A to Z

Once you've settled on your design, you're ready to make a plan and put it into action. Here are some steps you should follow when planning a new tile installation:

1. Make sure the subfloor can accommodate the tile you're considering. Tile and stone are heavy and require a rigid subfloor to support the added weight.

2. Draw a scaled layout of the room on graph paper. Include all obstructions, such as pipes or heating units.

3. Calculate the square footage of all tiled surfaces by multiplying the length and width. You'll need these figures to shop around before you select a supplier.

4. Order the materials. Order 10 to 20 percent more than you think you need to account for mistakes, broken or warped pieces, color variations, or complex patterns. Store unused pieces for later repairs.

5. Give yourself plenty of time to complete the project. Don't plan to have a new kitchen floor and countertops by Thanksgiving if you start thinking about them on November 10.

6. Remove any old surface materials if necessary. Before you tear out the old wall or floor, however, wait until you have the new tile on-site so you can examine it to make sure you're getting what you ordered and that it's in good condition. Make sure the color, size, and texture are what you ordered and that the materials match your expectations.

7. Have a plan for disposing of the old materials. Order a trash container if necessary.

8. Prepare the subfloor and the drywall or plaster. It's essential that the tile base be in good condition and made of the materials recommended by the tile manufacturer. Proper preparation is the most important factor in a successful tiling installation—so important that warranties can be voided if a material is installed incorrectly.

9. Install the tile. Carefully follow the step-by-step instructions for the project you choose. Consult with experts if you need advice, and be sure you understand the manufacturer's recommendations for installation. Take your time: If the adhesive requires a certain amount of time to set up before installing the tile, wait patiently. Carefully follow all the steps recommended for finishing the project. Make sure the job is done properly before you move furniture and family back into the room.

Building codes and common sense

Building codes can be confusing. They establish and enforce consistent methods of installation to ensure safety. If your project involves electrical work or altering plumbing, new construction building codes may apply and must be followed. The practices shown in this book meet relevant national codes, but local codes can sometimes be more stringent. If you have concerns about your project, check with a local building inspector.

Common sense is more difficult to define because it involves instinct and experience. Practices that are common sense to a seasoned pro aren't always perfectly obvious to a do-it-yourselfer. Putting glazed floor tile in a bathroom or on a staircase, for instance, is not a good idea—somebody might slip when the tile gets wet. Industry standards, good construction practices, and manufacturer's requirements for honoring warranties are important too. Planning carefully and asking questions can help balance a lack of experience.

Maintenance

▲ **Tile is the perfect choice for this laundry room. It is durable, impervious to water, and easy to clean and maintain. Flooring choices for high-traffic, heavy-use areas such as this can be both beautiful and functional.**

Any tile surface will need cleaning and maintenance on a regular basis. Regular care lengthens its life, guarantees that warranties will be honored, and keeps the surface looking its best. For example, once a floor is in use, dirt, stains, scratches, and tears are inevitable. The longer the time between cleanings and repair, the worse the problem becomes.

How much are you willing to do?

Consider the amount of care your tiled project will need after installation and the amount of time you are willing to spend taking care of it when you choose materials.

■ Choose materials appropriate to use of the room. High-traffic and heavy-use areas such as entrances, staircases, landings, and kitchens might stand up to the wear and require less maintenance when covered in durable materials such as nonslippery ceramic tile, natural stone, vinyl, indoor/outdoor carpeting, or laminate. Softer coverings, such as carpet tile, work well in more lightly used areas, such as living rooms and bedrooms, where comfort is desired over durability. Keep in mind that wear varies from one area to another across the floor; edges tend to get less wear than major traffic areas, such as in front of a sofa or at an entrance.

■ Decide how much time you want to spend on care and maintenance. Pick your tile to fit your lifestyle. Some materials are more maintenance-intensive than others. Avoid carpet tile if you loathe vacuuming. Light-color tile will probably require more frequent cleaning in a home with children or pets.

■ Maintenance requirements vary even among similar materials. Ceramic tile requires less maintenance than natural stone, which must be resealed and polished occasionally. Cork and hardwoods also require reapplication of sealers and finishes as they wear.

Safety

Safety is a primary concern when choosing floor tile. Falls are dangerous for everyone but especially so for the elderly, children, and those who are physically challenged. The majority of slips and falls that occur inside households are caused by improper installation and maintenance of materials, a buildup of grease and grime, extensive wear, and the properties of the flooring material itself. You can avoid many accidents if you put the right flooring materials in the right places and properly maintain them. Here are some common potentially slippery areas.

■ Hard surfaces, especially those that are polished or glazed.
■ Grease or liquid spills left unattended in a kitchen or water puddled on a kitchen or bathroom floor.
■ Area rugs without a slip-resistant backing.

■ Carpet on stairs that is improperly installed or loose.
■ Highly polished ceramic tile or plush carpet on a staircase or entry floor.
■ Loose tiles or floorboards, as well as protruding nails or staples.
■ Carpet with extensive wear, such as holes or tangles of fiber.
■ Uneven transitions between rooms or types of flooring.
■ Flooring materials that visually obscure transitions between levels.
■ Wooden floors that are not properly sanded and sealed. (They present the risk of splinters for bare feet.)

▶ **The least slippery surfaces are rubber, textured surfaces, low-pile or indoor/outdoor carpet, surfaces with low-gloss or no-gloss finishes, such as this tile, and surfaces that absorb water.**

Evaluate your skills

Store associates will do their best to qualify customers for tiling projects by asking some basic questions to get a sense of their abilities and interests. These associates are more than curious—they want you to succeed.

Here are some questions you should ask yourself before tackling a home improvement project.

- Do you enjoy working on your house? If the answer is yes, move on to the next question. If the answer is no, pass this book on to someone who does.
- Do you mind getting dirty? Tiling projects can be messy and require considerable cleanup.
- How about heavy lifting? Cartons of tile and bags of mortar are heavy. Tolerating physical labor is part of installing a floor.
- Do you like working with tools? Do you have any? Most tiling projects involve a variety of hand and power tools. You may need to add tool purchase or rental costs to the cost of your project.
- Can you visualize level and vertical surfaces and compute dimensions (including fractions)? You'll need to know basic geometry and math for most tiling projects.
- Are you willing to do some research and make a plan? Doing your homework so you understand the process and scope of a project is essential. Learn the skills and understand safety issues before you begin.
- Do you know your limitations? It's OK to admit that a particular project is a little beyond your current skill level. It's better to pay a professional to do a job you're not comfortable with than to pay extra for someone to fix a mistake.

■ Tiling calls for skills such as mixing and spreading mortar as well as tough physical work such as ripping up old flooring.

Ready for the mess?

You never know what's under an existing floor or behind a wall. Even the experts can't tell you what's there without looking. If you live in a newer home, it may be a subfloor, and it may be in good shape. If your home is older, it could be a couple of other floors, the last of which might be solid oak strip flooring. No matter what it is, in most cases it will either have to come up or be repaired in some way—and repair and replacement mean dust.

Home remodeling projects are not only time-consuming, they're messy, and you'll avoid frustration if you take some steps to minimize the infiltration of the mess into the rest of your home.

First find out if and when your trash service takes remodeling debris. Then plan your job so you're doing any rip-it-up work in warm weather. That way you can use an open window as an exit for the debris. For first-floor jobs you can either bag or tie up the stuff indoors or pile it outdoors and dispose of it later. For second-story projects build a plywood chute and hang it on the window. If you're tearing up a large area, let the chute empty into a trash container.

Keep another window open and put a window fan in it to exhaust the dust. Even if you can close the workspace off with a door, hang a plastic sheet on the work side to keep the dust from being sucked out when you open and close the door. Put a rug or carpet sample just outside the work area to take the dust off the bottom of your boots when you leave. And leave the boots on the rug at the end of each workday.

Choosing floor tile

F loor tile comes in astounding variety. The next 14 pages will survey the different kinds available, starting with ceramic tile.

Ceramic tile was first used far back in history. Roman ruins have tiled floors that are still intact, and 4,000-year-old ceramics have been found in ancient Mesopotamia. This long history gives tile a reputation for durability—a material that's lasted for thousands of years is likely to hold up in the bathroom.

Ceramic tiles are slices of clay fired at high temperatures—usually between 1,900 and 2,100 degrees. The clay may be coated with a glaze that colors the surface, or it may be mixed with dye and fired. Glaze is applied directly to untreated clay when it is single-glazed, whereas double-glazed tiles are fired, coated with glaze, then refired. Single glaze is more vivid; double glaze shows patterns better.

Because tile comes in so many colors, shapes, and textures, the challenge in designing a tile floor is to make the right choices. A good way to start is to look at every magazine you can and tear out any tile photo that appeals to you. You'll soon see a trend developing and begin to get an idea of what attracts you, be it large handmade saltillo tiles or intricate mosaics. Modern mosaics are small tiles mounted on mesh sheets that are laid like larger tiles. You can lay them quickly, but you can also follow the traditional, but time-consuming, mosaic method of laying individual tiles (any under 2 inches) to create elaborate patterns.

As you plan, remember two things: First, ceramics last a long time. Avoid trendy colors and designs unless you're sure you'll like them 40 years from now. Second, think about how the floor interacts with the walls around it. Because of their shape and color, tiles are a stronger design element than wood or carpet. Select tile that agrees with the style of the room. A multicolor floor made of several different-size tiles, for example, might not work well with busy floral wallpaper. Buy sample tiles and take them home and live with them for awhile to make sure the color, scale, and texture add up to something you want in your home.

Porcelain tile

Porcelain tiles are ceramic tiles made from highly refined white clay. They are fired at an extremely high temperature—around 2,500 degrees—for nearly twice as long as other ceramic tiles. The result is an extremely dense, waterproof tile with a glossy surface. Their density makes them wear extremely well, even under heavy traffic and in constantly wet and freezing conditions. Porcelain comes as surface-colored and through-bodied tile, in which the color is uniform throughout the tile. The color of the surface-colored tile can wear or chip off. The color of through-bodied tiles won't. Which one should you buy? Make your decision according to what you can afford and how much traffic the floor will get.

▲ **Porcelain floor tiles perfectly suit this country-style kitchen. The texture of the surface and the pattern convey the feeling of a manor house kitchen and complement the plain wood cabinetry.**

Design choices and maintenance

From a design standpoint, you can do almost anything with porcelain tile. It comes in many colors. Porcelain tiles are made with textures that imitate stone tiles, tumbled marble, terra-cotta, polished marble, travertine, and many other materials. Their density also means that porcelain tiles don't need mass for strength. They are thinner than other ceramic tiles so they can be installed where thicker tiles would raise the floor level too much. Porcelain tile is easy to maintain.

Glazed ceramic tile

Unlike porcelain tile, glazed ceramic tile is a soft-bodied molded ceramic tile. The glaze sheds moisture, but the tile is not impervious. The combination of molding and glazing gives this tile a multitude of shapes, colors, and sizes. Because glazing can produce an extremely slippery surface, floor tiles are usually finished with a textured surface or a raised design to increase traction. Glazed tile (with a thinner body) is commonly used as wall tile.

▲ When you want stone but need something a little less expensive, porcelain tile is a good choice. Here several colors, shapes, and textures create an old-world look.

■ You can create countless patterns with ceramic tile, from the traditional checkerboard, above, to the colorful ornamented pattern at right.

Terra-cotta and saltillo

Terra-cotta tiles are made of unrefined natural clay that has been baked (not fired) at low temperatures or dried in the sun. These tiles are comparatively low in cost and high in rustic charm. Because of their low density they absorb water, so you'll need to seal them often.

Saltillo tile is a terra-cotta tile named for the area in Mexico where it originated. It is a large colorful tile, handmade and dried in the sun. Because it is handmade, the tile colors and sizes aren't entirely uniform. This lack of uniformity produces a rustic look and requires grout lines of about ¼ inch to accommodate the irregularity. As demand for saltillo has grown, factories have begun to produce machine-made look-alikes. While not a true saltillo, the new tile retains much of the charm of the original.

These tiles are easily stained too, so you should seal them (usually every year) to keep them from getting grimy. They will not withstand freezing temperatures and should not be used outdoors except in climates where they won't freeze.

▲ Saltillo tiles have a universal rough-and-ready appeal, and from a design standpoint are well suited to any room, especially when you want to create a rustic or Southwestern theme.

▲ The rough texture of terra-cotta tiles makes them an ideal choice on floors where safety is a factor. No material is completely slip-proof, but these tiles are more slip-resistant than many others.

Quarry tile

Quarry tile is a thick tile made from natural clays and shales. The name originally referred to stone tile cut from quarries, but now is applied to these high-fired tiles that resemble the stone tile.

Quarry tile is usually earthy in color, ranging from brick red to various shades of tan, off white, and gray. Some quarry tiles are fired at temperatures high enough to make them vitreous so they are more water-resistant than their semivitreous counterparts. The semivitreous tiles are considered highly slip-resistant—spilled water soaks in instead of remaining on the surface. This means stains will soak in too, but you can alleviate some of that problem by applying a penetrating sealer to the tile. Penetrating sealers soak into the body of a tile and do not form a coating on the surface. Thus they allow the tile to retain its original character.

▲ **Because quarry tile is slip-resistant, it is often found in work areas like this kitchen.**

Deciphering the label

Cartons of tile now have labels with a series of icons that tell you important facts about the tile you're buying. This chart shows what the numbers and symbols mean.

- **Grade:** Grade 1 is suitable for walls or floors; Grade 2 is similar but has slight imperfections; Grade 3 is thinner tile designed for walls. You can use floor tiles on walls, but not wall tiles on floors. They'll crack.

- **PEI (Porcelain Enamel Institute) Wear Rating:** the tile's resistance to abrasion. I and II—not suitable for floors (walls only); III—all residential; IV—residential and light commercial; IV+—commercial and heavy traffic.

- **Water absorption:** proportion by weight: nonvitreous, more than 7 percent; semivitreous, 3 to 7 percent; vitreous, 0.5 to 3 percent; impervious, less than 0.5 percent. Only vitreous and impervious tiles should be used outdoors or in wet locations.

- **Coefficient of friction:** Resistance to slip, measured by the force required to move an object across the tile divided by its weight. The lower the number, the slipperier the floor.

- **Tone:** A multishaded grid indicates variations in tone from tile to tile. This variation is found in most tile, except for pure colors such as black and white.

- **Frost resistance:** Irrelevant indoors. An indication of whether tile not directly exposed to the elements will crack because of freeze-thaw cycles. If a tile is frost-resistant, you'll find a snowflake on the label.

What should you get?

- For a floor, purchase tiles that are Grade 1 or 2. Grade 3 tiles are for walls and will crack on a floor.
- Look for a PEI, or wear rating, of III or more.
- Make sure the coefficient of friction is 0.6 or more.
- Water absorption standards vary. Tiles with a water absorption rate of less than 7 percent (semivitreous) are best for any floor installation. Tile for areas that are frequently wet should have a water absorption rate of less than 3 percent (vitreous or impervious). Elsewhere, water absorption is unimportant.
- Frost resistance is a consideration for outdoor installation only.

Mosaics

Any tile less than 2 inches wide is considered a mosaic. Although you can still find installers who lay mosaics one tile at a time, most mosaics now come attached to mesh-backed sheets that are laid like larger tiles. Within the world of sheeted mosaic tile, you'll find a vast array of colors, designs, shapes, sizes, and materials—glass, porcelain, clay, and even metal. Some mosaic patterns are regular, not varying from sheet to sheet. Other patterns are random, which can make for an unusual floor design. With random sheets, you must take care not to bunch similar sections of the pattern together, creating unsightly splotches of color or shape. Whatever the pattern, mosaics can create a stunning display of variety and form—this is a material that will be a major element in the design of your room. Designing with mosaics, therefore, takes a little more forethought than planning a floor with standard tiles in a neutral color. With this material everything from wall colors and decorations to lighting and furnishings has to work together so the elements do not compete for attention.

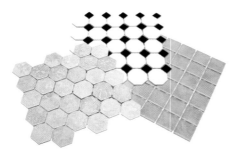

Cement-body tile

▲ Inexpensive cement-body tile is especially useful in room designs with a rustic flavor. It is also good for Southwestern themes, with fireplaces or wood stoves, or in rooms such as covered porches and sunrooms that provide a transition to the outdoors.

Cement-body tiles are made of mortar (a sand-and-cement mix) instead of clay and are cured instead of fired. The result is a hard, durable flooring material that is excellent for adding a touch of the rustic to your room. They are made to resemble brick, glazed tile, or stone, but because they're a concrete product, you get the look of a fancier material at a considerable cost saving.

You'll find a wide variety of cement-body tile. Surfaces come smooth or porous, dull or shiny, and in a surprisingly large number of colors and tints, even the appearance of veined marble. And because the color runs all the way through the tiles, chips or wear spots are less noticeable.

These tiles are an economical choice, and although they have certain design limitations (you'll never get them to look like highly polished marble, for instance), they're tough and long lasting. They are not vitreous, however, and many porous tiles will crack in freezing climates. Check with your distributor if you're considering cement-body tile for a patio.

Accents

Decorative accent tiles can turn an otherwise plain installation into a work of art. Inset at regular or random intervals across the surface, they add interest and excitement. Hand-painted or embossed (or both), they can be expensive, but just a few can enhance your design without costing you a bundle. You can choose a relatively inexpensive tile for the field of your tiling project and spice it up with some accent tiles without straining your budget.

Accent tiles are available in seemingly endless varieties. The wide range of choices can make it difficult to pick out accents for your project. In general you can safely add accents that have at least one color similar in tone to the general color of the rest of the tile. Another option is to be outrageous and choose accent tiles with a striking contrast.

Consider your walls. You can use accents to frame a range hood or the sink when tiling a kitchen backsplash, for example. Accents are ideal for creating a focal point in an otherwise plain expanse of tile. You can set off sections of the wall tile with a glass-tile border. On the floor, accent tiles can draw attention to dimly lit areas and effectively brighten the area without actually increasing the light.

Some accent tiles are molded in relief patterns; others are hand painted. Glass and metal tiles are glossy and easy to clean. Antique tiles can bring unusual effects to a tiled installation. You can find them at flea markets and antiques shops. Because you're not likely to find complete sets and probably won't be able to find specific designs or colors, it's usually better to choose these tiles first, then find field tiles that provide a complementary background.

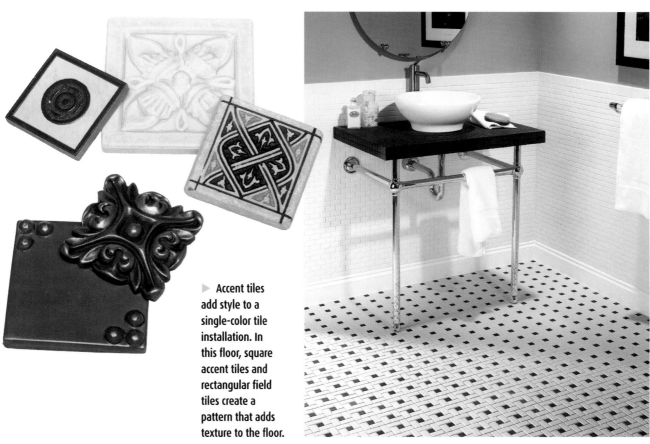

▶ Accent tiles add style to a single-color tile installation. In this floor, square accent tiles and rectangular field tiles create a pattern that adds texture to the floor.

Stone tile

Stone tile includes minerals such as granite, marble, slate, sandstone, limestone, and quartzite. You'll find stone tiles generally in one of three categories, depending on how it is surfaced—polished, tumbled, or cleft (natural). No matter what its finish, stone soaks up stains, which are then impossible to remove. Sealing will help minimize stains, but because nothing beats the unrivaled natural beauty of stone, you may find it worth the risk of stains. Be sure to use white thinset on lighter color translucent stones. Gray thinset will show through.

Polished stone

Polished stone varieties were once limited to granite and marble. Recently onyx, quartzite, and travertine have become increasingly popular. All these materials display an unmatched individuality. Marble has hazy veins or creamy colors; granite, mottled colors; and onyx, shades of light and dark spread throughout. Quartzite and travertine have a pebbly visual texture, with fine veins in the travertine. These stones are expensive but properly cared for will last a lifetime. In general they look best with very thin, almost nonexistent grout lines.

▲ **Field tiles, which are usually 4×4-inch squares, can be dressed up with borders, listellos, or a predesigned and mesh-backed medallion, shown creating a classic focal point on this marble floor.**

Tumbled stone

Tumbled stone tiles, with their characteristic rounded edges and rough-hewn look, present an elegant option for a tiled installation. The tiles, usually marble or granite, are tumbled in abrasives and sometimes bathed in acid, which accentuates the natural veining and leaves an open, porous surface.

Each tile is unique. Flaws such as open veins, chips, and depressions are part of the charm of these materials. Colors are natural, ranging from neutral tans to reds, browns, greens, and blacks. Tumbling imparts a soft texture to this otherwise hard material, an already aged and ancient aura that is reminiscent of old Mediterranean villas. Tumbled tiles must be sealed before grouting to prevent the grout from staining the body of the tile.

▲ **Stone tile brings a touch of old-world charm to a tiled room. Stone can be formal or informal, elegant or rustic.**

Natural stone

Natural stone tile is split (cleft) from larger deposits then cut to size with saws. The split face gives the tile a rough texture. Slate and bluestone (a regional stone specific to the Northeast) are among the most common varieties. Limestone and sandstone, formed from sedimentary deposits, are among the softest stones.

Because they are soft, both limestone and sandstone should be installed in light traffic areas, as they will wear quickly. Slate comes in hard and soft varieties and in many choices of greens, grays, and blues. Plan your installation to form a patchwork of these colors. The surface of slate is naturally ridged, which makes it a good choice for floors where safety is paramount. Bluestone has a distinctive deep blue-gray hue, with hints of green, yellow, and other colors throughout its surface. Its fine-grained surface wears extremely well.

▶ **Slate makes an excellent floor for entryways because it is classic in appearance, durable, and extremely slip resistant. Hard varieties are easy to maintain. Softer varieties, called Indian slates, require sealing.**

Rating ceramic tile for residential floors

Conditions/typical areas	Grade	PEI	Water absorption	Coefficient of friction	Tone	Frost proof yes/no
Interior, light traffic (sunroom, living room, dining)	1 or 2	3+	any	any	any	no
Interior, heavy traffic (entrance, stairs, hall)	1 or 2	3+	any	0.6 minimum	any	no
Interior, occasionally wet (bathroom, kitchen)	1 or 2	3+	less than 7%	0.6 minimum	any	no
Interior, frequently wet (tub, shower, pool)	1 or 2	3+	less than 3%	0.6 minimum	any	no
Exterior, warm climate (patio, walkway, stairs)	1 or 2	3+	less than 7%	0.6 minimum	any	no
Exterior, freeze/thaw (patio, walkway, stairs)	1 or 2	3+	less than 3%	0.6 minimum	any	yes

Ceramic borders, baseboards, and thresholds

▶ **Check out the selection of border tile at your home center. Borders with complex patterns and mosaics can be purchased preassembled and attached to a mesh backing that makes installation easy.**

Borders, baseboards, and thresholds have practical functions, but they also have design potential and can be stylish additions to a room. Borders help separate one area of a floor (or wall) from another, baseboards hide the expansion gap at the edges of the floor, and thresholds provide a smooth visual and physical transition from one flooring material to another. Chosen carefully, they all enhance the appearance of a room. Even though they are often among the last pieces you install, you should not treat them as an afterthought.

When planning a border, draw out the pieces on a scale drawing of the room. The drawing will help you get a clear idea of how the border looks and whether its scale and location fit the overall design of the tiled surface.

There are several ways to deal with baseboards. You can, of course, replace the original baseboard in the room (first consider repainting or refinishing it). You can enhance the appearance of the room, however, by installing either straight bullnose tile or a decorative tile baseboard. Bullnose tile has one rounded edge and is often available to match the color or style of tile you've chosen for the floor. If the manufacturer doesn't make bullnose pieces to match your tile, you can make your own by cutting a whole tile to width and rounding the cut edge with a mason's stone. You can install a baseboard in a color different from the floor to define the edges of the room in a dramatic fashion.

Although some tiled installations result in a floor the same height as the one in the adjoining room, most do not. In this case, you need a threshold. From a design standpoint, a threshold milled from wood might be a better choice than an aluminum one. Marble thresholds are available and add a rich look, although they are somewhat more expensive.

▲ Baseboards can be as simple as rounded bullnose tile (if it's available from your manufacturer) or molded decorative pieces, which are usually designed to be used as the cap piece in a multipart baseboard.

▲ Extreme contrasts create high drama. This wood baseboard is the original from the bathroom with a new coat of paint. Use caution when removing a baseboard like this if you're going to reuse it. Old wood, especially yellow pine, splits easily.

▲ Marble thresholds add a touch of class to a tiled floor. They are slightly more expensive than wood thresholds, but for many installations the look is worth the cost.

▲ Mixing shapes, sizes, and colors of granite floor tiles creates a strong visual movement. Carrying the tile up the wall acts as a unifying element. Contrasting grout emphasizes the variety of forms in this composition.

Vinyl tile

Vinyl tile is an easy floor tile to install. Whether you lay it in adhesive or use self-stick tiles, it goes down one piece at a time. It's easy to trim, and if you make a mistake, you've wasted only a single tile. Vinyl tile is also extremely versatile when you want to exercise your individual creativity and create patterns of your own. You can also use it to generate a wide variety of effects. You can mix and match tiles to create patterns, or you can buy tiles with patterns that are almost identical to those on ceramic or stone tile.

Underlayments

Vinyl must be installed over a plywood underlayment designed specifically for that purpose. Unapproved plywoods with rough surfaces create nothing but trouble—the roughness will eventually show through. Natural pigments contained in woods like lauan eventually bleed through some tile and become visible. Unstable or poorly manufactured plywood may warp and lift your floor.

If the underlayment ruins your floor, it's covered by the underlayment manufacturer's warranty, not the vinyl manufacturer's warranty. Purchase an underlayment that's approved by the Engineered Wood Association (formerly American Plywood Association) for use under vinyl tile. Appropriate plywood is stamped to identify it as certified underlayment.

▲ To create a patterned surface that functions as a backdrop for the rest of the room, choose a ceramic pattern in a light color.

▲ Some tiles are as vivid as others are tame. The pattern on the tile above mimics patterns in sheet vinyl, and once the tiles are down, they are virtually indistinguishable from sheet goods.

Printed vinyl and inlaid vinyl

The pattern on vinyl tile is either printed or inlaid. Printed vinyl, sometimes called rotovinyl because of the printing process used to produce the pattern, is protected by a wear layer. It is available in a wide range of patterns and colors. Inlaid vinyl is made of millions of tiny granules of vinyl that are deposited in precise patterns and fused into a solid sheet. Inlaid vinyl's pattern and color go clear through the tile. Most inlaid tiles require periodic sealing to keep dirt from migrating deep into the tile where you can't remove it.

Peel-and-stick tiles are printed tiles, and their surfaces are usually embossed to help create a three-dimensional effect. The quality of these tiles varies widely from manufacturer to manufacturer. Avoid tiles so flexible that you can bend them almost edge to edge. They won't hold up.

Vinyl tiles of contrasting colors are a great way to bring contrast to a room. Alternating tiles with the same dominant color creates a unified look. Alternating contrasting colors can help create a modern or retro look.

Cork for floors

Once used only in the most expensive homes, cork tile is finding increasingly wider use. It's soft, resilient, dampens noise more effectively than other resilients, and looks elegant. Cork comes from the bark of the cork oak, but stripping it does not damage the tree. In fact, the tree regenerates new bark at a regular cycle of several years. Once harvested, the cork bark is ground and mixed with resins and dyes to create different tones. Tiles glue down like vinyl tiles.

Linoleum

Linoleum, the original resilient floor covering, is gaining new popularity. It is composed of linseed oil, cork, wood, and sometimes stone chips. The resurgence of interest in linoleum is due in part to the muted colors and tones that it is associated with. Linoleum has practical benefits too—it is naturally resistant to bacteria and has antistatic qualities that make cleaning easier because it repels dust.

Linoleum tiles are installed using the same techniques as for vinyl flooring.

1

Laminate tile

Laminate flooring has been popular in Europe for more than 25 years but is a relatively new product in the U.S. It's a synthetic product through and through, from its tough melamine wearcoat to its kraft paper (or MDF) core. Laminate can be made to look like any material—stone, ceramic tile, wood—at a fraction of the cost of the real thing—because its second layer contains a photographic representation of the material. Early laminate looked unrealistic, but today's laminates convincingly reproduce the look and texture of wood, tile, or stone. Laminate flooring is stable and can be installed below grade.

Laminate flooring installs easily—most products simply snap together and float on a layer of plastic foam underlayment. You can install it without spreading adhesives because it doesn't attach to the subfloor at all. The underlayment provides some resilience as you walk on it, which makes a more comfortable surface than hard tile. The underlayment also helps deaden sound in the floor.

Some laminate floors can be glued together for bathrooms or other areas where watertight joints are required or for hard-use areas like recreation rooms. Most installations snap together to make a floor that's one large piece, held down around the edges by a baseboard or shoe molding. Because no nails are needed, laminates make a great floor covering for concrete.

Laminate wear layers are tough and durable—made from the same polymer as laminate countertops but thicker. They stand up extremely well to dents but not as well to scratches, and scratches in laminate can't be rubbed out or repaired. That makes them a less than ideal floor for backdoor mudrooms and other rooms that are likely to receive rough abrasive treatment and get scuffed up from shoes coming indoors. The melamine finish is hard, resists dirt, and requires only periodic damp mopping.

▲ **One advantage of laminate flooring is its durability. Another plus is that laminates look like stone or ceramic tile, as shown here, but cost less and are easier to install**

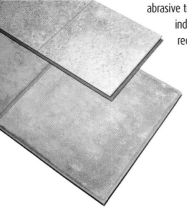

Parquet

Parquet tile is one of the most subtle flooring materials. It brings an understated pattern to a floor, providing interest without becoming overwhelming. Parquet was once the standard flooring for mansions of the wealthy, with each strip (or fillet) of wood laid separately. Parquet today is sold as tiles of preassembled fillets that can be laid like other tiles.

Fillets can be cut from a wide range of wood species and in several configurations—in wide parallel strips and narrower angled patterns. The beauty of parquet is enhanced by its changing geometries as well as the range of slightly different wood tones across each tile. It's easy to install in an adhesive made specifically for this purpose. In higher grade parquet, tongues and grooves are milled along the edges to give each corner a perfect fit. Don't scrimp on the cost; inexpensive parquet may have a thin veneer layer, which won't wear well, and its glues may deteriorate, resulting in loose or curled fillets.

▲ Parquet is a tile made of contrasting pieces of wood. It installs like a vinyl tile and gives you the opportunity to create the visual effects typical of other tiles.

Carpet tile

On a cold day, there's nothing like getting out of bed and stepping onto a warm carpet. And the same goes for carpet tile. Carpet tile is now much better than the ones that first hit the market years ago.

It's one of the easiest kinds of tile to install. It comes in two varieties—peel and stick and dry-backed, for installation in an adhesive. And for all this simplicity, you can create some surprising design effects with carpet tile. This tile has a directional nap and arrows on the back that show which way the nap lays. Installing the tiles with arrows pointing in the same direction will create a broadloom effect. Placing the arrows at right angles will result in an understated checkerboard pattern.

Choosing wall tile

Wall tiles are available in a variety of sizes, colors, shapes, patterns, and textures. The biggest challenge may be narrowing your selection from thousands of available designs. Because wall tile doesn't have to stand up to the heavy loads of floor tile, you'll find tile made specifically for walls is generally thinner. Some wall tile (but not all) is less expensive than floor tile. You can install any floor tile on a wall, but do not lay wall tile on a floor. The traditional tile size for wall tile is a 4-inch square, but a number of sizes and shapes are available.

Glazed ceramic wall tile

Glazed ceramic wall tile has long been the mainstay of wall tile. It's a soft-bodied tile and is generally less expensive than dense high-fired tiles. Because its bisque is molded (extruded), it comes in all kinds of shapes and sizes, and with a wide range of textures—some resembling rough stone, others crazed with tiny lines. And even though it has a nonvitreous body, its glaze helps it resist water penetration.

Most wall tile is prespaced with small lugs molded on the sides of the tile. These allow you to set the tile without the annoyance of adding spacers by hand. Prespaced tiles usually leave a gap for the grout a little less than ¼ inch wide.

The variety of color, size, shape, and surface sheen makes this the ideal tile for designing pattern on the wall. If you're choosing tiles from different manufacturers for your pattern, they may be different sizes and thicknesses. Make sure they will all fit together for your pattern.

▲ A tiled wall design does not have to be composed of the same size and same color tiles. Vary the size, the shape, the colors, add listellos and pattern tiles, and you'll create a wall design that sets the tone for the rest of the room.

Porcelain wall tile

Except for a slightly thinner profile, porcelain wall tile shares the same characteristics as porcelain floor tile—dense, hard, impervious to water, and a wide assortment of colors, sizes, and shapes.

Like most wall tile, manufacturers usually make a supply of trim and border tile complementary to their lines of wall tile. That will save design time because you won't have to figure out so many finishing details when you design your installation.

With through-color porcelain tile, you won't have to worry as much about chips and scratches. The color is uniform throughout the body and surface of the tile, making chips and scratches less noticeable. Porcelain tile is less prone to staining and easy to keep clean.

▲ Porcelain tile is perfect for bathrooms and other locations with surfaces that will get wet because it's impervious to moisture. Grout joints must be sound to keep water from getting in between the tiles or at the edges.

Stone tile for walls

All the stone species used on floors—marble, granite, slate, travertine, and more—can be applied to walls. And like their floor-tile counterparts, you can choose from polished stone, cleft stone, stone with a matte finish, and tumbled stone tile.

Thinner tile is better for walls; the thinner pieces are lighter and easier to install. The critical concern when installing stone tile on walls is keeping the joint lines straight. You won't be able to hide imperfect grout lines or an unsquare tile, especially if the tile is polished.

Matching trim tile is often unavailable for stone. You may have to cut your own and polish the edges with a masonry stone or increasingly finer grits of sandpaper. On rough-stone projects, you can omit the polishing step. Polished edges are rarely seen on rough-stone walls.

Tumbled stone tiles, with their characteristic rounded edges and rough-hewn qualities, are an elegant option for walls. Flaws—open veins, chips, and depressions—in tumbled tiles are part of the finished look. Tumbled stone is usually available in 4×4-inch squares with borders, listellos, or preassembled mesh-backed medallions.

Stone tile must be sealed before grouting to prevent stains. Deep veins in the surface can fill with grout as well. Stone enhancers can be applied to accent natural veining and color. All unfinished stone will absorb water and is subject to staining. The tile must be sealed; ask your tile retailer to recommend appropriate sealers and cleaners.

▲ **Tumbled stone set in a band along the backsplash adds a unique custom touch. Lay out the pieces on a flat surface to arrange the design, then set them individually.**

▲ Stone tile adds elegance to small areas where the patterns and color variations are easier to see up close. An installation like this is expensive.

BUYER'S GUIDE

TILE CHARACTERISTICS

TYPE OF TILE	COST	RELATIVE DURABILITY	WATER ABSORPTION	MAINTENANCE
Glazed wall	Low to medium	Low to high	Medium	Low
Glazed decorative	High	Low to medium	Medium	Low
Porcelain	Medium	High	Low	Low
Quarry	Low to medium	High	Medium	Low
Terra-cotta	Low to medium	Low	Medium to high	High
Natural stone	Low to high	High	Low to high	Medium to high
Cement-body	Low	High	Low	Low to medium

Glass and metal tile

Glass tile has been in use for centuries. It was used to decorate Roman homes and residences of the Egyptian hierarchy. Modern manufacturing methods have brought a consistency of color, size, and pattern that would have been unknown to earlier artisans. Nonporous glass tile (some glass tile is made porous on purpose) is easy to clean, but all varieties scratch relatively easily. Glass is a good candidate for use as accent tiles on walls but not floors and countertops.

Metal tile, by comparison, is a relatively new invention. Already stainless steel, aluminum, copper, brass, bronze, and even titanium are finding their way into modern design. No other tile fits quite as well into contemporary design schemes. These tiles are susceptible to scratches. Metal tile is usually installed sparingly as an accent, mostly due to its cost.

▲ Glass and metal tiles may be expensive, but where their use is limited by the size of a small area, such as a kitchen backsplash or vanity border, they can provide the perfect embellishment at a reasonable cost.

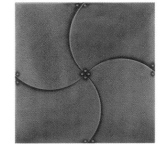

Murals

A mural is a mosaic design made with large pieces. More specifically, murals are tiled pictures displayed generally on walls. Depending on the picture, a mural can be composed of 50 or more pieces. Schedule enough time to install the one of your choice in one session. It is difficult (but not impossible) to stop midway though the application of a mural and resume later.

Murals are often used in kitchens but can look equally good in a home office, family room, or bedroom. If you can't find a commercial pattern you like, some artisans will create a tile mural from a photograph or sketch that you provide.

▲ A mosaic mural is a stylish feature that can be installed on a floor or wall. This kind of mural requires careful work.

▲ This screen-printed mural is easy to install and adds a point of interest to the plain white backsplash.

Listellos

A listello is a narrow tile used to accent field tiles. You'll find most listellos made for floors in the form of mesh-back mosaics with repeating patterns. The repeating pattern and modular dimensions simplify installation, allowing you to install in a few hours a design that would otherwise take days. You can make a wider border for a large area by installing a double course of listellos separated by a single course of contrasting floor tiles.

Listellos for walls often have a raised relief and are used for cornice moldings, mural frames, chair rails, or borders to outline wall sections for visual interest. If you're looking for a way to embellish an expanse of wall tile and are put off by the price of handcrafted decorative tiles, consider a listello border.

Listellos are also effective for breaking up large expanses of tile. You can install them as frames for contrasting tile fields or other decorative features, such as murals. Many attractive installations are possible using a row of listellos set into or around a background of inexpensive field tiles.

■ Listellos add character to the tile wainscoting around this bathtub (above) and along this backsplash (right). The listellos at left are examples of the styles you'll find. Some wall or floor tile has matching or coordinating listellos, but you will often have to choose listellos separately from the body tile for your installation.

Tile for countertops

When selecting tile for a countertop, consider whether it will be subject to standing water. Surfaces that are frequently exposed to water should be covered with vitreous tile or a nonporous natural stone. The grout and adhesive must also be nonporous (latex- or acrylic-modified).

Mechanical abuse, such as cutting, slicing, and abrasion from china and cast-iron cookware, calls for a hard surface. To keep nicks, scratches, and chips from showing, pick tile in which the color extends through the body of the tile.

Glazed wall and decorative tiles are unsuitable for countertops. The best choices for hard-working surfaces are porcelain tile, quarry tile, and granite.

- Porcelain tiles are made of highly refined clay and are fired at very high temperatures. As a result, they are dense and hard and highly resistant to wear and scratching. They are also among the most water-resistant tiles; they don't absorb water or oil and harbor mold and bacteria.
- Natural stone includes granite, marble, and slate. Granite and marble are available in polished (shiny and slippery) and honed (dull and less slippery) finishes. Both slate and marble are fairly soft and porous

CLOSER LOOK

INSTALL A CUTTING BOARD

Rather than chopping or cutting directly on a tile countertop, install a wood or plastic cutting board. Cut a maple cutting board to fit in place of the tiles in one area and set it into the gap with silicone adhesive. Because the board shrinks and swells, caulk the board and tile joints with silicone.

Countertop trim

Make sure there are trim pieces that coordinate with the tile you choose. If these are not available, or if your tile is natural stone, your dealer can supply oak L-trim in 5-foot and 8-foot lengths.

If you have a dishwasher, be sure the bottom of the trim is at least 34¼ inches above the finished floor. Otherwise you may not be able to open the dishwasher or remove it in case of a plumbing problem.

The best way to increase the clearance is to install a thicker plywood base.

▲ Tiling a moderately sized countertop can be accomplished in a three-day weekend if you plan the work thoroughly. You need enough time to remove the old countertop, install a new base, lay backerboard and let the thinset dry, then install the tile the next day.

V-CAP is designed for edging countertops. Its raised lip prevents spills from running over the edge.

L-SINK TRIM also has a lip to keep liquid spills on the countertop and off the floor.

WOOD TRIM goes with any color tile, but you must caulk the joint between trim and tile to keep out water.

compared to granite. In addition, marble is vulnerable to common kitchen acids such as vinegar and citrus juice. Polished granite is a good choice for kitchen countertops.

- Quarry tile originally was quarried stone. Quarry tile today is clay extruded through a die, cut to size, and fired in a kiln. The tile is extremely hard and stands up well to abuse. It is fairly nonporous, (absorbs little water). Color selection is limited.

- Glazed tiles are generally machine-made of clay, pressed in a die, and fired in a kiln. The glaze adds color and a hard but easily chipped surface. Most glazed tiles are intended for walls and are too soft and too water absorbent to be used on kitchen countertops. If you decide to use them because of their bright colors, provide wood or plastic cutting surfaces in or on the countertop (see "Closer Look" on page 46).

Porcelain tile

Quarry tile

Glazed tile

Stone tile

Tile characteristics for countertops

TYPE OF TILE	COST	RELATIVE DURABILITY	WATER ABSORPTION	UPKEEP
Porcelain	Medium	High	Low	Low
Quarry	Low to medium	High	Medium	Low
Natural stone	Low to high	High	Low to high	Medium to high

Tile for the outdoors

Patios are outdoor floors that may be exposed to standing water as well as freeze-thaw cycles. Consider these four qualities when selecting patio tile:

- **PEI WEAR RATING:** The tile's resistance to abrasion (suitability for foot traffic).
- **WATER ABSORPTION:** The percentage of water the tile can absorb (suitability for wet locations).
- **COEFFICIENT OF FRICTION:** Slip resistance on a scale of 0 to 1.0. Look for a rating of at least 0.6.
- **FROST RESISTANCE:** Warranty against damage by freezing and thawing (a requirement in freeze-thaw regions). Beware that in some rating systems, the term "frost resistant" may not mean that tile is warranted against frost damage.

Most floor tiles at your home center will display rating labels. If you have any questions about the suitability of a certain tile for a patio, ask the salesperson for advice.

Terra-cotta tiles are popular for patios in the South. Made of natural clay fired at low temperature, most terra-cotta tiles are produced in Mexico. Their appeal comes from low cost, earth-tone colors, and rustic handmade charm. Low density and high water absorption require frequent sealing to prevent staining and prohibit use in freeze-thaw areas.

Natural stone is available as square-cut tile and as random-shape cleft stone. Tiles include granite, marble, and slate. Granite and marble are available in polished (too slippery for patios) and honed (less slippery) finishes. Tumbled marble tiles, slate, and cleft stone are the least slippery. Most stone, except granite, is porous and can be damaged by water and freeze-thaw cycles.

Cement-body tiles made of mortar are commonly used in patios. Durable versions are available that resemble brick, glazed tile, or stone. Cement-body brick, a variety of cement-body tile made to look like brick, comes in common brick face and side. These tiles can be used on concrete patios and concrete block fireplaces.

Quarry tile is popular for patios because of its earth tones and low cost. The extremely hard, unglazed tile is ideal for flooring. Most quarry tile can be used outdoors, even in freeze-thaw areas; check the frost resistance rating of the particular stock you consider for your project.

▲ **Stone tile gives this patio a rugged, timeworn look. The style complements casual furnishings like these, but stone tile can also convey a more formal feeling.**

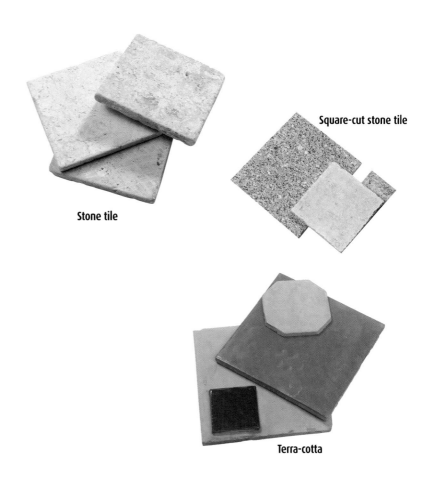

Square-cut stone tile

Stone tile

Terra-cotta

Cement-body tile

Quarry tile

▲ Natural variations in color and texture among stone tiles make each patio unique. Mixing tile sizes and shapes adds another dimension to the patio's style.

▼ Cement-body tiles set in a basketweave pattern make an attractive patio that's easy to install. The versatile tiles are available in a variety of colors and textures that resemble other materials.

Underlayments and membranes

What goes under your flooring can mean the difference between a successful installation or a troublesome one. Each kind of tile and installation situation will have different requirements.

An **isolation membrane** covers cracks in the slab and keeps them from cracking the flooring material.

Cement backerboard and **fiber-cement board** provide a sturdy, inflexible surface for ceramic tile and stone.

Underlayment plywood is smooth and ensures that there won't be defects that telegraph into resilient materials.

Structural plywood is a sturdy subfloor for all flooring materials.

A **waterproofing membrane** (either troweled or sheet formed) keeps moisture from wicking through a slab and into the finished floor. In wet locations such as bathrooms and showers, 15 lb. felt paper is often used as a waterproofing material.

PVC membrane waterproofs the floor of a custom shower, protecting both the subfloor and the framing from water damage.

Foam underlayment acts as a cushion under laminate flooring and helps deaden the sound in floating floors.

Fiberglass reinforcing tape reinforces the joints in backerboards.

Backerboard screws anchor cement backerboard to the framing and won't rust.

Embossing leveler smooths out the embossed pattern in vinyl tile and sheet goods so you can overlay new tiles.

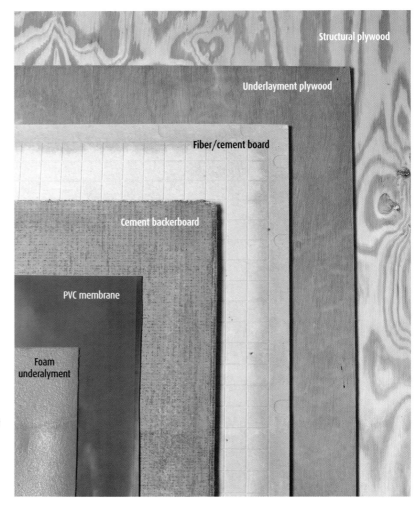

Structural plywood

Underlayment plywood

Fiber/cement board

Cement backerboard

PVC membrane

Foam underalyment

Waterproofing membrane

Trowel

Embossing leveler

Backerboard screws

Fiberglass reinforcing tape

Adhesives, grouts, and sealers

Adhesive holds a tile installation together and firmly attaches the tiles to the substrate. Grout keeps moisture from working its way into the adhesive and also has a decorative function, adding color and definition to a tiled surface. Sealer keeps dirt and moisture from getting into and under the tile and grout.

Almost all tile requires a specialized type of adhesive, grout, and sealer. Consult with your retailer to find out what is best for your tile and installation situation.

Thinset mortar is the adhesive of choice for most ceramic tile and stone.

Organic mastic is the usual adhesive for wall tiles up to 6×6 inches. It comes premixed in a can and cures by drying. Mastic is fine for wall tile but should not be used for floors.

Latex additives of various kinds increase the adhesion, flexibility, and water resistance of thinset mortar.

Sanded grout is designed to fill joints from ⅛ to ½ inch wide.

Unsanded grout is used for thin joints, less than ⅛ inch wide, chiefly in stone tile.

Sealer, either penetrating or topical, helps protect tile from water and stains.

Floor tile adhesive is formulated for vinyl tile, sheet goods, and parquet.

Carpet adhesive holds down carpet in glue-down installations.

Seam sealer prevents carpet from fraying where two pieces meet.

Hot-melt seaming tape is a heat-sensitive tape placed across the back of carpet at the seams. It comes in different widths for different applications.

Carpet edging, or binder bar, is a metal strip placed at an exposed carpet edge to protect it and act as a transition.

Tack strip grips the edge of carpet in a stretch-in installation.

Sanded grout

Cleaner and sealer

Unsanded grout

Latex additive

Sealer

Floor tile adhesive

Sanded grout

Sanded color grout

Prep and demolition

Preparation is the part of a tiling project you may want to avoid thinking about, but it's where every tiling job starts. If you're putting in a new floor, you'll probably have to remove the old flooring. This is also the time to assess the strength of your subfloor if you're putting down ceramic tile. The combined weight of backerboard, thinset mortar, and tile is significant, and many existing subfloors will need to be shored up to keep them level and intact. If you're tiling a wall, you might have to remove wallpaper or at least rough up

the paint. Some of these jobs are easy, some not so easy. For example, different flooring materials come up in different ways: You can usually release stretched carpet along the edges and roll it up. But you'll have to scrape off old vinyl tile or sheet flooring. On a wall, newer vinyl wallpaper might pull right off while older paper will require a liquid remover.

New tile will hide an old surface, but it won't fix structural problems. Inspect the floor or wall before you start tiling and correct problems before the new material goes down. The repairs

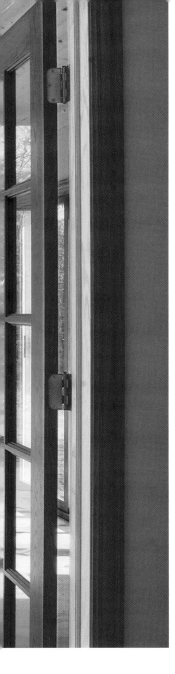

Chapter 2 highlights

most often necessary are usually relatively straightforward jobs, often involving only driving a few nails, pouring some leveling compound, or patching some holes in drywall.

Whatever preparation is required, do it carefully. Once you've completed the repair work, you'll have a smooth, stable, and flat surface, and your new tile should go down without problems.

Keep your preparation work organized in sections. It always helps to ease into a job, especially if you're not familiar with all the details, so do the easy stuff first. Most prep starts with the removal of fixtures and appliances, then the baseboard and shoe molding; these jobs all proceed in a fairly logical manner. After the room is cleared, go ahead with removal of old surface coverings and necessary repairs.

The basic home-repair toolbox

Tools are available in a wide range of prices. Usually price is a good indicator of quality and durability. Many home centers carry different grades of tools for most jobs. Low-cost tools are intended for small jobs and infrequent use; better ones will generally last longer, but the best tools are the ones the pros use. They'll last a lifetime if you care for them properly. When buying tools, follow this simple principle: Buy the best tools you can afford.

Buy or rent?

A hammer is a tool you'll use often, so it's a good idea to buy a high-quality one. On the other hand, renting makes more sense than buying for some tools. If you need a wet saw to cut a few tiles for a project, rent one. Buying one probably doesn't make sense unless you're going into the business. Whatever you rent, wait to rent until you're ready to use it. That way, you will not pay for time the tool is sitting idle.

ADJUSTABLE WRENCH
Use an adjustable wrench to remove nuts and bolts or loosen some plumbing fittings.

CARPENTER'S LEVEL
Use a carpenter's level to level and plumb long sections of framing and for evaluating the condition of subfloors.

CAULKING GUN
You'll need a caulking gun for caulking joints and for applying construction adhesive in tubes.

CHALK LINE
A chalk line makes long, straight lines—essential when laying out a job.

CIRCULAR SAW
Use a circular saw to cut lumber and sheet goods as well as old flooring and underlayment when you need to remove them.

COMBINATION SQUARE
A combination square allows you to mark boards for crosscutting.

COMPASS
You'll find a compass useful when scribing the cut line for the flooring you lay next to the wall. The scribed line will follow any irregularities in the wall surface.

COPING SAW
A coping saw is necessary to correctly cut moldings at inside corners. Equipped with a carbide blade, it can cut curves in tile.

CORDLESS 18-VOLT DRILL/DRIVER
A cordless 18-volt drill/driver keeps the workplace free of extension cords. Use it for drilling holes and for driving screws.

DIAGONAL CUTTERS
You'll need diagonal cutters to cut electrical wiring when necessary. Always make sure the power to the circuit is turned off.

HACKSAW
A full-size hacksaw cuts pipes and helps in removing rusted fittings and old sections of pipe.

JIGSAW
For cutting access panels, flooring, and holes for sinks, use a jigsaw.

MITER BOX
For cutting miters in trim, you'll need either a miter box or a power mitersaw.

FRAMING SQUARE
Use a framing square to square large framing members.

HACKSAW—MINI
Use a close-work hacksaw in tight areas. Most use full-size hacksaw blades as well as shorter metal-cutting blades.

LAYOUT SQUARE
A layout square does many of the same tasks as a framing square and can serve as a guide when crosscutting with a circular saw.

NAIL SET
You'll find a nail set handy for driving finishing nails below the surface of moldings.

GROOVE-JOINT PLIERS
This tool can grip pipes and fittings or loosen connections when removing fixtures.

HOLE SAW
Use with a drill to bore big holes in wood and other materials.

MAGNETIC SLEEVE AND SCREWDRIVER BITS
Use this with your cordless drill/driver. The magnetic tip holds the screw, and the sleeve slides down over it to hold it steady for driving.

PLUMB BOB
A plumb bob hangs at the end of a line and provides a vertical reference.

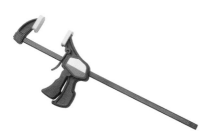

QUICK CLAMP

Quick clamps tighten with one hand—a real advantage. You'll need several sizes to hold flooring stock securely to a work surface when cutting it.

T-BEVEL

Set a T-bevel to transfer angles from one surface to another.

TORPEDO LEVEL

Use a torpedo level where a carpenter's level won't fit.

QUICK-CHANGE SLEEVE

The holder chucks into your drill or drill/driver. You can then switch quickly between twist drills and screwdriver bits.

TAPE MEASURE

A tape measure is a compact ruler made for all measuring tasks. Get a 25-foot model with a 1-inch-wide blade.

UTILITY KNIFE

A utility knife does everything from sharpening pencils to cutting drywall.

SPADE BITS

These bits bore rough holes through framing or subflooring for pipes and cables.

TOOLBOX HANDSAW

A toolbox handsaw packs a lot of cutting power into a compact size and makes quick work of cutting things down to size.

16-OUNCE FRAMING HAMMER

A 16-ounce framing hammer is essential—heavy enough to drive framing nails yet light enough for trim work. Add a 22-ounce framing hammer for heavy work.

Demolition tools

CAT'S PAW
For pulling nails nothing beats a cat's paw.

COLD CHISEL AND SMALL SLEDGE
To cut away a small section of concrete or to remove or replace ceramic tile, a small sledge and cold chisel may be all you need.

FLAT PRY BAR
A flat pry bar will disassemble most framing joints and is also handy for prying off moldings.

FLOORING SCRAPER
Use a flooring scraper to scrape up residual adhesive after removing vinyl flooring.

PUTTY KNIFE
A wide-blade stiff putty knife will come in handy for removing flooring adhesive.

RECIPROCATING SAW
A reciprocating saw cuts through studs and nails. It is useful for demolition work and floor removal.

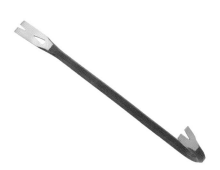

RIPPING BAR
For heavy-duty demolition, you may need a long ripping bar.

STUD FINDER
A stud finder will locate studs in the walls. Get one that locates the stud by sensing its density, not the presence of nails.

Tools for tile

ABRASIVE STONE FILE
An abrasive stone file helps shape tiles to fit special configurations.

CARBIDE GLASS BIT
A carbide glass bit will drill small holes in tile.

CARBIDE ROD SAW
A carbide rod saw makes intricate cuts in tile.

CARBIDE SCORING TOOL
A carbide scoring tool is made especially for scoring backerboard.

GROUT BAG
Use a grout bag for filling wide (more than 1/2-inch) joints and joints between rough tile.

GROUT FLOAT AND TROWELS
Different jobs require different trowels, and filling the joints properly calls for a grout float.

HEAVY-DUTY DRILL AND MIXING PADDLE
To mix thinset mortar, use a heavy-duty drill and a mixing paddle.

MARGIN TROWEL
A margin trowel will get mortar into tight spaces and is a handy tool for scooping mortar from a bucket.

MASONRY STONE
A masonry stone removes rough or sharp edges.

NONABRASIVE PAD
A nonabrasve pad will remove stubborn grout residue.

RUBBER MALLET AND BEATER BLOCK
Use a rubber mallet and beater block to set tile in mortar.

SNAP CUTTER
A snap cutter scores and snaps tiles in straight lines.

SPONGE
You'll need a sponge to clean the grout off the surface of the tiles.

STRAIGHTEDGE
Use a metal straightedge to keep tile courses straight.

TILE NIPPERS
Use tile nippers to chip away small pieces of tile when cutting circular or unusual patterns.

WET SAW
A wet saw makes quick work when you have lots of cuts to make.

Concrete tools

BROOM
Use a stiff-bristled broom to roughen the surface of a slab.

JOINTER
A jointer cuts control joints in fresh concrete to help minimize surface cracking.

MATTOCK
A mattock will loosen clay and compacted soil, making excavation easier.

ROUND-NOSE SHOVEL
A round-nose shovel is used to excavate patio sites and to move concrete from a wheelbarrow to the site.

BULL FLOAT
With its long handle a bull float can reach across larger areas than a darby or wooden float.

MASON'S HOE
The holes in a mason's hoe are designed to let concrete flow through when mixing in a wheelbarrow.

POINTED TROWEL
Various pointed trowels are used to smooth concrete, cut it away from forms, and place small amounts in low spots on the slab.

SQUARE TROWEL
A square trowel is used to smooth concrete after using a darby.

DARBY
A steel or magnesium float imparts a smooth surface to concrete.

MASON'S LINE
Mason's line is tightly woven nylon string used for laying out concrete projects.

PORTABLE CEMENT MIXER
A portable cement mixer allows you to mix concrete closer to the site.

WOODEN DARBY
A wooden darby is a tool used to carry out the initial smoothing of concrete after pouring.

EDGER
An edger rounds off the edge of a concrete slab, making it less prone to chipping.

MASON'S WHEELBARROW
A mason's wheelbarrow is made deep enough to mix concrete with minimal spillage.

POWER TAMPER
Rent a power tamper to compact soil and gravel in a slab bed.

PREP AND DEMOLITION

TILING 1-2-3   59

Tools for wood and laminates

FLOORING NAILER
A flooring nailer sets flooring nails at just the right angle to penetrate the tongue and anchor the board to the subfloor.

INSTALLATION CLAMP
For some glued laminate installations, the rows must be pulled together with straps and clamps while the glue sets.

LONG-HANDLED ROLLER
You'll need a long-handled roller and roller pan to apply some primers and adhesives.

PULL BAR
A pull bar snugs laminate materials together in hard-to-reach places.

ROLLER PAN
Use a throwaway pan or pan liner for adhesives so you won't have to clean it.

TAPPING BLOCK
To make sure that each piece of laminate is set tightly against its neighbors, use a tapping block. It is made of a material that will withstand light hammer blows without breaking the tongue or groove of the flooring.

Safety gear

DUST MASK
Wear a dust mask or respirator to keep from inhaling airborne dust.

EAR PROTECTION
Wear ear protection when using power tools or with any activity that produces loud noises.

KNEE PADS
A pair of knee pads will save wear and tear on your knees.

LEATHER GLOVES
Leather gloves will help protect your hands from scrapes and splinters.

SAFETY GLASSES
Wear safety glasses when carrying out any activity that produces dust or flying debris.

 **BUYER'S GUIDE**

Tool	Use for	Relative price	How important
MEASURING AND LAYING OUT			
Chalk line	layout, cut lines	$	must have
China marker	marking tile cuts	$	or felt-tip or pencil
Combination square	marking tile cuts	$$	nice to have
Framing square	establishing square	$$	must have
Tape measure	measuring	$$	must have
4-foot level	establishing level, vertical	$$	can use small level
CUTTING AND SHAPING			
Abrasive stone	smoothing cut edges	$$	nice to have
Carbide (glass) bit	small holes in tile	$$	only for small holes
Carbide hole saw	large holes in tile	$$	must if hole is inside tile
Carbide-grit rod saw	curved tile cuts	$$	nice to have
Rotary grinding tool	smoothing cut edges	$$$	nice to have
Snap cutter	straight tile cuts	$$$	must, or wet saw
Spiral saw	cutting soft tile	$$$	nice to have
Tile nippers	intricate tile cuts	$$	must, or wet saw
Wet saw	straight tile cuts	$$$	nice to have
SETTING AND GROUTING			
Caulking gun	caulking joints	$	must have
Foam paintbrushes	applying sealer	$	must have
Grout bag	grouting more than ½" joints	$	must for large joints
Grout float	spreading grout	$$	must have
Margin trowel	mixing and spreading grout	$	nice to have
Mortar mixing paddle	mixing grout	$$	must have
Nonabrasive pad	removing excess grout	$	must have
Notched trowel	applying mortar	$$	must have
Round-corner sponge	removing excess grout	$	must have
½-inch drill	mixing adhesives	$$$	must have
DEMOLITION			
Bricklayer's chisel	removing tile, old adhesive	$$	nice to have
Claw hammer	striking chisels, punch	$$	must have
Cold chisel	breaking tile	$	must have
Grout saw	removing old grout	$	must have
Point punch	breaking tile	$	nice to have
SAFETY GEAR			
Ear protection	protecting ears	$	nice to have
Knee pads	protecting knees	$	nice to have
Rubber gloves	protecting hands	$	must have
Safety glasses	protecting eyes	$	must have
Respirator	protecting lungs	$$	nice to have

 WORK SMARTER

RENTING CAN BE SMART

No matter how much you love buying tools, the cost of a specialty item, such as a floor sander or power stripper, is a little extravagant for a one-time job. Still, having the right tool can often prevent a weekend of drudgery. Visit a tool rental store to see what they have that will make the job easier and safer. Make sure you get the right attachments and equipment for your task, the proper safety equipment (including respirators, safety glasses, hearing protection), and the instruction manual. Ask the rental agent to show you how to use the machine effectively and safely.

When you get home, read the manual and try out the tool so you'll be confident and at ease when the job starts.

Removing baseboard and trim

2

PREP AND DEMOLITION

If there are appliances or fixtures in the room, it's usually better to remove them before tackling the baseboards and trim. That way you'll have clear access to the baseboard. But if your room is free of such obstructions, get the trim off first.

Take the shoe molding off carefully if you plan to reuse it. Shoe molding is relatively thin and probably brittle after being installed for years, and if you don't remove it by prying right at the nail locations, you'll almost certainly split it.

To make removal easier, drive the nails deeper into the wood with a nail set. That way they don't have as much wood holding them and the shoe molding will pop off the nailheads. If you plan to reuse the shoe, number the pieces as you take them off. In most cases, moldings will only fit in their original position without cutting.

REMOVE SHOE MOLDING AND BASEBOARD
Hold up a piece of scrap to protect the baseboard and insert a wide putty knife or flat pry bar behind the shoe molding at the nail locations. Gently pry the shoe loose—but not completely, to avoid splitting it. Then move to the next nails and pry again. Pull off the shoe and repeat the process for the baseboard.

REMOVE VINYL COVE MOLDING
Push the corner of a wide-blade putty knife behind the corner of the cove molding, and holding the putty knife as flat against the wall as possible, loosen the adhesive. Don't try to pry the molding off. Push the blade until you have enough molding loose to work with, then push the putty knife along the wall, breaking the adhesive bond.

Removing a threshold

 REAL WORLD

PRY, PRY AGAIN
Removing baseboard isn't as easy as it seems. It's usually nailed top and bottom with the nails angled toward each other. More than one customer has had to buy a replacement baseboard because the old one broke. Take your time. Do most of your work with a pry bar, and pry close to the nails that are creating the problem. If you still have trouble with the board, drive the nails through the molding into the wall.

1 **CUT THE THRESHOLD**
If the threshold is screwed down, remove the screws and slide the threshold out from under the trim. If the threshold is nailed, use a handsaw or backsaw to cut through the threshold at about midway along its length. Cut all the way to the surface of the floor.

2 **PRY UP THE PIECES**
Insert the flat end of a pry bar under the pieces and pry them up. Be sure to work from the side of the room in which you'll be installing the new flooring—to avoid damaging flooring you want to keep.

Removing toilets and sinks

I n one sense, removing toilets and sinks before a flooring job might seem optional. But removal is the most practical option in almost all cases. First, the absence of the fixtures will give you more clear working room. Second, with the toilet out of the way, you'll only have to cut the flooring for the drain hole. If you don't remove the toilet, you'll have to make many more cuts. In the long run, removing the fixtures will take less time than making all the cuts in the flooring.

Before you remove the toilet, pour a quart of bleach into the tank, flush it, and let it refill. Close the supply valve and flush again, holding the handle down until the tank empties. Push the water out of the trap with a plunger and stuff the bowl with rags.

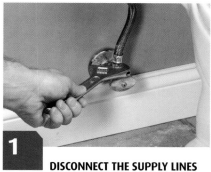

1
DISCONNECT THE SUPPLY LINES
Loosen the supply line nut with a wrench, unscrew the nut until it's completely loose from the threads, and pull the line from the valve seat.

Bolt cap

2
UNBOLT THE BOWL
Pull off the bolt caps (or pry them loose with a screwdriver) and remove the bolts with a wrench or groove-joint pliers. If the bolts spin, cut them with a hacksaw.

3
REMOVE THE TOILET
The toilet trap fits snugly over a wax ring that seals it. You'll have to break the seal by rocking the toilet body gently as you lift it. Lift the toilet off the floor and carry it to another room. Get help carrying the toilet to avoid injuring your back.

Removing a sink

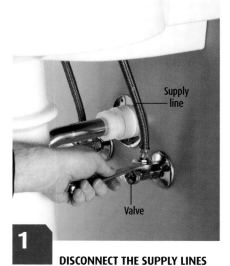

Supply line

Valve

1
DISCONNECT THE SUPPLY LINES
Shut off the hot and cold water valves, loosen the compression nuts with a wrench, and pull the supply line out of the valve.

2
DISASSEMBLE THE TRAP AND REMOVE MOUNTING BOLTS
The trap will contain a small amount of water, so set a bucket under it. Loosen the fittings on both ends of the trap with groove-joint pliers and pull the trap off the tailpiece. Dump the water in the bucket and remove the mounting bolts.

3
REMOVE THE SINK
If your sink has a pedestal, remove the bolts attaching it. Grasp the sink near the wall and pull it up off the mounting bracket. Unbolt the pedestal from the floor and lift it off.

Removing carpet

Removing glue-down carpet

Carpet glued to the floor is harder to remove than that held with tackless strips. Pulling up foam-backed carpet leaves a layer of foam stuck to the floor. To remove glued carpet, you can use a floor scraper—a tool like a wide putty knife on a long handle—or a floor stripper, a machine with a vibrating blade that peels the carpet off the subfloor much more quickly. First pull up whatever you can by hand. To use the floor stripper, start by cutting the carpet into long strips about 12 inches wide. Then cut a strip in the center of the carpet perpendicular to the long strips. Remove the center portion with the stripper, then remove the rest of the carpet piece by piece.

⊘ SAFETY ALERT

PROTECT YOUR HEARING
A floor stripper blade vibrates up to 5,000 times a minute. Put on high-quality hearing protectors while you're using the machine.

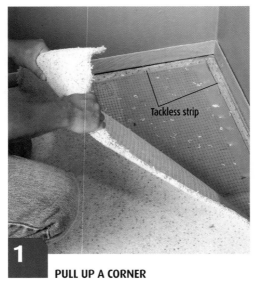

1

Tackless strip

PULL UP A CORNER
Carpet is generally held in place by tackless strips, which are nailed to the floor around the edge of the room, as shown here. To remove the carpet, first pull the corner loose by grabbing it with a pair of pliers.

2

PULL UP THE CARPET
Grab the loose corner of the carpet and pull. The carpet will begin to come loose from the rest of the tackless strips. Work your way around the wall, pulling on the carpet until it is completely free of the strips.

3

CUT AND ROLL
Once you have the carpet pulled away from the tackless strips—and if you're not going to reuse it elsewhere—cut it into strips 2 or 3 feet wide. Cut from the back of the carpet with a hook-bladed carpet knife, keeping your hands well away from the blade. Roll the strips one by one, tie them with cord, and haul them out of the room.

4

REMOVE THE PAD
When you've disposed of the carpet, pull at the padding to break it loose from its staples. Remove the staples from the floor with a pair of pliers. Make sure you've removed them all by pushing a wide putty knife or floor scraper across the floor. It will catch on any remaining staples. If the tackless strips are damaged or the new floor won't be carpet, remove the strips with a pry bar.

Removing/repairing a wood floor

1 f your existing floor is a solid wood floor and it's in good condition, you can probably lay tile right over it. The key question is whether the new floor level will be higher than the old level by more than 3/4 inch. If the new floor will be thicker than that, you may want to remove the old one. Removing the old floor will also reveal hidden faults.

Before you start tearing out old flooring, however, make sure that it's necessary. To find out whether you can install the new tile over your existing flooring, check the information at the beginning of each project. You can also ask your tile dealer or the tile manufacturer. The manufacturer's customer service telephone number is usually listed in the instructions.

Removing a hardwood floor

1

PLUNGE-CUT THE FLOOR

Set your circular saw so it cuts only through the thickness of the flooring and not into the subfloor. Starting in the center of the floor, rest the saw plate at an angle, start it, and lower it into the wood. Cut a section at least a foot wide.

2

PRY UP THE FLOORING

Tap a flat pry bar under the flooring at the nails and pry it up, working your way along each piece until you can pull it away. Be sure to push the pry bar under the board beyond the tongue or groove. Otherwise you'll simply snap off the tongue or groove and not remove the flooring.

Removing parquet

TAP AND PRY THE PARQUET LOOSE

Using a wide wood chisel (at least 1 inch), tap the blade under one edge of one parquet tile. Work a pry bar under the tile and remove it. Then continue prying the remaining tiles loose with the pry bar.

Repairing a wood floor

INSTALL A PLYWOOD PATCH

Using the same techniques shown above for removing a wood floor, make a series of plunge cuts until you have a rectangle larger than the damaged area. Remove the flooring in this area and cut a plywood patch of the same thickness and dimensions as the rectangle. Fasten the patch to the subfloor with construction adhesive and screws.

Removing vinyl sheets and tile

I f you're certain your vinyl flooring is asbestos free (see the Safety Alert below), removing it is straightforward. Usually the entire sheet is glued down to underlayment or a subfloor. Sometimes it's glued only around the edges. If you're lucky it lies flat on the floor with no adhesive at all. Whatever is there must be removed until you have a solid surface for the new floor—subfloor, concrete, or old flooring. Underlayment applied over the subfloor is usually in bad shape by the time you remove whatever was over it—take this off as well.

Start by testing your luck in the middle of the floor. Remove a section with a utility knife to see if it's glued down. If so rent a floor stripper. If the flooring pulls up freely until you reach the edge of the room, pull up what you can and scrape up the rest by hand or machine. If you lift up the sheet and don't run into any glue, cut the vinyl into manageable sections and toss it.

⊘ SAFETY ALERT

BE CAREFUL: OLD VINYL FLOORS MAY CONTAIN ASBESTOS

You can't tell just by looking whether flooring contains asbestos. If it does that doesn't mean you and your family are in danger with every step across the floor. Asbestos in old flooring is encapsulated in the material around it and isn't released into the air unless the material is damaged. Cutting through vinyl with a knife won't release asbestos fibers if done correctly. Sanding it, sawing it, scraping it, or removing it with a mechanical chipper, however, will. With an old vinyl floor, assume it contains asbestos unless you know otherwise. If possible lay the new floor right over it.

Laminate flooring and new vinyl flooring can be installed over existing vinyl that's in good condition. You can also apply a 1/4-inch underlayment over the vinyl, especially if the surface is uneven. Install carpet tile or vinyl tile over the underlayment. Ceramic tile can be laid on backerboard set over old vinyl.

Have suspect vinyl removed only as a last resort—if the vinyl is damaged, flaking, or has been pulverized in spots, for example. Hire a flooring installer who has taken the 8-hour training seminar offered by the Resilient Floor Covering Institute. (Contact information follows.) Make sure the installer is using the proper equipment, including a HEPA vacuum and a detergent that contains anionic, nonionic, and amphoteric surfactants.

If you must remove suspect vinyl, contact the Resilient Floor Covering Institute, 401 E. Jefferson St., Suite 102, Rockville, MD 20850; 301-340-8580; www.rfci.com and ask for their booklet "Recommended Work Practices for Removal of Resilient Floor Coverings." The booklet is available for downloading in pdf format at www.rfci.com/int_arf-techinfo.htm.

1

SEE WHAT'S UNDER THE FLOOR

This is where you'll find out if you have potential asbestos issues. Cut out a section in the floor with a utility knife or, better yet, pry off the metal cap in a doorway. Examine the edge of the flooring to see what's under the vinyl. Starting from the bottom, the subfloor is covered with vinyl that may or may not contain asbestos; the suspect vinyl is covered with 1/4-inch underlayment, which is, in turn, covered with the top layer of vinyl. If you suspect asbestos, hire a certified pro to remove the old flooring. If you are sure none of the layers contain asbestos, set the blade of your circular saw to the thickness of the layers and cut the flooring into 4×4-foot sections.

2

REMOVE VINYL AND UNDERLAYMENT

If the sheet vinyl is glued to an underlayment that is, in turn, nailed to the subfloor, remove the vinyl and underlayment at the same time. Put a pry bar underneath the corner of the underlayment and pry it loose. Move along both edges that form the corner, prying until you can lift off the underlayment and the vinyl on top of it. Pull up the underlayment one piece at a time. You'll encounter many nails; using a long-handled floor scraper as a pry bar may give you the leverage you need. If the underlayment was glued to the subfloor, remove both with a floor stripper.

3 USING A FLOOR STRIPPER

If the vinyl or underlayment is glued to a subfloor, try removing it with a hand scraper. First cut the floor with a utility knife into strips as wide as the scraper blade. If the floor won't come up, rent a floor stripper. With some strippers, you tilt the machine back; with others, you run the machine flat on the floor. Follow the manufacturer's directions, using a blade designed for the subfloor material. Push the stripper along between knife marks, scraping up the surface as you go.

4 CLEAN THE SUBFLOOR

Whatever is under the vinyl, whether it's adhesive or another layer of underlayment, remove it entirely. Unplug the machine and put in a new, sharp blade. Go over the entire floor again to remove the adhesive. Keep scraping until you have a clean floor. When you're finished, the floor may need some repair. If so, refer to pages 70–73.

Removing vinyl tile

1 SOFTEN THE ADHESIVE

Vinyl tile will come up much quicker if you soften the adhesive before you start scraping. Warm the adhesive with a heat gun or a hair dryer set on high heat. Start at a corner, insert a floor scraper or wide putty knife, and lift up the tile. Scrape the adhesive from the floor with a floor scraper.

2 REMOVE THE TILE

Continue softening the tiles, removing them one at a time until you have cleared the floor. If the tiles tend to tear as you remove them, keep the heat on the tile as you lift or scrape it.

3 CLEAN UP THE ADHESIVE

Once you have removed all the tile, clean the adhesive from the subfloor. Spray the floor in sections with an adhesive remover. Let the solution work according to the directions, then use a scraper to peel the residue from the floor.

Using ceramic tile as a substrate

2 PREP AND DEMOLITION

Before you start tearing out old ceramic tile for your new floor, consider that some flooring can be installed over existing ceramic floors— if the resulting increase in the height of the floor does not interfere with other elements in the room, like doors, appliances, and safety. In some cases you can apply the new material directly over the tiles. In other cases you'll have to do some prep work, but in no case is the prep work as exhausting or as messy as removing the tile. If the new floor is vinyl tile, fill any irregularities (grout joints and surface texture) that might make impressions in the new floor. If the new floor is ceramic tile or laminate, you can apply it over tile with a minimal amount of fuss.

Laminate tile over ceramic tile: easy as pie

Because laminate tile planks are a rigid material, you can install them over ceramic tile quite easily. In some cases, laminate tile can be installed directly over ceramic floors with no additional preparation. This makes it easy to replace a ceramic pattern you don't like with a laminate tile pattern that better matches the new decor of your room.

First inspect the floor carefully to make sure it contains no cracks in the tile or grout lines. Cracks might be an indication of a structural problem under the tile—make repairs if necessary. If the grout lines are deeply indented, skim-coat them with self-leveling compound, smoothing the grout lines level with the rest of the floor. That will provide solid support for any laminate joints that fall on the grout lines. Roll out any underlayment required for your laminate tile product and install the tile planks (see page 118). If your laminate flooring comes with its underlayment already attached, simply assemble the flooring and install it over the ceramic tile.

SMOOTHING CERAMIC TILE FOR SUBSTRATE
The ceramic floor must be sound, clear, dry, and dust-free. Rough up the surface by belt-sanding with a 40-grit aluminum oxide belt. Vacuum and wipe with a damp rag. Patch holes with a fast-setting patch-and-underlayment compound. Spread the compound with a straight-edged trowel to create a smooth surface. Some compounds require application of a primer first.

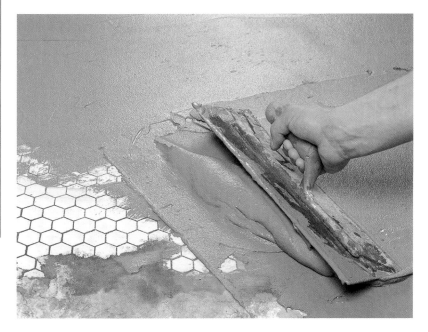

INSTALLING CERAMIC TILE OVER CERAMIC TILE
Ceramic tile can be laid directly over an existing tile floor, as long as the existing floor is sound. Clean to remove soap scum and other residue. Rinse well and let the floor dry. Then spread thinset and lay the tile.

Removing ceramic floor tiles

Ceramic floors do not come up easily. If you must remove the floor, remember that the edges of broken tiles are razor sharp. Protect yourself with long sleeves, safety glasses, and gloves. If the walls will stay as they are, protect them by leaning sheets of tempered hardboard against them.

If the tiles are set in mastic, they can be removed with a long-handled floor scraper. Older mastics could contain asbestos, however, and unless you know otherwise, always assume asbestos is present. Removing asbestos-laden mastic requires special precautions, special respirators, and other equipment. For complete guidelines, contact the Resilient Floor Covering Institute, 401 E. Jefferson St., Suite 102, Rockville, MD 20850; 301-340-7283; www.rfci.com.

Removing tiles set in thinset or mortar is a lot more work and will usually require removal of the subfloor also.

Removing tiles set in mastic

1 BREAK UP THE TILE
Break loose the grout between the tiles with a sledgehammer and cold chisel. Once the grout is loose, put the chisel against the edge of a tile and hit it with a sledgehammer to break it free. You may have to hit the tile several places to break it loose. If the tile is especially stubborn, rent an electric chipping hammer.

2 SCRAPE OFF THE TILE
If you're certain the mastic is asbestos-free, scrape away the tile fragments and mastic with a long-handled floor scraper. If the floor is rough when you're finished, level it with a patching compound.

Removing tiles set in thinset or mortar

1 CHIP OFF THE TILE
Rent an electric chipping hammer and break the tile loose from the thinset or mortar bed. Start by chipping away a grout line, then break loose a tile. Once you've removed the first tile, work your way across the floor.

> ⊘ **SAFETY ALERT**
>
> **SHARP EDGE AND DUST ALERT**
> Wear safety glasses, gloves, and long sleeves to protect yourself from the sharp edges of broken tile. Wear a dust mask when breaking up tile and mortar.

2 OPTION A: REMOVING BACKERBOARD
If the tiles were set on backerboard, cut through backerboard with a circular saw and a carbide blade. Set the saw just deep enough to cut through the backerboard (and not the subfloor) and cut it into sections. Remove the screws, pry up the backerboard, and break loose the thin layer of mortar underneath.

OPTION B: REMOVING A MORTAR BED
If the tiles were set in a thick bed of mortar, remove the subfloor along with the mortar bed. A mortar bed is thicker than a backerboard base, and the combined thickness of the floor may be more than an inch. It's a durable installation, and if the tile was set in mortar, you won't be able to salvage the subfloor. Put an old carbide blade in a circular saw and set it deep enough to cut through the mortar and subfloor but not into the joists. Pry up the sections with a pry bar. Install a new subfloor as recommended by the manufacturer.

Reinforcing a wood subfloor

PROJECT DETAILS

SKILLS: Basic carpentry
PROJECT: Inspecting and repairing an 8'×10' subfloor

TIME TO COMPLETE

EXPERIENCED: 1 hr.
HANDY: 1.5 hrs.
NOVICE: 2 hrs.

STUFF YOU'LL NEED

TOOLS: Wood shims, flooring nails, common nails, metal crossbracing, self-leveling compound and primer
MATERIALS: Hammer, nail set, level, screwdriver, drill, rectangular mixing paddle, 5-gallon bucket, circular saw, squeegee with handle, safety glasses

Almost everything that goes wrong with a subfloor shows up as a squeak. The sound you hear could be the floor flexing; it could be the floorboards or the sheets of plywood subflooring rubbing against each other. It could be the sound of the bridging pieces rubbing against each other below the floor; it could even be water pipes or air ducts squeaking as they rub against floor joists or flooring.

Most often, the root of the problem is a loose board, and the solution is a few well-placed nails. When possible, fix squeaks from underneath the floor or staircase. If the bottom of the floor is covered by a finished ceiling, work on squeaks from above. On hardwood floors, drive finishing nails into the seams between planks to silence squeaking. Check pipe hangers, heating ducts, and bridging for rubbing problems. Loosen tight pipe hangers and remove and reinstall wooden bridging members, leaving a small space between them.

Fixing a squeak

1
ONCE YOU'VE LOCATED A SQUEAK...
Stand above it and shift your weight up and down to see if the squeak is caused by a loose seam or poor support underneath. If the boards flex along the seam, look for an area where one side is higher than the other. Drive 8d flooring nails into the high side to pull it down.

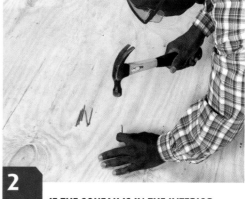

2
IF THE SQUEAK IS IN THE INTERIOR OF A SHEET...
The problem is either the subfloor or the joists that support it. Check the floor with a straightedge. If the straightedge rocks back and forth over the problem area, the subfloor has probably separated from the joists. Nail it into the nearest joists with 8d flooring or spiral-shank nails.

Water damage

Water damage caused by leaking sinks, bathtubs, and toilets is often unseen. Because leaks may continue for months or even years before they're discovered, the damage can be extensive, even if the leaks are small. Look for water damage before you install your new tile. Obvious signs include stains and perhaps plaster or drywall damage. Look for warped, rotten, or damp floors and subfloors.

If you find damage, fix the leak before making other repairs. (The leak may be some distance from the damage.) Cut out blistered or damaged subflooring with a circular saw. Set the blade so it's just deep enough to cut through the subfloor. Make the cuts down the center of the joists so that the replacement piece can rest on them.

Once you have removed the subfloor, check the joists for damage by poking them with a screwdriver. If it penetrates rotten wood, put in a shorter version of the sister joists described on the opposite page. Cut a patch out of the same material as the subfloor and nail it to the joists with 8d flooring nails, driving the nails every 3 inches.

3
IF YOU SEE A GAP BETWEEN THE STRAIGHTEDGE AND THE FLOOR...
Or if the floor is flat but still flexes downward, the floor joists have sagged. Shimming usually solves the problem. Wedge shims into the gaps between the joists and subfloor and tap them into place, driving them no farther than is needed to close the gap. Driving them too far will lift the floor and cause more squeaking.

Cleating and bridging a floor

CLEATING A FLOOR

If the flexing in the floor is limited to a small area, a cleat may solve the problem. Cut a 2×4 cleat that is 3 or 4 feet longer than the springy area and apply construction adhesive to one side. Put the side with the adhesive against the joist that supports the springy area and wedge it against the subfloor with another 2×4. Nail the cleat to the joists with 8d common nails spaced every 16 inches.

BRIDGING THE FLOOR

If the floor flexes or squeaks over a large area, it's often because the joists beneath the floor are shifting slightly as people move about above. In turn the joists are providing inadequate support to the subfloor. Nail steel bridging to the joists to stabilize the floor.

Installing sister joists

1 MEASURE AND CUT THE SISTER JOIST

If bracing fails to do the job, you may need to install a sister joist, a full-size joist of the same width and length as the problem joist. Remove any braces that are in the way and cut the sister joist to length, guiding the cut with a layout square as shown.

2 TEST-FIT THE SISTER JOIST

Often existing pipes, ductwork, and the narrow space between existing joists make it difficult to get the sister joist in place. You can take out a few extra inches by chamfering the sister joist's ends (see inset). If this fails, try cutting the board a little shorter, keeping it long enough to sit on whatever surface supports the joists. If this won't work, cut the joist in half and butt the two cut ends tightly against each other when you install them.

3 APPLY CONSTRUCTION ADHESIVE AND NAIL

Apply construction adhesive to the inner surface of the sister joist. Place the sister joist against the existing joist and nail through the sister with 8d common nails spaced every 16 inches. Drive two rows of nails, each about 1 inch from the edge of the joist. If you had to cut the sister joist to make it fit, apply a 4-foot-long cleat across the cut. Reinstall any braces you removed.

Leveling a subfloor

1   **TEST FOR HIGH AND LOW SPOTS**
Working in 4-foot sections, set a 6-foot level on the floor, then measure any low spots to determine if they exceed the manufacturer's requirements.

2   **MARK THE HIGH AND LOW SPOTS**
Wherever the floor shows high and low spots that exceed the manufacturer's specifications, mark these areas with a carpenter's pencil.

3   **PRIME THE HIGH AND LOW SPOTS**
If the leveling compound requires it, you will need to prime the areas you intend to repair. Don't overapply the primer. Let it set according to the manufacturer's instructions.

4   **SEAL OFF DOORWAYS**
If you're leveling the entire floor, nail strips of wood across doorways to keep the compound from flowing into other rooms. The strips don't have to be thick or high but should fit snugly into or across the doorway. They must fit firmly against the floor. Close openings around pipes with self-adhering weather stripping.

5   **MIX THE COMPOUND**
If you're leveling the entire floor, find out whether the brand you're using requires you to staple sheets of metal lath to the floor first (inset). Mix up the material in a 5-gallon bucket according to the directions on the bag. Have two or three buckets and always clean them out and scrub them thoroughly before mixing more compound. Compound that has set up in the bucket can make the fresh compound dry almost immediately.

6   **POUR THE COMPOUND**
If you're filling a dip, pour some compound into it, spread it with a float, and let it seek its own level. If you're leveling an entire floor, start against a wall and pour the compound over an area near the corner. Have a helper spread it with a tool called a long-handled gauge spreader, shown here. The spreader has guides that keep it slightly above the floor so that you spread the compound instead of wiping it off. Work your way across the wall, then apply in rows parallel to the first.

Repairing problems on the second floor

Problems on the second floor, or those over a finished basement, can be harder to fix than those above an unfinished basement. You can still nail down uncooperative subflooring, and you can still level the floor if you must. Cleats and crossbracing are out of the question, however, because there's a ceiling in the way.

The standards for flooring are the same on the second floor as they are on the first. Ceramic tiles installed over a springy floor are still going to crack; the joints in unglued laminate floors may work loose; floating floors are likely to develop problems; and manufacturers won't guarantee any flooring installed over a floor that doesn't meet their standards. So what do you do?

You work from above by cutting away flooring. You'll need to install sister joists, and as you'll see, doing so can turn into a major job. If you have to install more than one sister joist, consider hiring a carpenter. If you have only one joist to sister, make sure it's worth doing. Tell your flooring dealer what the problem is, ask whether it will affect installation, and ask about any alternative solutions.

1 REMOVE THE SUBFLOOR

Locate the problem and remove the subfloor above it. Walk over the floor and check it for problems as described on pages 70 and 71. If you find a problem joist, locate the joists on either side of it. Snap a chalk line down the center of these two joists and remove any nails along or within 1/4 inch of the line. Set your circular saw just deep enough to cut through the subfloor. (If you're not sure, start with a cut 1/2 inch deep and increase it by eighths until you've cut through.) Cut along the lines, guided by a straightedge you've nailed to the floor. When you reach the walls, make a crosscut between the lines, using the wall as a guide. Pry up the flooring between the cuts.

2 CUT A SISTER JOIST

Use a joist that's as thick, wide, and long as the existing joists. Once you've made the cut, drill two rows of 1/4-inch holes in the sister joist for bolts you will use to hold it in place. Space the holes 16 inches apart and 1 inch from each edge. If you drill the holes on the subfloor, protect it with pieces of scrap.

Measure the length of the problem joist and make sure you can get a 2× that long into the room.

3 DRILL THE BOLT HOLES

Put the joist in place and clamp it. Then drill holes through both joists. Remove the sister joist and apply construction adhesive to the face that adheres to the existing joist.

4 BOLT THE ASSEMBLY

Slip a washer over a 1/4-inch hex-head bolt and put the bolt in one of the holes. Slip another washer over the bolt and hand-tighten the nut until it's snug. Further tighten with a wrench. Then install bolts in the remaining holes. Replace the subflooring you cut out, cutting new pieces if necessary, and nail them in place.

📖 **WORK SMARTER**

HOLD IT RIGHT THERE, SISTER

Sister joists are used most often to shore up sagging joists—those with a bend toward the floor. Sometimes, however, a joist bows up instead of down. If this happens, have a carpenter check to see if it's caused by a structural problem. Ask what might have caused the problem, what can be done to fix it, and how much it will cost. Get the opinions and estimates of at least three carpenters before deciding what to do.

Preparing a concrete floor

PROJECT DETAILS

SKILLS: Mixing, measuring, and using a level
PROJECT: Preparing an 8'×10' floor

TIME TO COMPLETE

EXPERIENCED: Variable
HANDY: Variable
NOVICE: Variable

Variables: Prep time depends on the condition of the floor.

STUFF YOU'LL NEED

TOOLS: Duct tape, polyethylene sheeting, calcium chloride moisture test kit, self-leveling flooring compound for concrete
MATERIALS: Level, gloves, safety glasses

Preparation of concrete subfloors requires steps similar to those required for wood-floor preparation. Like wood subfloors, concrete slabs must be clean, dry, and flat. They need to be oil free, and any cracks need to be repaired. You may even have to test the pH to find out if the concrete is compatible with the flooring that will cover it.

Is the slab clean?

Concrete that is oily, dirty, or waxy is a disaster for a floor that requires any kind of adhesive, including mortar. The adhesives just won't stick to such a surface. To test for trouble, first sweep the floor clean. Then dribble some water onto the floor. If the water beads up, you'll need to clean the floor. Ask your supplier for the appropriate cleanser. Some strippers leave behind residue that weakens the adhesive you put down. Rinse the floor thoroughly once you've cleaned it to remove all traces of stripper. Then, just to be on the safe side, test it again.

Most of the tests are easy. Work in sections with a carpenter's level and mark areas that are higher or lower than the main body of the floor. A glass of water is all you need to test for oil, and most moisture tests require nothing more than a piece of plastic.

Most cracks are easy to repair, but the work can be messy. Wear gloves: The lime in concrete compounds causes extensive skin damage.

CLOSER LOOK

A SEALED DEAL
Concrete is often coated with a clear sealant to protect it and keep out moisture. Unfortunately, sealants will prevent mastics and mortars from sticking to the concrete. To test for sealer, dribble some water on the surface of the concrete. If it beads up, the surface is sealed. Depending on the sealer, you may or may not be able to remove it. Check with your flooring manufacturer for details.

Let a new concrete floor cure 3 to 4 months before installing flooring.

Leveling a concrete floor

1

TEST FOR MOISTURE

Water can wick up through concrete and damage or ruin your new floor. If you have a moisture problem, you'll need to fix it before leveling the floor. To test for moisture, tape several 2×2-foot pieces of polyethylene to the floor about 2 feet from each other. Put a light on the floor near the poly and turn it on to help create natural convection. If the concrete is dark after 72 hours or if the poly is cloudy or covered with condensation, the floor is too damp. Ask the flooring manufacturer for installation advice.

2

CHECK FOR SLOPE AND FLAT

Typically a floor should slope no more than about 1 inch in 4 feet, but again, check your manufacturer's specifications. Place a 6-foot level on the floor and lift one end until the bubble is centered in the vial. The gap between the floor and the level shows how far out of level the floor is: In this case, the floor slope is an acceptable 1/2 inch out of level over a 6-foot span. Working in sections, rotate the level across the surface and mark high and low spots.

3 POUR LEVELER

If much of the floor is marked with high and low spots or is sloped more than 1 inch every 4 feet, you may have to pour leveler across its entire surface. Nail 2×4s between the door jambs to keep the leveler from flowing into adjacent rooms. Start in the corner that is farthest from the door, always pouring the next bucket so the material flows into wet leveler.

4 FILL LOW SPOTS

If you find low spots at random locations in the floor, repair them with spot applications of self-leveling compound. Mix up a small batch of compound according to the manufacturer's directions. Pour it into the low spot and spread it with a trowel or squeegee. The compound will flow out to a feathered edge. Let the patch dry for six days before applying the new floor.

Installing a waterproof or isolation membrane

Water is the chief enemy of most building materials, including ceramic tile and other flooring materials. Water that penetrates a tile bed weakens the adhesive, promotes rot, and nourishes organisms destructive to the wood subfloor. Bathrooms, kitchens, and surfaces that require frequent cleaning are especially vulnerable. And even though many ceramic tiles and their mortars are waterproof, you can't be absolutely sure your installation is waterproof without a waterproofing membrane.

Waterproofing membranes come in several forms. There are fiber membranes and trowel-applied membranes. One of the easiest materials to install relies on an adhesive you spread with a roller.

An isolation membrane (also called a slip sheet) is a kind of bandage for cracks in concrete. It is designed to lay across a crack to allow the concrete to move without telegraphing those movements into the flooring.

ROLL ON THE ADHESIVE
Apply the adhesive with a roller, starting at a wall opposite the doorway. Work in sections. apply an even coat of adhesive on both sides of the crack. .

TOOL TIP

TO BE PRECISE...

If your flooring manufacturer has set a precise moisture requirement for your subfloor, you'll have to do a calcium chloride test. You'll need three kits (from your flooring distributor) for the first 1,000 square feet, and at least one for every additional 1,000 square feet. The kit contains a sealed container of calcium chloride and a protective plastic dome. Clean the floor of all adhesives and residue with a scraper and wire brush 24 hours prior to the test, and keep the heat and humidity at

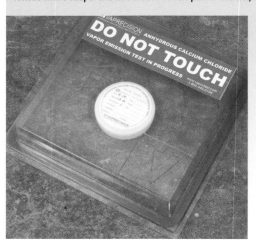

whatever levels the directions indicate. To conduct the test, you weigh the container of calcium chloride, remove the seal, and set it under the plastic dome for 60 to 72 hours. Then you'll reweigh the calcium. Based on the results, you can calculate how much moisture is present.

You'll need a scale that measures to the tenth of a gram. If you don't have such a scale, you can find one at an electronics store, scientific supply store, or on the Internet for well under $50.

Testing the pH

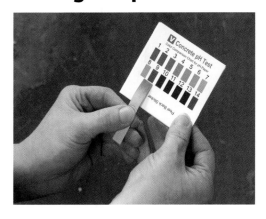

CONDUCTING THE TEST

On some jobs—especially those that involve adhesives—you need to be very careful about the acidity or alkalinity of the floor. Check manufacturer's directions to see if you need to run a pH test. If so, purchase a pH test kit from a flooring distributor. Pour a small amount of water on the floor as directed and let it sit for about a minute. Dab the litmus paper in the water. Compare the test strip to the color key to determine the pH of your floor.

Evaluating cracked concrete

All concrete floors are almost certain to crack. Some cracks, called inactive cracks, aren't getting any wider and have stabilized themselves. They are almost always caused by shrinkage in the concrete and they're no big deal. What affects your flooring installation are active cracks—those that keep widening or that create one level of concrete higher on one side of the crack than the other. Set a level across the crack. If the crack is active, you'll see a gap underneath one side of the bottom edge.

An active crack can indicate structural problems in the concrete, will defy most attempts to repair it, and will crack or pull apart any flooring installed over it.

If you have active cracks in your concrete subfloor, it's time for a consultation with a professional flooring contractor.

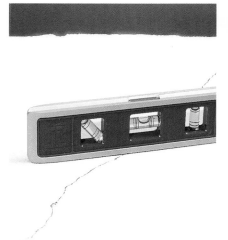

AN INACTIVE CRACK

A harmless shrinkage crack is indicated if there is no vertical displacement across the crack. This crack probably occurred during the first year as the slab dried out.

AN ACTIVE CRACK

A troublesome active crack is indicated by vertical displacement—a difference in height—across the crack. The cause is movement of the soil beneath, which will continue and damage your flooring installation.

Repairing cracked concrete

Fixing large cracks

1 KEY THE CRACK

With a hammer drill or small sledge and masonry chisel, reshape the crack so the bottom is wider than the top (called "keying the crack"). Keying helps anchor the patching material. Chisel out any weak or crumbling spots too. If the crack is deeper than $1/2$ inch, paint it with a bonding adhesive made by the company that manufactures the patching compound you'll be using. Let it dry thoroughly before applying the patch.

2 PATCH THE CRACK

On cracks up to about $1/2$ inch deep, trowel in a vinyl concrete patch. Mix according to the directions on the bag or pail, and trowel a $1/4$-inch layer into the crack. If more layers are necessary, let the patch dry according to the manufacturer's recommendations before applying a new layer. Trowel the final layer smooth and flush.

3 FILLING DEEP CRACKS

On deeper cracks, prepare some sand mix according to the directions on the bag. Trowel it into the crack, filling it flush with the surface. When the sheen dries off the surface, work the patch so it matches the rest of the concrete. If the existing surface is slightly porous, smooth the surface with a wooden float. If the existing concrete is very smooth, even out the surface with a metal finishing trowel. If the surface is covered with swirls, pull a whisk broom across the patch.

Fixing a small crack

Blow dust from the crack with a shop vac. If the crack is deep, fill it partially with sand, leaving a space about $1/4$ to $1/2$ inch deep. Squeeze some crack sealer into the opening until it forms a layer $1/4$ inch deep. Let it dry overnight, then apply another layer. Repeat until the surface is flush with the floor. Be sure not to overfill.

Installing underlayment

2

PREP AND DEMOLITION

 PROJECT DETAILS

SKILLS: Basic carpentry
PROJECT: Installing an 8'×10' sheet of underlayment

 TIME TO COMPLETE

EXPERIENCED: 15 min.
HANDY: 20 min.
NOVICE: 30 min.

STUFF YOU'LL NEED

TOOLS: Tape measure, circular saw, hammer or power nailer, safety glasses, trowel
MATERIALS: Underlayment, flooring nails, underlayment joint patch

Many floors require both a subfloor and an underlayment, and since these terms are often used interchangeably, you need to make sure of your definitions when talking to your flooring retailer. To make things even more confusing, the word "substrate" is often used as a substitute for both underlayment and subflooring.

The subfloor is structural, made of $3/4$-inch plywood or oriented strand board (OSB). It holds up the floor and provides a solid base for the underlayment and the flooring material.

Underlayment (commonly some form of $1/4$-inch plywood, but also cement board for ceramic tile floors) performs several functions: It provides a puncture-resistant base for the floor, with a smooth surface that will expand and contract very little. Whatever you use as underlayment, you'll need to leave small gaps in between sheets because plywood expands slightly as humidity rises. Some floorings require that you fill the gaps with an elastic filler; others don't.

You will want to be especially fussy about what goes underneath vinyl flooring. The vinyl conforms to underlayment defects over time, and you'll be able to see their outline in the vinyl. That's why underlayment for vinyl must be perfectly smooth. Some, but not all, lauan plywood has pigments that bleed through the vinyl, staining the floor, so be sure to inquire about the kind you need for your flooring.

Removing old underlayment

1 **CUT UNDERLAYMENT INTO SECTIONS**
Snap a grid of 2×2 chalklines (or any manageable size) on the underlayment. Set your circular saw so it cuts through the underlayment but not into the subfloor. Cut the underlayment on the lines.

2 **REMOVE THE UNDERLAYMENT**
If the underlayment is nailed to the subfloor, pry it up with a pry bar. If it's screwed down, you may be able to pop it loose with a crowbar, if the screws are not very long. Otherwise, you'll have to remove the fasteners before the underlayment sections.

Installing new underlayment

1

ACCLIMATE THE UNDERLAYMENT

Before installation your underlayment needs to reach the same temperature and relative humidity as the subfloor. If it doesn't it is liable to expand or contract once it's installed, resulting in gaps between sheets or even buckling. Bring the underlayment into the room at least three days before installing it. Stand the panels on edge and lean them against the wall.

2

INSTALL THE FIRST SHEET

Starting in a corner set the underlayment so its length is perpendicular to the joists. Trim the panels, if necessary, so the edges are offset from the edges of the subfloor panels by at least 2 inches. Nail the panel in place with uncoated 4d ringshank or spiral-shank nails. Start about $3/8$ inch from the long edge and nail every 3 inches along it. Then work your way across the panel. Drive nails on a 6-inch grid across the face of the plywood and every 3 inches along the edges. If necessary relocate individual nails to avoid nailing into the joists.

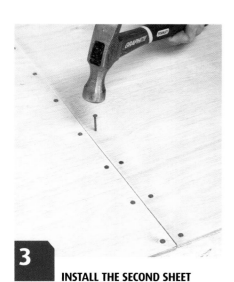

3

INSTALL THE SECOND SHEET

Put the next panel down, leaving a $1/32$-inch gap between the sheets to allow for the minor expansion that may occur. As before drive the nails every 3 inches along edges and on a 6-inch grid across the rest of the surface. Continue laying sheets in the same row, trimming the last sheet as needed.

4

OFFSET THE JOINTS

Cut the first sheet of the next row in half so the end seam is offset from the end seam of the first row. (The allowable offset may be considerably less, depending on the floor that will go above it. Always follow the manufacturer's directions.) Nail it down as before, leaving $1/32$ inch between long edges of the sheets. Continue along the row, leaving $1/32$-inch gaps between sheets. Lay the rest of the underlayment the same way, alternating between full and half sheets at the beginning of each row.

5

FILL THE SEAMS

Some manufacturers require you to fill the gaps between sheets; others direct you to leave them open. If you need to fill the gaps, use a filler made especially for underlayment, applying it following the manufacturer's directions. Fill just the gaps—don't build up and feather out the surface the way you would mud a drywall seam. Make sure the trowel leaves a smooth surface without any ridges or gaps.

Installing radiant heat

2

PREP AND DEMOLITION

 PROJECT DETAILS

SKILLS: Wiring, plumbing, masonry, and carpentry skills
PROJECT: Installing radiant heat in an 8'×10' floor

 TIME TO COMPLETE

EXPERIENCED: Variable
HANDY: Variable
NOVICE: Variable

 STUFF YOU'LL NEED

TOOLS: Crimper, scissors, stapler, right-angle drill with ½-inch chuck and bit (Forstner or similar), hammer, safety mask, safety glasses, leather gloves, tubing cutter
MATERIALS: Low-voltage underfloor mats, 14-gauge tinned copper sleeves, staples, insulation, electrician's tape, PEX tubing, aluminum plates, nails

The principle behind radiant heat is simple: Instead of blowing hot air through a vent or pumping hot water to a baseboard along the wall, radiant heat warms up the entire floor. No more huddling around the register on cold winter mornings. No matter where you stand on a radiant floor, you're always directly above the heat source.

It's an energy-efficient system: In order for you to feel warm, the system only needs to heat the floor up to about 85 degrees. Studies show that, as a result, your energy costs may be 25 to 50 percent lower.

You can heat the floor in two ways: One is through pipes embedded in or directly below the floor; the other is via electric mats, also in or below the floor.

Each has its advantages. Electric systems are thinner and, as a result, good for retrofits. Some wires are designed to double as thermostats, simplifying installation. You needn't buy a separate furnace, so the initial cost is lower and no pipes will freeze or spring leaks.

Nonetheless, hot water seems to have become the standard for larger installations. It's generally more economical to operate and uses gas, propane, oil, solar energy, or geothermal energy (a heat pump) as a heat source. Because the flow can be minutely controlled, this system provides heat in the right amount exactly when and where you need it.

While there is a good deal of work you can do yourself, a hydronic floor is no less complicated than a zoned-baseboard heat system. It requires a boiler heated by gas, oil, or electricity. It requires valves and manifolds to distribute the water, as well as sophisticated thermostats to control the heat. While an electric system may be less complicated, certain systems involve some heavy-duty wiring, and, in some cases, a new electrical panel.

If you're a hands-on person, find an installer who will work with you. Because running tubing or installing electrical elements is simple and time-consuming, it's the perfect job for a homeowner. If you're interested in saving a little money, let someone else design the system, then do the heavy lifting yourself.

 CLOSER LOOK

ABOVE OR BELOW?
You can install radiant heat systems either above or below the subfloor. Ideally, it's placed above the subfloor so the heat source is actually heating up the flooring material and not the subfloor. In a retrofit, however, this can raise the floor a couple of inches, creating problems with appliances and doors.

In an existing home installation is usually below the floor—as long as the area beneath the floor is accessible. You can install the heating elements right against the floor. With a hydronic system you'll attach aluminum plates beneath the floor to spread and store heat.

Whether the system is electric or hydronic, install insulation beneath it. If you don't, half of the heat you generate will seep away into the room below the one you're trying to heat.

Picking the right flooring

Radiant heating works great with some types of flooring, but not as well with others.

- Ceramic tile has long been a favorite candidate for radiant heat flooring. You can lay the wires or tubes in a mortar bed underneath, and the tiles themselves conduct heat quickly. Wood has been considered a problem flooring in this arena because heat dries out wood, causing cracking and creating gaps between boards. Properly installed, wood does work over a radiant heat system.
- Vinyl works well. It can be applied directly over a mortar, concrete, or gypsum base that covers the heating elements. Because it is thin, the floor heats quickly.
- Carpet may or may not work, depending on the type. Thick carpets, or those with thick pads, won't work well because they act as insulation. Heat generated by the system stays trapped in the floor.

Installing underfloor electric radiant heat

There are two basic electric radiant heat systems: low-voltage mats and high-voltage cables. Cables are usually embedded in concrete and require some electrical skills to install. Mats, however, are easy to install and wire. The wires in some double as thermostats: As the floor temperature rises, the ability of the wire to produce heat drops.

Mats made for above-the-floor installation need a layer of mortar for protection. Under-the-floor installations have to be insulated but otherwise need no protection.

Before starting an installation, check with an electrician to be sure your existing electrical system can handle the new circuit, if it needs one. As a guide, figure that you will need between 8 and 12 watts per square foot of heated floor. Make sure the floor you're installing under is radiant-heat friendly, and make sure the system is designed to account for climate and building insulation.

The system shown here is one of many available, and installation procedures will vary from manufacturer to manufacturer. The low-voltage system shown uses a wire that acts as its own thermostat. Other systems might require either a wall thermostat or one mounted directly in the floor. Always follow the manufacturer's recommendations.

Installing underfloor mats

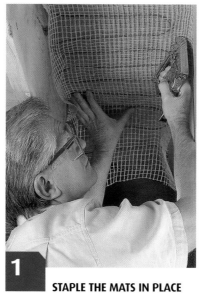

1 STAPLE THE MATS IN PLACE

Unroll the mat material and cut it to length with scissors. Strip the insulation off an end of the two wires that run the length of the mat. Turn the mat so those ends are facing the wires that will bring power to it. Have a helper hold the mats against the bottom of the subfloor while you staple them in place. Don't install the 2 feet or so of mat to which you'll be attaching wire.

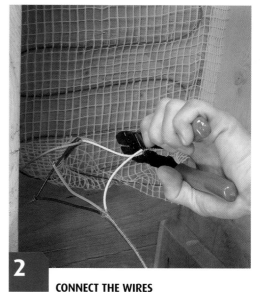

2 CONNECT THE WIRES

Crimp a black wire on one mat wire and a white wire on the other. You'll need a tinned copper sleeve for the job and a tool called a crimper. Slip the crimping sleeve over the wire at the end of the mat and put a 14-gauge stranded, tinned copper wire inside. Squeeze the crimping tool to crush the sleeve tightly over the wires. Cover the connection with electrician's tape.

Installing above the subfloor

If you can't get to the underside of a floor, install electric mats above the floor. Keep in mind that they will have to be covered by a protective layer of gypsum or concrete. Staple the mats on top of the subfloor and wire as directed.

While some manufacturers advise spreading thinset over their mats, it can be difficult to keep the floor flat and level. Have the work done by a company that pumps a self-leveling gypsum mixture over the mats. Let it dry the appropriate length of time, then cover it with flooring as if you were installing the flooring over a concrete base. In bathrooms and kitchens, you'll need to install a moisture barrier to protect the gypsum.

3 INSTALL INSULATION

Once all the mats are in place, install insulation between the joists, keeping it the recommended distance from the heating mats.

Installing an underfloor hydronic system

PEX tubing, the heart of a hydronic heating system, carries the hot water along the length and width of the floor. PEX is short for cross-linked polyethylene, a plastic that has been manufactured specifically to remain flexible and withstand heated water.

Unlike electric mats, hydronic systems aren't prepackaged. Installation, however, is fairly simple. Work in the room below the floor you're going to heat. Start at a corner of the room and run tubing to the other side between the joists. Feed it into the bay between the neighboring joists through predrilled holes. When you've snaked tubing from one side of the room to the other, hold it in place with aluminum plates stapled to the subfloor. Some companies prefabricate the plates; others require you to bend your own. It's not all that difficult, but prefab is definitely quicker.

Have a professional design the layout: PEX comes in various diameters, and you want to make sure your system is properly sized. In addition, large areas or those with small spaces between the joists may require two sets of loops under the floor.

1 **DRILL THE HOLES FOR TUBING**

Drill a hole at one end of each bay so you can feed the tubing into the neighboring bay. Plan where each hole needs to be and drill them all before installation. Drill an oversize hole, as directed by the manufacturer, using a Forstner or similar bit. Spade bits aren't durable enough for a big job like this. Space will be tight and the drill bit will have a thick shank, so use a right-angle drill with a 1/2-inch chuck.

2 **THREAD THE TUBING**

Lay a coil of PEX on the floor at one end of the first bay. Have a helper stand at the other end of the bay. Pull one end of the tubing to the helper's end and push it through the hole in the joist. While your helper pulls tubing off the coil and feeds it through the hole, pull the end back to the starting side. There, feed the tubing through the hole in the next joist. Have your helper continue to feed tubing through the first hole as you feed it through the second one. Continue until you've run tubing under the entire floor.

Above-the-floor installation

Like electric systems, you can install hydronic systems in a concrete, mortar, or gypsum bed. It's easier to install the tubing in specially made plywood with precut channels. Nail the plywood in place as you would a subfloor or underlayment. At the wall, install pieces with curved grooves that make a U-turn and send the tubing back across the room in another groove.

You can install carpeting and wood flooring directly over the plywood. Vinyl requires underlayment, and ceramic and stone floors should be set in a mortar bed or on cement backerboard.

3 **FASTEN THE DISSIPATION PLATES**

Once the tubing is in place, go back to the beginning of the job. Hold the tubing against the underside of the subfloor and put an aluminum plate over it. Staple the plate to the subfloor. Space the plates along the tubing as directed by the manufacturer. If you have multiple loops, put a piece of tape on the ends of the tubing and label which end is connected to the heat source and which returns to the heat source. Have an installer connect the valves, manifolds, and pipes required to finish the job.

Preparing vinyl floors

Some resilient flooring (linoleum, vinyl, or vinyl-asbestos sheet and tile) can be used as a substrate for new flooring if it's well adhered to the subfloor or underlayment. In most cases, however, it will require some minor preparation as shown here.

The word on resilients

Resilient flooring can serve as a base provided it is of a single layer, is not of the cushion-vinyl variety, is not cracked, and is firmly adhered. Cushioned vinyl and multiple layers are too compressible to provide adequate support, while cracks may indicate an instability, which will cause failure in the flooring material as well.

To determine the nature of the existing flooring, remove a small sample from under a refrigerator or dishwasher and take it to a flooring store for identification. The existing flooring needs to be firmly adhered and installed over exterior-grade plywood at least ⅝ inch thick. If the subfloor is inadequate, screw a layer of ½-inch, CC-plugged, exterior-grade plywood over the flooring.

You also need to determine whether the flooring contains asbestos. Don't start sanding until you are sure (see the Safety Alert, right). If subfloor and sheet flooring are OK, then remove any wax from its surface and roughen with 40-grit sandpaper. Remove the sanding dust with a damp sponge.

SAFETY ALERT

ASBESTOS TILE
Resilient flooring installed before 1986 may contain asbestos. It doesn't pose a problem until you try to remove it. Then the loose fibers can get into your lungs and cause serious health problems. Consider all other possibilities before you decide to remove old resilient flooring—you will have to have the asbestos tile removed professionally. See the Safety Alert on page 66 for additional information.

1 ROUGHEN THE SURFACE

Roughen the surface of soundly adhered, wax-free resilient flooring with 40-grit sandpaper. Be sure to wear a tightly fitting dust respirator.

2 REMOVE THE DUST

Remove the dust of sanding with a damp sponge. To test whether the adhesive will adhere, give the surface the "water-bead" test on page 74.

USING EMBOSSING LEVELER

Embossing leveler is a modified mortar product designed specifically to level out embossed patterns in vinyl flooring. With the surface levelled, well-adhered vinyl can be used as an underlayment for new vinyl without risking the old embossed pattern showing through.

Spread the leveler in a thin coat and remove the excess—all you want is to level the depressions in the surface. Work quickly—this stuff sets up fast. When it's dry go back and lightly scrape off your trowel marks to smooth the surface.

Preparing walls for tile

Preparing drywall

If the wall is in a moist location, staple 4-mil polyethylene to the wall as a moisture barrier; then cover it with ¼-inch backerboard as a base for the tile. Fasten the backerboard to the studs through the drywall. In areas where there will be no moisture, sound drywall is an adequate base for wall tile.

Small dings and scratches don't matter; they will be filled and covered with thinset mortar. Wallpaper is another matter. The moisture in the thinset will loosen the wallpaper adhesive, and the wallpaper—tile and all—may come tumbling down.

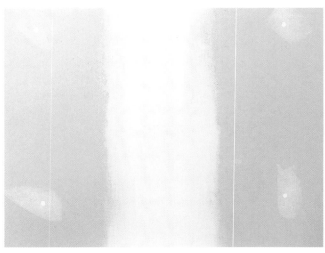

CLEAN AND TAPE
Drywall needs to be clean and solid without loose paint, wall, or wallpaper adhesive residue. If you can, hang new drywall and tape it.

REMOVE WALLPAPER
Wet (or steam) the paper and remove it with a 4- to 6-inch scraper. If the scraper is metal, round off the corners to avoid damaging the drywall. Sand off any adhesive residue with 80-grit sandpaper; then remove the dust with a clean, damp cloth.

ROUGHEN UP PAINTED WALLS
Paint must be sanded with 80-grit sandpaper in order to remove loose paint and to give the paint a "tooth" that the mortar can grip. Don't sand through the paint. Wear a dust respirator when sanding.

REMOVE THE DUST
Remove sanding dust with a clean, damp sponge. Kitchen walls are often greasy from cooking; wash them with TSP and let dry before sanding.

Repairing damaged drywall

1 **OUTLINE THE AREA**

Using a square, outline the area surrounding the hole. Score the drywall on the lines with a utility knife, then cut through the drywall with a drywall saw. Pry out the damaged area or knock it into the wall recess.

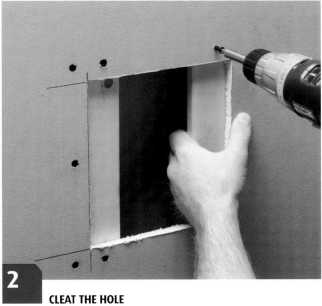

2 **CLEAT THE HOLE**

Cut a couple of 1×3 cleats about 6 inches longer than the area you're going to patch. Work a cleat into one side of the recess and cinch it to the rear of the drywall with 1-inch screws. Repeat for the other side. These cleats will keep the drywall patch from falling into the wall.

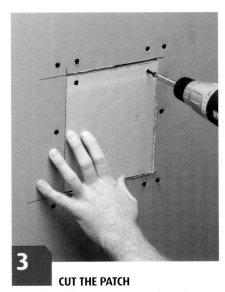

3 **CUT THE PATCH**

Cut a piece of drywall to the same dimensions as the hole you've cut. Set the patch in the recess against the cleats. Use 1-inch screws to fasten the patch to the cleats. Tape the joint around the patch with fiberglass drywall tape.

4 **MUD THE PATCH AND FINISH**

Finish the joints by applying a thin coat of drywall compound over the tape. The edges do not have to be perfectly smooth because you will cover them with thinset, but do not leave high spots of drywall compound. Sand smooth if necessary.

Find studs in the wall

One or more of your preparation activities may require you to find the location of the studs behind a finished wall. Electronic stud finders make the job easy. Get the kind that senses the presence of a stud by its density, not the presence of nails. Mark both edges of the first stud, then its center. The remaining studs should be found at 16- or 24-inch intervals. Check with the stud finder to be sure.

2

PREP AND DEMOLITION

Repairing holes in plaster

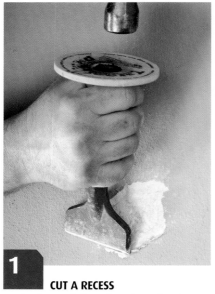

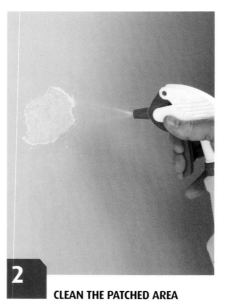

1 **CUT A RECESS**
Cut the damaged plaster from the wall with a wide cold chisel. Cut away till you reach plaster that's soundly adhered to the wall. Remove any small pieces clinging to the edge of the hole.

2 **CLEAN THE PATCHED AREA**
Clean out the recess with a brush or vacuum, then moisten the lath and exposed edges of the plaster with a spray bottle.

3 **REPAIR WITH PATCHING PLASTER**
Push patching plaster into the recess with a wide putty knife, forcing the material slightly into the lath. If the plaster is thick, apply a thin coat first, let it dry, and apply another coat. Thick patches tend to dry with cracks if applied all at once.

Removing water-damaged drywall

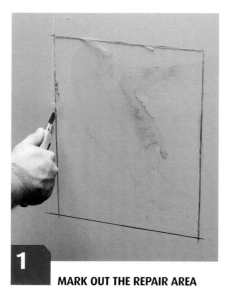

1 **MARK OUT THE REPAIR AREA**
Use a carpenter's pencil to line out the area you need to patch. Then score the line with a utility knife. Cut through the drywall with a drywall saw. Protect the area below with heavy paper.

2 **PUNCH A HOLE IN THE DRYWALL**
Punch out the damaged area with a hammer. Enlarge the hole until you can get your hand or a pry bar behind the edge of the drywall.

3 **REMOVE THE DAMAGED SECTION**
Grab an edge of the drywall and pull it off the studs or pry it away with the pry bar. To remove large sections, space your hands as far apart as possible. Then pull the nails from the studs and patch the area as shown on page 85.

Repairing large damaged areas in plaster

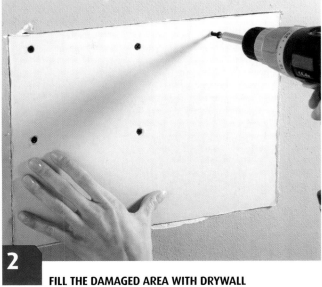
1 PREPARE THE DAMAGED AREA

Outline the area you need to repair, making sure it extends well beyond the damaged area. Score the edges of this outlined area with a utility knife. Remove the plaster with a wide cold chisel. Work in small sections; tap gently to avoid cracking the remaining wall. Measure the depth of the recess and, if necessary, attach $1/4$-inch plywood strips to the lath so a $1/4$-inch drywall patch will be flush with the surface.

2 FILL THE DAMAGED AREA WITH DRYWALL

Cut a piece of $1/4$-inch drywall to the dimensions of the cutout and apply a $1/4$-inch bead of construction adhesive to the shims or lath. Press the drywall into the area. Starting at the corners, drive 1-inch drywall screws around the perimeter of the patch. Space the remaining screws about 6 inches apart. Tape the joints with fiberglass drywall tape and spread a thin, level coat of drywall compound over the tape. Sand level when dry if needed.

Patching plaster

📖 WORK SMARTER

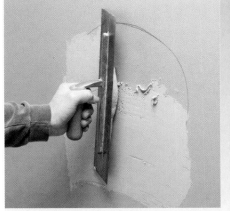

Many areas of a plaster wall will not require the extensive repair work shown elsewhere on these pages. What you will find, however, are a number of cracks. Clean out these cracks with the edge of a putty knife and dust out the crack with an old paintbrush. Moisten the crack and apply spackling compound.

Pack joint thinset into the recess with a wide putty knife or drywall knife. When you have filled the crack, draw the putty knife across the surface to smooth it.

LEVELING AND PLUMBING WALLS

Fill minor depressions with thinset. Mark the perimeter of the depressions with a carpenter's pencil and apply the thinset with a mason's trowel. When the thinset is dry, recheck the area with a level or straightedge.

You shouldn't have to fix the entire surface of an out-of-plumb wall. The slant is most noticeable at corners. Apply a skim coat of thinset along the corner to bring adjacent surfaces plumb. If the condition is severe, replace the wall before tiling.

Floors

Once the preparation is done, tiling a floor should prove to be a much more enjoyable experience. Not that it's really any easier than preparation, of course—it's just that now you can begin to see progress.

Like any other material, all tile products need to acclimate themselves to your work space, so whatever you use—ceramic tile, vinyl tile, parquet, or laminate—bring it into the room for the period specified by the manufacturer. And once you've started spreading thinset mortar, pay close attention to its working time (that's how long it takes to set up). After the time expires, you'll have to throw the batch away and mix a new one. The same goes for grout and the mastics and solvent- or water-base adhesives used to set other tile. Setting tile once required specialized skills. Today, however, it requires only that you choose a tile appropriate to the purpose and that you follow the manufacturer's directions exactly.

Chapter 3 highlights

Laying out a floor

No matter what kind of tile you're installing, layout procedures will generally be the same. The keys to success in tiling are the guide lines (called layout lines). They show you where to start laying the tile and are arranged so the tile is evenly centered in the room. Centering the tile ensures that the tiled edges are the same width around the perimeter. A tile floor that isn't centered—or that is roughly centered—looks unbalanced because the tiles at opposite walls are different widths and any irregularity in the walls is magnified.

Your on-site layout tasks will be more successful if you lay out the tile on graph paper first. That will give you an idea of where to start and how the finished installation will look.

1
FIND THE CENTER OF THE ROOM
Snap chalk lines between the midpoints of opposite walls. The center of the room is where the chalk lines cross.

CLOSER LOOK

AS EASY AS 3-4-5
When you're trying to lay out lines that are perfectly square, tools will ultimately fail you. A combination square is too small and a framing square is never perfectly reliable. To determine whether two lines are square with each other, use a 3-4-5 triangle. Mark one of the lines 3 feet from the point where the lines cross. Mark the other line 4 feet from the crossing. Measure the diagonal distance between the two marks. The lines are square if the distance between the points is exactly 5 feet. This method works with multiples of 3, 4, and 5 (6, 8, and 10, for example, or 9, 12, and 15). It works whether you're measuring in feet, inches, yards, centimeters, or any other unit.

If the measurements tell you the lines aren't square, adjust one of the lines slightly and remeasure. Repeat as needed until you get a perfect 3-4-5 triangle.

2
MEASURE FOR SQUARE
Measure and mark one layout line 3 feet from the intersection of the lines. Measure and mark the other layout line 4 feet from the intersection. If the layout lines are square, the distance between the marks will be exactly 5 feet. If not, use a pencil to sketch the diagonal on the floor for reference.

Original chalk line

3
ADJUST THE LINES IF NECESSARY
If the lines are not square (see As Easy As 3-4-5 above), moving one end of either line will fix the problem. Whichever line you choose, move the end that's closest to the pencil line you sketched on the floor. If the diagonal measured more than 5 feet in Step 2, move the end toward the 90° angle. If the distance between points was less than 5 feet, move the end away from the angle.

4

TAKE A TRIAL RUN

Lay tiles along the chalk lines in both directions without mortar but with spacers. Stop when the remaining space is smaller than a full tile.

5

READJUST THE LINES

If the space between the last full tile and the wall is less than half a tile width, move the line parallel to that wall until the tiles at both ends are of equal width, and if possible, more than half a tile wide. Repeat the process for the tiles on the other axis. Make sure the lines are still square.

6

MAKE A JURY STICK

When you actually lay the tiles in mortar, you will find it easier to set them in sections or grids. An easy way to lay out the sections with chalk lines is to make a jury stick. Lay out a section of tiles with spacers and set a length of 1× stock along an edge. Mark the jury stick at the edges of the tile.

7

MARK THE LAYOUT

Set the jury stick along the wall and mark the floor at each mark on the jury stick. Repeat at each wall, then snap chalk lines between the marks to lay out the grid.

Small room

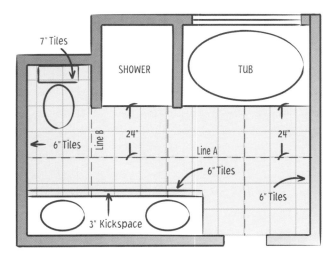

7" Tiles

SHOWER

TUB

6" Tiles

Line B

24"

Line A

24"

6" Tiles

6" Tiles

3" Kickspace

Bathrooms are generally too small to make use of the 3-4-5 triangle to establish reference lines. Lay out a single reference line on the center of the floor on its longest dimension. Dry-lay a row of tiles along this line and adjust the placement of the line so that tiles will be the same size at the edges on both sides of it. Snap lines to indicate the placement of the center tiles and the edge tiles. Repeat the process on the other dimension.

In this small bathroom, full tiles are used at the entrance and along the tub and shower. The layout was adjusted to avoid having a 2-inch strip of tile at the end of the vanity.

Multipurpose rooms

Kitchen/dining rooms and other multipurpose rooms may require special layout techniques.

If the rooms are joined by a doorway, separate the field tiles at the doorway with a threshold. Full tiles may be installed on both sides of the doorway without visually disturbing the pattern. The joints that carry through the doorway must, of course, line up.

In the kitchen and dining room shown here, the layout accounts for cut tiles along the peninsula counter as well as the perimeter of the room. The width of the bay allows the installation of full tiles if the $1/2$-inch to $3/4$-inch gaps along the walls are covered with baseboards.

Most of the cut tiles are obscured by the cabinet toe-kick. The only place a design principle is violated is at the kitchen door, where there's a tile less than half the width.

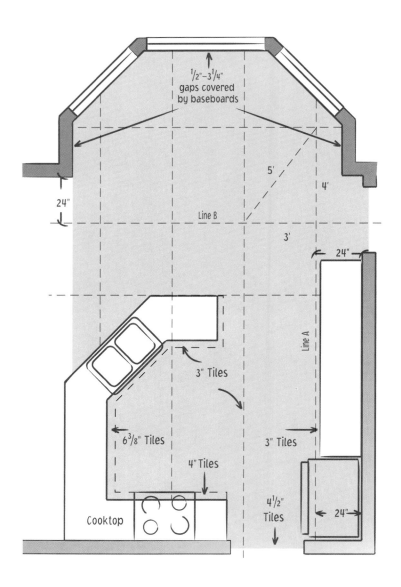

$1/2$"–$3 1/4$" gaps covered by baseboards

5'

4'

24"

Line B

3'

24"

Line A

3" Tiles

$6 3/8$" Tiles

3" Tiles

4" Tiles

$4 1/2$" Tiles

24"

Cooktop

Connected rooms

Uninterrupted joint lines are the key to laying a tile design through multiple rooms. The method is simple: Run the primary reference lines through the doorways into the adjacent rooms.

In Option A below, Line A runs vertically through the kitchen and the dining room. Using a 3-4-5 triangle, lay out reference Line B 90 degrees to Line A through both the dining room and the utility room. A second 3-4-5 triangle establishes reference Line C in the utility room. This allows full tiles to be set through the utility room doorway, which leaves 6-inch border tiles along both walls.

Option B shows a wood or marble threshold installed in the width of the wall in the doorway, allowing full tiles to start in the utility room.

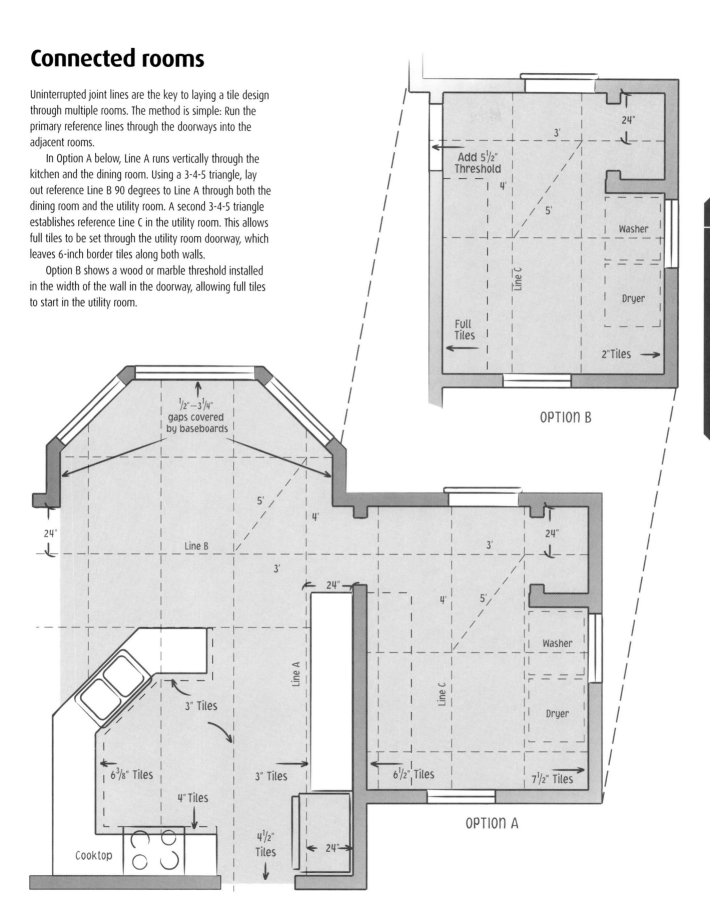

OPTION B

OPTION A

3

FLOORS

Installing backerboard

PROJECT DETAILS

SKILLS: Basic carpentry
PROJECT: Preparing an 8'×10' area

TIME TO COMPLETE

EXPERIENCED: 2 hrs.
HANDY: 2.5 hrs.
NOVICE: 3 hrs.
VARIABLES: Time includes mixing and spreading mortar, positioning sheet, cutting, screwing, and fitting around obstructions.

STUFF YOU'LL NEED

TOOLS: Tape measure, straightedge, mortar mixing paddle and ½-inch drill, trowel with ¼-inch square notches, margin trowel, drill with screwdriver bit, carbide scoring tool, carbide-tipped hole saw, dust respirator, safety glasses, knee pads
MATERIALS: Latex-modified thinset mortar, backerboard, backerboard screws, fiberglass backerboard tape

The quality of your finished ceramic tile project depends on the quality of the surface beneath it. For best results use backerboard to create a smooth and level underlayment.

To avoid cracking, tile needs a rigid bed to rest on, and backerboard is it. Backerboard, a rigid panel that creates a solid substrate for tile, is made of cement, fiber-cement, gypsum, plywood, or plastic depending on the manufacturer. Use the manufacturer's recommended thickness and application.

Backerboard and thinset mortar make the tile bed. The backerboard is set in mortar spread on the subfloor, then screwed to the subfloor. Gaps between sheets of backerboard are taped and mortared. Once this has dried, a layer of mortar is applied on top of the backerboard and the tiles are set in it.

When you buy fiberglass tape for the joints, make sure you get backerboard tape. Drywall tape can't stand up to the lime in the mortar. Backerboard screws are also a must; drywall screws will rust.

TOOL TIP

CUTTING BACKERBOARD
- The sand in mortar quickly dulls a utility knife, so use a carbide scoring tool designed for the job.
- Score the board on both sides instead of just one. If the board has a mesh surface, cut all the way through it when you score.

Tiling translated

- **Admix:** A liquid added to mortar for more strength.
- **Backerboard:** A ½- or ¼-inch-thick rigid panel sometimes reinforced with fiberglass mesh that provides a substrate for tile.
- **Latex-modified mortar:** A mortar mix with latex added to improve adhesion, increase strength, and give the mortar greater flexibility.

- **Polymer-modified mortar:** Similar to latex-modified, except that long-chain molecules (called polymers) are added.
- **Thinset:** Mortar designed for use over backerboard and applied in a thin layer. Thinset is available in several grades and with additives. Always follow the manufacturer's recommendations for use.

Cutting backerboard

1 LAY OUT THE CUT

Measure and lay out each end of the cut with a felt-tip pen or with a carbide scoring tool. Draw a line on each side of the panel. Use a straightedge to guide the carbide scoring tool along the layout line. Score several times with moderate pressure on one or both sides of the panel, depending on the manufacturer's instructions.

2 SNAP THE PANEL

After scoring, press down with your hand and knee near the score line. Lift the edge to snap the panel. Cut through the backside if you haven't yet scored it.

Drilling holes in backerboard

1 LAY OUT HOLES

Measure and lay out the center of the hole. Or, if you and a helper can manage the board fairly well, you can mark the hole with lipstick. Rub some lipstick on the stub of the pipe (or other obstruction), then carefully align the backerboard above it. Lower the backerboard gently onto the stub to make a mark where you'll need to drill. For best results, use one method and double-check it with the other.

2 DRILL THE BACKERBOARD

Drill the hole with a carbide-tipped hole saw. Drill slowly and press lightly to avoid cracking the panel. Cut only about halfway through, then turn the piece over to finish cutting the hole. (The drill bit in the center of the hole saw is longer than the cutting arm itself.) When you flip the board you'll see the hole to use as a guide to finish the cut. Wear safety glasses and a respirator to avoid inhaling crystalline silica, which is harmful to your lungs.

3 MAKING LARGE HOLES

If you need a large hole, start by laying it out on the panel. Put a 1/2-inch-diameter carbide bit in your drill and drill a series of holes as close together as possible just inside the layout line. (Instead of drilling, you can drive a screwdriver through the surface along the layout line.) When you've made all the holes, knock out the waste piece with a hammer. Wear a respirator and safety glasses.

Laying backerboard

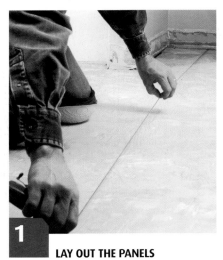

1

LAY OUT THE PANELS

Plan the layout so the backerboards span the joints in the subfloor and reinforce them. Start every other row with a half panel so the corners of panels never meet. Snap chalk lines to show where each panel will go.

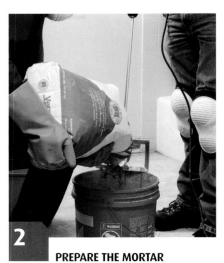

2

PREPARE THE MORTAR

Use latex-modified thinset mortar. Mortar has a working time of about 2 hours once it's mixed, so mix about half the bag following the manufacturer's directions. Start by putting the water (or the recommended liquid admix) in a large bucket and have a helper slowly pour in the mortar.

3

MIX THE MORTAR

As your helper pours in the mortar, mix it with a paddle specifically designed for mortar—don't use a paint paddle. The paddle has a lot of work to do, so the shank is $1/2$ inch in diameter, and you'll need a drill with a $1/2$-inch chuck to power it. Mix slowly to a smooth paste consistency. The mortar is properly mixed when you can form a ridge in it with a trowel. If the ridge slumps add more mortar to the mix. If it crumbles add water. Once it's mixed let it slake, or rest, for about 10 minutes, then mix again.

4

MORTAR THE SUBFLOOR

Pick the best spot to start your installation and cut a panel to fit within the layout lines, if necessary. Apply mortar within the layout lines for the panel, using a $1/4$-inch square-notched trowel. (The notches control how much mortar you apply.) Follow the backerboard manufacturer's specs when choosing a trowel. Press the mortar into the plywood with the face of the trowel, holding it at a slight angle, then start building the bed. When you've applied a bed about $3/32$ to $3/16$ inch thick (depending on the manufacturer), hold the notched edge 45 degrees to the subfloor and rake out the mortar.

5

BED THE BACKERBOARD

Put the backerboard in the mortar bed as soon as you've laid the bed. Put spacers at the walls to leave a gap between the walls and backerboard. (The size of the gap varies depending on the manufacturer.) Walk gently on the panel to set it in the mortar. If you don't put the panels into a wet mortar bed, gaps between the floor and the panels will form in some places, and the tiles will crack when you walk over the voids.

6

FASTEN THE PANEL

Fasten the panels to the floor with 1¼-inch backerboard screws. Place the screws across the face of the panel as recommended by the manufacturer and drive the heads flush with the surface. Keep screws at the perimeter of the panel ½ inch away from the edge, spacing them as recommended by the manufacturer.

7

INSTALL THE SECOND PANEL

Apply mortar within the lines for the second panel just as you applied it for the first. Put the panel in place, using spacers at the wall to leave the proper gap. Leave a ⅛-inch gap between panels using 16d nails as spacers—you'll fill the gap with mortar later to tie the panels together. Screw the panel in place.

8

LAY THE REMAINING PANELS

Work your way around the room spreading mortar, laying panels and screwing them in as you go. Continue to leave ⅛-inch gaps between panels and a ¼-inch gap at the wall. Remove the spacers once the panels are installed.

9

MORTAR THE JOINTS

When you've laid all the panels, fill the spaces between them with mortar. Smooth it on with a margin trowel, forming a 3-inch-wide band that's centered on the joint.

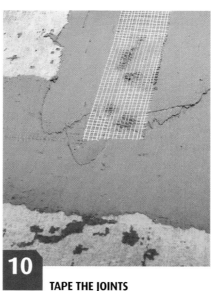

10

TAPE THE JOINTS

Put tape across all the seams and embed it firmly in the thinset.

11

MORTAR THE TAPE

Apply the mortar, then smooth it out with a trowel. You won't be able to get it flat without exposing the tape, so simply smooth the mortar with the trowel. Feather the edges. When the mortar has dried, lay out the floor, using the techniques shown on pages 90–91.

Setting ceramic tile

 Ceramic tile is the most durable flooring you can install. It stands up well to water, making it popular in kitchens, baths, and entry halls. It's also low maintenance, making it popular with all those who clean floors.

Installation is labor-intensive. Even if you don't have to install backerboard (not necessary on a slab floor or patio), there's mixing mortar, setting tile, applying grout, and sealing the tile.

Tile installers are a skilled lot, but patience is a good substitute for skill. Read the directions here carefully, then read all the directions that come with the grouts and mortars you buy. Mix them carefully, and once you're ready to go, follow your layout lines with precision.

 WORK SMARTER

AVOIDING COLOR PROBLEMS WITH GROUT
Don't assume you can just mix a colored grout and it will be consistent over the entire floor. Read the recommendations and directions on the grout bag carefully to ensure that you know the proper method of application. Avoid mottled colors and grout lines that change by:

- Mixing the powder before you add water to distribute the pigment uniformly. If you're using more than one box, mix the boxes.
- Using the same ratio of water to grout in each batch. Changing the mixture can change the color.
- Making sure the grout dries for about two hours after you buff the haze off the tile with a rag. (And remember to buff immediately.) Wipe the floor with a clean rag, lightly dampened in clean water. Immediately cover the floor with kraft paper, making sure neighboring pieces overlap. Leave the paper in place for three days. If this is impractical, spray the floor with a fine water mist several times a day for three days.

Tile flooring prep at a glance

- **Location:** On, above, or below grade.
- **Level/flat:** Within ¼ inch over 10 feet.
- **Acceptable subfloors:** Minimum of $^{19}/_{32}$-inch exterior-grade plywood on joists spaced 16 inches on center. Cover plywood with mortar and set cement-based backerboard in the mortar while still wet. Screw to subfloor with approved screws. Spread mortar over backerboard and set tiles in mortar.
- **In bathrooms and other wet locations:** Install a waterproof barrier above the backerboard.
- **Trim:** Undercut door trim before installation. Remove baseboard, shoe molding, or both.

 CLOSER LOOK

GROUT LINES
You get to decide how much space to leave between tiles. A few guidelines follow:

- **Quarry tile:** Tiles are customarily spaced ¼ inch apart.
- **Large, uniform machine-made tile:** Space the tiles ⅛ to ¼ inch apart.
- **Large handcrafted tiles, such as saltillo:** Space the tiles ½ to ¾ inch apart so their irregular edges are less noticeable and less problematic when laying the tile.
- **Marble and granite:** Butt tiles and fill chamfered edges with unsanded grout.
- **Ceramic and porcelain:** Space them ⅛ to ¼ inch apart.

BUYER'S GUIDE

MASTIC ISN'T MAGIC
Avoid mastic adhesive when installing ceramic floor tile. The best installation is a plywood subfloor covered by a cement-based backerboard that bonds with the mortar and tile to create a single strong unit.

Always buy latex- or polymer-modified grout. It forms a stronger bond and is less likely to crack.

Laying ceramic tile

1 MIX THE MORTAR

Use the latex-modified thinset mortar specified for your tile. If you're installing porcelain tile, buy mortar made specifically for porcelain. It mixes and goes on like other mortar but sticks better to porcelain's nonporous surface. Pour about three-quarters of the recommended amount of water into a plastic mixing bucket and have a helper slowly add the mortar. While the helper is pouring, mix with a mortar paddle (a paint paddle will break) driven by a ½-inch drill. Add water as you mix until the mortar has a smooth, pastelike consistency. Wear safety glasses, a dust mask, and rubber gloves to protect your skin from the mortar, which is caustic.

Test the mortar. Put some mortar on a scrap piece of plywood or on the floor and use your trowel to form a peak. If the peak holds its shape, the mortar contains the right amount of water. If the peak slumps add mortar to the mix; if it crumbles add water. Continue adding, mixing, and testing until you achieve the right consistency.

2 SPREAD THE MORTAR

Start in the center of the room and spread mortar right up to the edge of one of your layout lines. Apply the mortar first with the straight edge of the trowel, then comb it with the notched edge. Use a trowel with the notch shape and size recommended by the manufacturer—the notches control the amount of mortar on the floor. Comb the mortar into straight lines.

Water, water everywhere: Installing waterproof barriers

Although water has little effect on ceramic tile, ceramic tile doesn't necessarily stop water from leaking to the subfloor. This is OK for the floor that gets only the occasional mopping, but it can be a real problem in other places, especially around bathtubs, where water can warp the subfloor or even leak through to the ceiling below. In places that are likely to see a substantial amount of water, put a good moisture barrier beneath the floor. Choose from two ways to do it: with a waterproof sheet or with a trowel-on moisture barrier.

On walls you can use tar paper or plastic sheeting, which must be installed behind the backerboard in order to work correctly. On floors the backerboard must be mortared directly to the subfloor; consequently tar paper and plastic are out of the question. Instead a special membrane that is applied to the top of the backerboard is used. The membrane is made of a waterproof material sandwiched between layers of polyester.

It doubles as an isolation membrane, helping to prevent cracks in concrete floors from working their way into the tile. To apply install the backerboard as you normally would, then trowel on latex thinset with the recommended trowel. Unroll the membrane into the mortar. If you need more than one width of membrane, overlap the strips and glue them together with glue used for PVC. (Use the manufacturer's brand.) Roll the membrane into the mortar with a floor roller. Let the mortar dry and apply mortar and tiles on top.

Trowel-on membranes are exactly what you'd expect them to be: flexible, watertight compounds that you trowel over the subfloor. Some are premixed; others must be mixed before application. Some require two coats; others require only one. The final coat is about $1/16$ inch thick. Tile can be installed in the normal manner once the membrane has dried, which usually takes 4 to 6 hours. Follow the manufacturer's directions.

3

SET THE TILE AND CHECK THE SPREAD

Put two tiles next to each other in the mortar, with a spacer in between. Press both firmly into the mortar. Double-check the consistency of the mortar by pulling a tile up and looking at the bottom. The back of the tile should be covered with mortar. If you see only parallel mortar lines, the adhesive is too dry. If mortar squeezes up between the tiles, the bed is too thick and you need to drop the angle of the trowel as you comb. If the ridges in the adhesive have left more or less solid lines on the tile, the bed is too thin and you need to raise the angle of your trowel. If the mortar on the floor fails to stay in ridges, it is too wet.

4

SET THE FIRST TILE

Set the first tile. Comb out the area of mortar that you tested, adding more mortar if necessary. Lay the first tile at the intersection of the guidelines. Twist the tile back and forth slightly to make sure it is embedded in the adhesive. If the tiles are 12×12 inches or greater, comb the mortar into straight lines with the trowel. Then put the tile in place and move it back and forth between $1/8$ and $1/4$ inch, perpendicular to the direction in which you combed. This helps fill any voids created by an uneven back.

 WORK SMARTER

WORKING WITH SALTILLO

Because they are handmade and fired at low temperatures, saltillo tiles need extra attention. Grout can stain saltillo, so begin by sealing the face of the tiles by brushing on a commercially made tile sealer.

Saltillo is especially porous, so once the sealer has dried, soak the tile in a bucket of water to which you've added two drops of dishwashing soap. This keeps the tile from absorbing all the water from the mortar and causing it to fail. The face of the tile may turn a whitish color as a result of soaking, but this disappears once the tile is fully dry.

Saltillo tiles have irregular backs with nooks and crannies that may be difficult to fill with mortar. Back-butter the tile: Wipe a coat of mortar onto the back, creating a smooth surface to get rid of any voids between it and the backerboard. Set the tile in the mortar just as you would any other tile.

5

SET THE SECOND TILE

Set spacers next to the first tile and place the second tile alongside the first, twisting it slightly. Continue laying tiles until you have filled the layout section. Twist each tile as you set it.

6

CLEAN THE TILES

Mortar that sticks to the top of the tiles will be difficult to remove. Wipe off the face of the tiles with a damp sponge as you go. Use a sponge that's just wet enough to wipe up stray mortar but not so wet that it leaves the rest of the mortar runny.

 CLOSER LOOK

EXPANSION JOINTS

Subfloors expand and contract with changes in weather, and the movement can force tile into the wall. Avoid damage by leaving a $1/4$-inch caulked gap between the tile and the wall. If you're installing a floor that's more than 36 feet in either direction, you'll need an expansion joint in the middle as well. To make the joint, leave one of the grout lines empty. Fill the void with a foam backer rod and caulk over it with caulk that matches the grout. For quarry and cement-bodied tile, make the joint the same width as a grout joint but no narrower than $1/4$ inch. For other tiles, $1/4$ inch is preferred, but you can make the joint as narrow as $1/8$ inch.

7 BED THE TILES

As soon as you've installed three or four tiles, lay a short length of 2×4 or a beater block on top of the tile. Tap lightly with a rubber mallet to level the tiles and embed them firmly in the mortar.

8 LAY THE NEXT SECTION

After you finish the first layout section, move on to a neighboring section in the same quadrant. Spread mortar in the grid and lay the tiles. When each section is finished, move to the next. Keep laying tiles until you reach a point where the space between the tiles and walls is less than a full tile width.

9 MARK THE EDGE TILES FOR CUTS

To lay out the proper size cut quickly and without measuring, put the tile you're going to cut on top of the last full tile near the wall. Put a second tile against the wall and slide a third tile against it. Trace along the edge of the third tile to draw a line on the first tile. Once you cut it, the tile will fit perfectly in the space and leave the proper expansion gap. To avoid confusion, lay out, cut, and install one tile at time.

10 SCORE THE TILE WITH THE SNAP CUTTER

Cutting a tile on a snap cutter is a two-step process: scoring and snapping. To score the tile put it in the cutter and align the cutting wheel with the layout line. Lift the handle to bring the scoring wheel down onto the line. Push or pull the cutting wheel along the top of the tile with a single firm stroke.

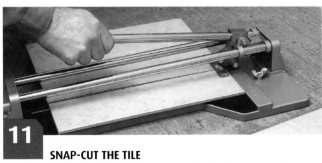

11 SNAP-CUT THE TILE

Put on a pair of safety glasses. Press down on the handle to move the cutting wheel out of the way. Press down farther to snap the tile.

12 SET THE EDGE TILES

If you haven't already done so, spread mortar between the last full tile and the wall. Put the tile in place and set it just as you set the others. Work your way along the wall, one tile at a time.

Marking cuts

1 f you're working in a room without obstructions or pipes, your tiling installation can be a breeze. But obstructions, even piping coming through the floor, doesn't need to intimidate you. You can work around obstructions with a few basic techniques. The key to a successful installation is to center the pipe in the flooring material and make a smooth cutout that will place the flooring square at the location of the pipe.

Edges are similar. In many cases, you will not have to worry about cutting the flooring at the wall to the same contour as the wall. If the gap between the flooring and the wall will not exceed 1/4 inch anywhere along its length, you can cut the edge piece straight and let the shoe molding cover the gap. If, however, the gap along the wall will at any point exceed 1/4 inch, shoe molding may not cover it. These situations call for cutting the flooring so it mirrors the contour of the wall.

Wear safety glasses when drilling.

Fitting laminate tile around pipes

1 MEASURE TO THE WALL
Cut the plank or strip so it would fit in the remaining space if the pipe weren't there. Then measure the distance from the wall (or spacer) to the center of the pipe. Mark the plank at this distance.

2 CENTER THE WIDTH
Measure the distance from the neighboring plank or strip to the center of the pipe and mark the plank at this distance. The intersection of the lines will give you a center point for drilling.

Drilling pipe holes

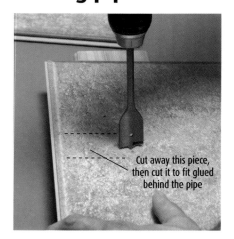

Cut away this piece, then cut it to fit glued behind the pipe

DRILL THE CUTOUT
Where the lines cross drill a hole 1/2 inch larger than the pipe diameter, drilling from the finished side of the flooring. Minimize the tearout on the reverse side by placing the flooring on a piece of scrap wood. Then finish the cutout with a coping saw and trim the cutout so you can glue it between the pipe and the wall.

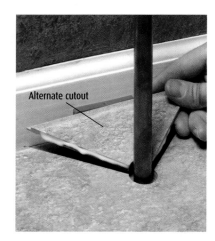

Alternate cutout

AN ALTERNATE CUTOUT
Instead of squaring the cutout, which will often leave a piece of flooring too small to work with, drill out the hole as shown in Step 3 and then cut the flooring on the diagonal as shown. This will result in a larger cutout, one that's easier to work with. Glue the edges of the cutout to the flooring.

Marking tile edge rows

1 **SET THE TRIM TILES**

When you've reached the edge of the installation and need to cut tiles to fill the remaining space, set out the tiles to be cut exactly on the last row of tiles already in place.

Tile to be cut

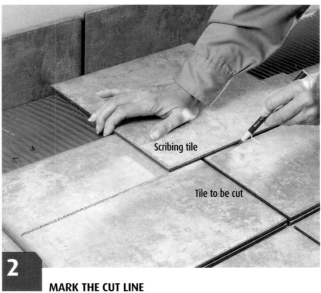

2 **MARK THE CUT LINE**

Set a full tile (a scribing tile) against the wall or against spacers if necessary (plywood or scrap tile as shown here). Taking care to not disturb the tile to be cut, draw a marker along the edge of the scribing tile. Move the scribing tile down the length of the wall and repeat the process until all the tiles are marked.

Scribing tile

Tile to be cut

Marking complex cuts

1 **MAKE A TEMPLATE OF THE CUT**

Mark the outline of the cut on a heavy paper stock or cardboard. Cut it out with scissors or a utility knife.

2 **TRACE THE CONTOUR TO THE TILE**

Trace the outline onto the edge of the tile. Apply masking tape to the edge of the tile and trace the outline onto it.

 **WORK SMARTER**

PRACTICE MAKES PERFECT

When marking a complex cut, take the time to get the pattern exactly right before you cut the tile. Transfer the pattern carefully to the tile and be sure to save the cutout in case you make a mistake and have to start over.

3

FLOORS

Cutting tile

PROJECT DETAILS

SKILLS: Using a snap cutter or wet saw, drilling, and grinding
PROJECT: Cutting floor tile for a kitchen

TIME TO COMPLETE

EXPERIENCED: 2 hrs.
HANDY: 3 hrs.
NOVICE: 4 hrs.

STUFF YOU'LL NEED

TOOLS: Snap cutter or wet saw, tile nippers, hammer, center punch (for holes), carbide hole saw, abrasive stone or rotary grinder
MATERIALS: Floor tiles

TOOL TIP

ROTARY GRINDING AND CUTTING TOOLS
High-speed rotary grinding and cutting tools are good multipurpose tools to have on hand. They come with a variety of attachments that make finishing work with stone, metal, or wood fast and easy. Wear goggles and a mask and work in a well-ventilated area.

nap cutters are great for straight cuts. They create sharp edges you must smooth on exposed edges.

A wet saw works like a tablesaw. Its circular blade cuts even the hardest tile. Wet saws can be used for straight cuts, L-cuts, and notches.

Cutting notches

Use a wet saw to make notches less than 1 inch wide by making two parallel cuts and tapping the inside piece with a hammer. Make wider notches by repeating parallel cuts about 1/4 inch apart and breaking off the interior pieces. Smooth the break with an abrasive stone or rotary grinder. Rod saws can also be used for small jobs.

Curved cuts

Curved cuts can be made three ways. Tile nippers nibble away tile in tiny bites. The smaller the bite, the less chance you will break the tile. The nippers produce a ragged edge that must be smoothed with an abrasive stone or rotary grinder. Use a wet saw to cut tightly spaced parallel cuts up to the curve and snap out the interior pieces. Rod saws have diamonds on the rod, enabling them to cut in any direction, but they are effective only for softer tiles.

Cutting holes

Make round holes in tile with a carbide hole saw. It works best in a drill press, but a 1/2-inch hand drill also can be used. In either case, clamp the tile and drill slowly to prevent breaking the tile.

Smoothing edges

Vitreous tile is as hard as glass. Cutting it with a snap cutter or with tile nippers produces a sharp edge. Unless the cut edge is hidden, it must be smoothed with an abrasive stone or a rotary grinder.

Using a snap cutter

1 **LINE UP THE CUTTING WHEEL**
Place the tile so that the cutting wheel lies on top of the cut line, then move the wheel back to the far edge of the tile. Pull the cutting wheel toward you, exerting light pressure on the handle. If the tile is thick (more than 1/4 inch), repeat to deepen the score.

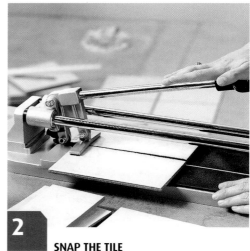

2 **SNAP THE TILE**
Lift the cutting wheel, lower the pressing tee, and strike the handle quickly to snap the tile along the scored line.

Cutting tile on a wet saw

A wet saw is a power tool that uses a water-cooled diamond blade to make quick work of cutting tile. Although you can cut tile with a snap cutter like the one shown on page 104, a wet saw better handles jobs that require lots of cutting. Wet saws usually have a sliding table that feeds the tile into an overhead blade. A pump shoots a stream of water over the blade while it's running. As you can imagine, the slurry created by the water and tile dust makes quite a mess. If possible, set up the saw outside or in a garage.

Professional-grade wet saws cost several hundred dollars, so rent instead of buying. For a few dollars more than the rental price of a professional's saw, however, you can buy a homeowner's wet saw like the one shown here.

1

ALIGN THE TILE IN THE SAW

Set the fence so that when the layout line is at the blade, the widest part of the tile is between the blade and the fence. This keeps your hands as far away as possible from the blade during the cut. Put on a pair of safety glasses, back the tile away from the blade, and turn on the saw.

2

CUT THE TILE

Holding the tile with both hands, feed it along the fence and into the blade. Push slowly, letting the saw do the work and keeping your hands away from the blade. Push the piece between the blade and fence until it completely clears the blade.

Cutting curves with a wet saw

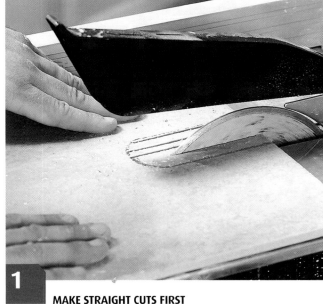

1

MAKE STRAIGHT CUTS FIRST

Outline the dimensions of the cut with a china marker. Make a series of straight cuts from the edge to the cut mark, stopping just at the curved line. Space the parallel cuts ¼ inch.

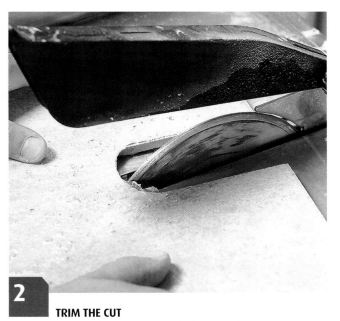

2

TRIM THE CUT

Break off the slivers, then trim the jagged edge with sideways pressure on the tip of the abrasive blade.

Cutting notches

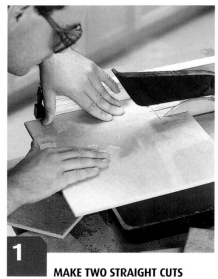

1

MAKE TWO STRAIGHT CUTS
Lay out and mark the sides and the end of the notch. Make a cut along one side of the notch. Reset the fence to make the other cut. Stop each cut when the blade reaches the line marking the end of the notch.

2

CUT AWAY THE WASTE
If the notch is wider than 1 inch, reset the fence to make a series of parallel cuts spaced about $1/4$ inch apart. Stop each cut when it reaches the line that marks the end of the notch.

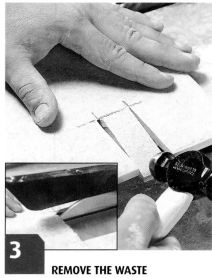

3

REMOVE THE WASTE
Break off the individual pieces between the sides of the notch. To trim the remaining jagged edge, put the tile back on the saw with the blade just touching the end of the notch. With the blade running, slide the tile sideways, keeping pressure on the tip of the blade to smooth the jagged edge. (See inset.)

Using rotary cutters and spiral saws

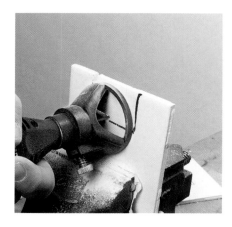

MARK THE CUT LINE
Mark the line with a china marker and guide the saw through the cut. Clamp the tile between wood strips in a vise.

USE TWO HANDS
Cutting tools tend to wander, so use both hands in intricate cuts and when you want a straight cut.

CUTTING CIRCLES
Cut circles with a spiral saw with the circle accessory. Locate the accessory's pivot at the center of the circle and swing the arc.

Cutting curves

When you're laying tile around pipes, the shortest distance between two points is a curve, no matter what your geometry teacher said.

If the pipe falls on the edge of the tile, you can cut the curve with a pair of tile nippers. If the pipe falls in the middle of the tile, you'll have to drill a hole with a carbide-tipped hole saw. Rod saws, which look like coping saws that have extra-thick blades, are great for cutting wall tile. Unfortunately they're not up to the job of cutting floor tile, which is thicker.

 TOOL TIP

WOOD SAWS WON'T CUT IT
The hole saw used to install a door lock isn't tough enough to cut through ceramic tile. You'll need a saw with carbide grit on the cutting edge. Such a saw fits in a standard 3/8-inch drill and costs just a little more than a standard hole saw of the same diameter.

Cutting curves with nippers

1 START THE CUT
Start at one end of the curve. Bite into the tile using about one-quarter of the jaw. Widen the cut by nibbling away at the tile.

2 FINISH FROM THE OTHER END
Once the cut is underway, move to the other end of the curve and make a cut. Work from both ends toward the middle until you've removed a strip of waste along the edge of the tile. Repeat the process until you've cut out all the waste.

Cutting holes

1 MARK THE CENTER
Drill bits wander on the hard, slick glaze on ceramic tiles. Prevent wandering by tapping a center punch ever so gently with a hammer to break through the glaze. This gives the bit enough purchase to start the hole.

2 DRILL THE HOLE
Drill the hole with a carbide-grit hole saw. Clamp the tile to a piece of scrap plywood. Put the center bit on the divot you made in the glaze. Drill slowly, exerting light pressure to avoid breaking the tile.

Smoothing the edges

Use an abrasive stone file or rotary grinder to smooth the edges of tiles cut with nippers or a snap cutter. Tiles cut on the wet saw are smoother and don't need grinding.

Cutting corners

Cutting outside corners

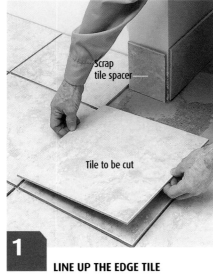

1 LINE UP THE EDGE TILE

Set the tile to be trimmed directly on top of the full tile opposite the outside corner. Set spacers (scrap tile or plywood) along the corners of the wall if necessary.

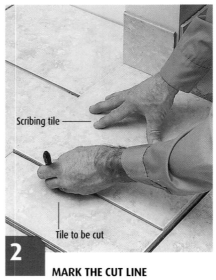

2 MARK THE CUT LINE

Put a full-size scribing tile against the scrap spacer and on top of the tile to be cut. Mark the cut line on the edge tile.

3 MARK THE CORNER

Once you've drawn the edge line, mark where the spacer tile meets the corner scrap, as shown.

4 TRANSFER THE CORNER MARK

Slide the scribing tile slightly away from the edge and transfer the corner mark to the tile you will cut.

5 MARKING THE CORNER CUT

Using a square, draw a line from the corner mark to the edge line. Cut out the corner on a wet saw, positioning the fence so the blade just removes the line. Stop when the blade reaches the corner of the cutout and finish with a carbide rod saw if necessary.

Marking inside corners

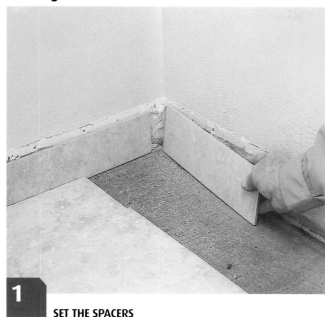

1 **SET THE SPACERS**
Set scrap tile in both sides of the corner to act as spacers. Then set the tile to be cut exactly on a tile already set in thinset.

2 **SET THE SCRIBING TILE**
Put a full-sized scribing tile against the scrap on one wall and over the tile to be cut. Trace along the edge of the scribing tile to lay out a line on the tile that you will be cutting.

3 **MARK THE OPPOSITE WALL**
Put the scribing tile against the other wall and mark the second cut line. Cut the corner on a wet saw.

Tiling doorways

UNDERCUTTING THE DOOR TRIM
In places where the flooring meets door trim, the standard practice is to cut away the bottom of the trim and install the flooring under it. Once you've installed the underlayment—building felt, rosin paper, plywood, or foam— put a piece of flooring (wood, laminate, or tile) upside down next to the trim. Set a trim saw on the flooring and use it as a guide to cut away the trim. This will create a recess into which the new flooring will fit snugly when you install it.

Installing mosaic tile

The tiny, individual tiles you often see on the floors in older homes used to be set individually. Now they are not, since the invention of mesh-backed mosaics. These are mosaic tiles mounted on a 12×12-inch mesh sheet that is laid as if it were a single tile.

This makes the job considerably easier, but you still need to take care. Make sure the entire sheet, not just some of it, is set in the adhesive. Make sure the sheets are properly aligned with their neighbors. If one sheet is a little bit crooked, every sheet after it will be equally crooked. It's also easy to install a sheet slightly higher or lower than its neighbor.

When you lay this kind of tile, some mortar will squeeze to the surface between tiles. Because you won't be able to successfully clean out the mortar, use a mortar that matches the grout. This way the color will be uniform.

1 **PREPARE AND MORTAR LAYOUT GRIDS**
Prepare the floor as you would for any tile job. Snap layout lines that divide the floor into quadrants and sections. Square the lines and make sure you have edges of equal widths.

2 **SET THE FIRST SHEET**
Spread mortar in one of the sections and set the first sheet of tile into one the corner formed by the layout lines. Press it into place with a beater block, a small rectangle that you tap with a hammer to set the tiles in the mortar.

3 **CHECK THE MORTAR SPREAD**
Lift the sheet up to see how much mortar is on the back. If parts of the back are bare, switch to a trowel with a larger notch. Recomb the mortar and reset the first sheet. Some mortar will squeeze up between the tiles; it's unavoidable. If it gets on the surface of the tiles, wipe it off with a damp sponge.

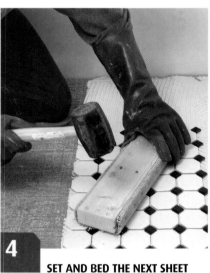

4 **SET AND BED THE NEXT SHEET**
Install the next sheet the same way. Then press on both sheets with the beater block to make sure they are flat and at the same level. Make sure the sheets are spaced properly and that gaps are equal in width.

5 **FINISH THE FIRST SECTION**
Continue across the mortar. Make sure each piece is flat, level with its neighbors, and properly aligned. When you've finished the first section of floor, lay mortar for the next. Work your way across the floor until you've covered it with tile. Grout and seal normally.

Installing a border

nstalling a border is easy and adds design interest to the floor. You can create your own border using tiles that contrast with or complement the rest of the floor, or you can buy commercially available patterned border tiles. The border need not travel along the wall. Place it several feet away to purposely emphasize one part of the room, or use it as a transition between differing tiles.

The key to borders is laying them out correctly. Never assume that the room is square and that you can simply run the border along the wall. If the room isn't square, and few are, the tiles that meet the wall will have to be cut to different sizes. This isn't obvious if they're plain tiles, but it's terribly noticeable in the case of border tiles. If the lines you draw during layout tell you you're going to have trouble, move the border away from the wall by a tile or two to hide the problem.

1 FIND THE CENTER OF THE ROOM
Snap a chalk line from the midpoint of one wall to the midpoint of the opposite wall. Repeat on the neighboring walls. The lines cross in the center of the room. Establish layout lines for the floor as explained in "Laying out a floor," page 90.

2 LAY OUT THE BORDER
With the tiles and spacers aligned along layout lines, choose a spot for the border that ends on a full grout line. Measure and snap a chalk line this distance from the layout line of this and the opposite side of the room. Repeat on the neighboring sides of the room.

3 TEST-FIT THE BORDER
Lay tiles and spacers for the border all the way around the room. Adjust as necessary. If the border is against the wall in a room that's badly out of square, the width of the border tiles will change noticeably along at least one of the walls. If the difference is objectionable, move the border at least one tile away from the wall but parallel to layout lines. Any tiles you have to trim will be in a less noticeable part of the floor.

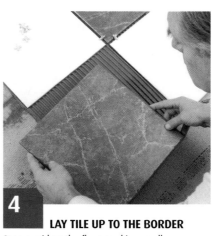

4 LAY TILE UP TO THE BORDER
Snap a grid on the floor, marking small rectangular sections that you'll lay one at a time. Trowel on mortar in a center rectangle and lay tiles in it. Working in one quadrant of the room, lay tiles across the floor until you've laid the entire quadrant inside the border. Move on to the next quadrant and repeat until you've laid all the tiles inside the border.

5 LAY THE BORDER
Trowel on mortar and lay small sections of the border. If there will be tiles between the border and the wall, install them as you go. Let the floor dry and grout and seal it.

Setting a pattern

3

FLOORS

1 TAKE A DRY RUN

Prepare the floor and install backerboard (see page 94). Then use graph paper to draw the pattern to scale, accounting for all the tiles. Use this drawing to guide you as you install the pattern. Snap layout lines that represent both the interior and exterior areas of the border and the tiles within the field. Using your drawing as a guide, dry-lay all the tiles, making sure that the layout will not produce tapered rows.

2 CUT A GUIDE BOARD

Cut a piece of ½-inch plywood to the dimensions of the interior of the border. Spread and comb thinset on the area just inside the border and across to the nearest wall. Set the plywood guide on its layout lines and arrange the border pieces in order on top of it. Set the border pieces in the thinset.

3 TEST THE INSETS

Dry-lay the centerpiece on its layout lines and dry-lay the surrounding tiles. Where there are inset cuts to make, cut cardboard templates, test fit them, and if they're right, use them to cut the tile itself.

4 CUT THE INSETS

For every diamond inset, hold the pattern tile centered on the corners of the cut tile and trace a cut line around the edges. Cut all these tiles at the same time.

5 INSTALL THE REST OF THE TILE

Pull up the plywood guide board and trowel thinset in the central area. Set the pattern in place, using your drawing as a guide. Let the mortar cure, grout and clean the tiles, and seal them if necessary.

Setting a tile base

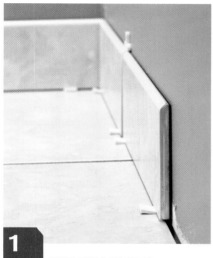

1 LEVEL THE BASE TILES
Even on out-of-level floors you'll have to install the tiles with their top edges on the same plane. Here's how. Lay the bullnose tile against the wall with spacers between them. Adjust the tile heights with plastic wedges (available at your tile supplier) until all tiles are level. Mark the wall at both ends of the line of tiles.

2 MARK THE LAYOUT LINE
Take up the tiles and snap a level chalkline between the marks you made. Mark all the walls with chalklines in a similar fashion. Mix up enough thinset to cover the area in which you'll be working. Back-butter each tile.

3 SET THE TILE
Set each tile in place, inserting spacers between them. Keep the top of the tiles level with the line using the plastic wedges. Gently remove excess mortar from the joints with a utility knife and clean the surface. Set and clean corner tiles and let the mortar cure overnight before grouting.

Setting tile corners

4 CAULK THE EDGES
Grout the trim tiles. Sponge-clean the surface at least twice and wipe off the haze with a clean rag. Caulk the joint at the floor and along the top edge of the trim. Smooth the caulk with a wet finger or sponge.

1 START AT AN OUTSIDE CORNER
Dry-set the tiles in place and mark a line to designate where the top of the tile hits the wall. Remove the tiles, spread thinset to the line, and starting with a full tile at the outside corner, reset the tiles. When you get within two tiles of the inside corner, decide whether the last tile will be less than a full tile. If it will be, cut the last two tiles larger than half but sufficient to fill the space.

2 CUT THE FOOT TO FIT
At the inside corner you will need to make an angled cut off the edge of the cove in order for it to fit against the foot of the tile on the adjacent wall.

Grouting ceramic tile

1 MIX THE GROUT

Mix the grout at slow speed in a plastic mixing bucket with a mortar paddle and a ½-inch drill. Some grouts have latex in the powder mix; others require a latex admix. If you fail to mix a required admix, the grout will eventually need to be replaced. After you've mixed the grout, let it rest, or slake, for 10 to 15 minutes, then remix.

2 SPREAD THE GROUT

Apply masking tape to protect baseboard, trim, and neighboring floors. Spread the grout with a rubber grout float. Hold the float at a shallow angle and work on three or four tiles at a time. Press the grout into the joints to fill them. For joints wider than ⅜ inch, use a grout bag (see Work Smarter on page 115).

 **WORK SMARTER**

SEAL OUT DIRT

Before you grout porous tile, unglazed tile, and stone, apply a sealer to prevent the grout from soaking into the tiles. This will prevent grout from staining the tile. Let the mortar cure for 72 hours (or as stated in the instructions) after you've installed the tile. Then apply the sealer with a new mop, brush, or sponge. Let the sealer soak into the tile for 10 to 15 minutes, then wipe off the excess. Apply a second coat. Test 2 hours later by dribbling water onto the tile. If the water soaks in, apply more sealer. If the water beads up, apply the grout.

Use nonsanded grout if the space between the tiles is less than ⅛ inch. Otherwise use sanded grout.

3 REMOVE EXCESS GROUT

Hold the float at a steep angle. Sweep it across the tiles diagonally to avoid dipping into the joints. Remove grout along the edge of the floor with a margin trowel.

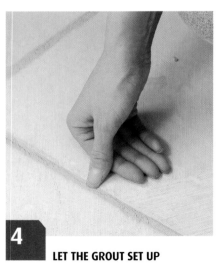

4 LET THE GROUT SET UP

Once you've removed as much grout as possible with the float, let the grout cure. Test it by pressing it with your thumbnail. When this leaves no impression, the grout is solid enough for the next step.

5 CLEAN THE TILES

Grout leaves residue on tiles. Use a damp sponge to wipe it up. Dip the sponge in clean water frequently and wring it out thoroughly before wiping up more of the residue.

6

REMOVE THE HAZE

Once the water from sponging has dried, most likely a slight haze will remain on the tiles. Buff it off with a clean, dry rag.

7

SLOW-CURE THE GROUT

Instead of drying, grout undergoes a chemical reaction called curing. A slow cure results in stronger grout. Twenty-four hours after you've applied the grout, spray it with water once or twice a day for three days to slow the cure.

8

APPLY TILE AND GROUT CLEANER

Sponge the cleaner on, then scrub the surface with a stiff brush. Rinse thoroughly and let the floor dry before applying sealer.

9

SEAL THE GROUT

Apply sealer after the grout has cured a minimum of three days. Some grouts need to cure much longer before being sealed, so follow the manufacturer's directions. Using a sponge, apply sealer to 6 to 8 square feet at a time. Wipe up the excess before it dries and move on to the neighboring tiles. Apply a bead of caulk in the gap between the tile and the wall.

 WORK SMARTER

SLING A GROUT BAG

A grout float works poorly on joints wider than ⅜ inch or on tile with irregular edges. Apply grout with a grout bag instead. The bag is like a pastry bag and has interchangeable tips. Pick one that's the same width as the joint. Fill the grout bag from the top by troweling in grout with a margin trowel. When the bag is about two-thirds full, roll up the top to close it, squeezing the rolled material firmly with one hand. Put the nozzle between the tiles and squeeze with your other hand. Smooth out the joint with the rounded end of a trowel or a similar object.

 TOOL TIP

SEALER APPLICATOR

Instead of applying grout sealer with a sponge or brush, use a sealer applicator. The applicator's wheel turns as you run it along the grout line, controlling how much sealer is applied and where it is applied, which cuts down on cleanup.

Before you grout your floor, make sure the grout won't scratch or dull the tile. See the Good Idea on page 165.

Installing stone tile

Applying stone tile is much like applying ceramic tile. Prepare the floor as you normally would (installing backerboard over a wood subfloor or applying directly to a concrete floor).

When choosing stones avoid black and green marble. They stain easily and require professional installation with epoxy-based mortars.

Other stone tiles are easier to install, but make sure you buy a mortar and an unsanded grout designed for stonework. Other mortars may show through the tile, and sanded grout may scratch the tile.

Because it is a natural product, stone tile is uneven. Using an ordinary tiling procedure, it is difficult to lay each tile at the same level. Compensating for this involves back-buttering the tile—applying mortar to the back of the tile in addition to what's already on the floor. The extra mortar provides a cushion that you can push a tile into, if necessary, to align it with its neighbors.

Stone tiles with a highly polished surface usually have a chamfer along the edge. Set them edge to edge, then fill the chamfer with grout. Set tumbled stone tiles, such as those shown here, with a wider space between tiles.

1 DUST OFF THE TILES

Stone tile often has a coat of dust on its back from the milling process. The dust keeps the stones from bonding as well as they should. Wipe off the backs with a damp cloth and let them dry.

2 SEAL THE TILES

Seal the tiles before you install them to protect them from stray mortar. Wipe on the sealer, wait 10 to 15 minutes, then wipe off the excess. Repeat. When the surface is dry, gather the tiles randomly to spread out any color variations and put them in piles or in boxes.

3 SET THE TILES

Mix the mortar and spread it one section at a time as you would for ceramic tile. To keep the surface of the floor flat, back-butter the tiles (put a coat of mortar on their backs) and put the tiles in the mortar bed.

4 **BED THE TILES**

Each time you put a tile in the adhesive, bed it with a beater block and rubber mallet. Make sure each tile is level with its neighbor, tapping with the mallet to adjust as necessary.

5 **GROUT THE TILES**

Let the mortar dry for at least 24 hours, then mix a nonsanded grout designed for use with stone. Spray the tiles with water from a spray bottle before you spread the grout to prevent the tile from absorbing all of the water from the grout. Apply and seal as you normally would.

Romancing the stone

Some tile lines come with bullnose and trim tile. Others don't. If your selection doesn't come with them, you can make your own by rounding the edges with a rubbing stone.

Hone the edge of a cut tile with a rubbing stone to duplicate the chamfered edge that comes from the factory.

Cutting stone tile

CUTTING EDGE TILES

When the mortar has set overnight, cut the edge tiles with a wet saw and lay them in a mortar bed, back-buttering each tile as you go. Measure the dimensions of each edge tile—it's unlikely they will all be the same size.

1 **CUTTING A HOLE**

Mark the outline of the hole (for an electrical outlet box, for example) with a china marker (not a felt-tip, which may bleed). Using a dry-cutting saw equipped with a diamond blade, lower the saw into the middle of the line. Work the saw forward to one end of the line, then back to the other corner.

2 **KNOCK OUT THE CENTER**

Knock out the cut piece with tile nippers and trim the corners. Don't worry if the cut line is slightly errant; it will be hidden under the wall plate.

Installing laminate tile planks

PROJECT DETAILS

SKILLS: Basic carpentry
PROJECT: Installing a laminate floor

TIME TO COMPLETE

EXPERIENCED: 3 hrs.
HANDY: 4 hrs.
NOVICE: 5 hrs.

STUFF YOU'LL NEED

TOOLS: Tape measure, level, saber saw or tablesaw, layout square, hammer, spacers, tapping block, pull bar
MATERIALS: Foam underlayment (if not already bonded to laminate flooring), laminate flooring, floor-leveling compound (if needed)

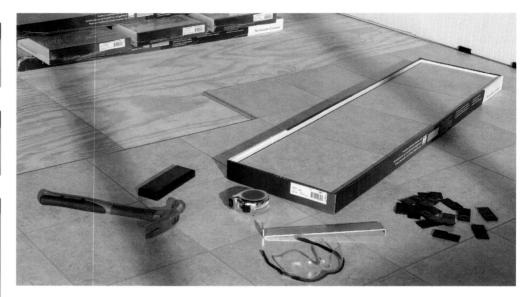

aminate flooring comes in many styles, and among the most common are planks with a ceramic tile pattern that looks like the real thing. A laminate floor is quick to put down (the planks snap together), durable, and easy to clean, and is ideal for installation over vinyl floors that may contain asbestos—you can install it without disturbing the original floor.

Because of its construction, laminate can be laid either perpendicular to or parallel to the flooring joists. For the best-looking floor, position the planks so they're parallel to the main light source. If light enters the room through a window on the north wall, for example, run the planks from north to south. If the window is on the east wall, run the planks from east to west. In narrow spaces, run the planks parallel to the long wall—in a hallway, for instance, run the planks the length of the hall.

WORK SMARTER

CUTTING LAMINATE FLOORING
Laminate chips when it is cut. To minimize chipping when cutting with a saber saw, use a laminate blade with the teeth pointing down and cut with the good side of the tile facing up. On a tablesaw or chop saw, cut the plank face up, causing the chipping to occur on the bottom of the plank.

Laminate prep at a glance

- **Location:** Use above or below grade. Glued planks are generally approved for use in full baths; snap-together planks are not. Seal edges of floor with caulk or sealant if used in bath. Seal edges of floor if likely to get wet in kitchen. Never install over any floor that has a drain or sump pump.
- **Crawlspaces:** Cover ground or underside of joists with 6-mil plastic.
- **Subfloor:** Fill any depressions greater than 3/16-inch. Floor must be level within 1 inch over 6 feet.
- **Concrete:** Tape plastic to surface for 72 hours. If dry, cover with 6-mil vapor barrier. If wet, contact manufacturer for advice.
- **Other subfloors:** All subfloors are acceptable except carpet. Wood and parquet flooring installed over concrete must be removed before installation.
- **Prep:** Remove baseboard and replace after installing floor. Undercut door trim so floor will fit underneath it. Acclimate boards at least 48 hours before installation.

Membranes and underlayments

Foam underlayment

Vapor barrier

When installing a laminate product on a concrete slab, you must provide a 6-mil plastic vapor barrier to keep moisture from wicking up into the laminate. (See "Laminate Prep at a Glance"). In addition, although some laminates come with their foam underlayment already adhered to the plank, others don't. If your laminate product requires a separate underalyment, roll it out before installing the flooring.

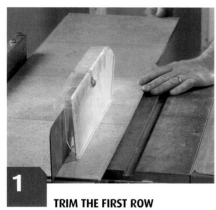

1 TRIM THE FIRST ROW

Divide the width of the room by the width of the plank. Add the remainder to the width of a plank and divide again by two. This is the width of your first and last rows. Cutting from the tongued edge, trim the planks for the first row to this width. Even if your computations resulted in planks you don't have to cut, trim the tongue from the first row.

First row
First plank of second row

2 INSTALL THE FIRST ROWS

Working a few feet away from the wall, snap the ends of the planks together to make the first row. When you no longer have space for a full plank, center the row between the walls, leaving equal spaces at each end. Cut and install plank sections to fit the end spaces. Snap the first plank of the second row as shown, offsetting it according to the manufacturer's directions.

3 SNAPPING THE ENDS

Snap the next plank in the second row into the end of the previous one, leaving a slight gap between the long sides.

4 SNAPPING THE SIDES

Kneel on the first row and lift the front side of the last plank about 1 inch off the floor. Pull the plank towards you and down, snapping the long sides of the planks together. Repeat until the second row is complete. Then assemble the third row.

5 FINISH THE FLOOR

Turn around and push the assembled three rows against spacers on the wall. Continue assembling the rest of the rows, offsetting the first plank in each row according to the manufacturer's directions, snapping the ends of the planks, then the sides. If you see a gap anywhere along the edges, close it by tapping the edge with a hammer and tapping block.

Scrap plank

Last row laid

Final row of planks

6 TRIM THE FINAL ROW

To trim the final row so its edge follows the contour of the wall, assemble a complete row of planks and line it up exactly on top of the last row laid. Set a piece of scrap plank against the wall and hold a spacer against the other edge. Hold a pencil against the spacer, and pull it and the spacer to mark the final row, moving the scrap as you go. The line will follow the contour of the wall. Number the order of the planks in the final row, disassemble them, and trim them on the pencil line. Then reassemble the final row in the numbered order.

 CLOSER LOOK

USING A PULL BAR

When you get to the last plank in a row, put a spacer against the wall, and cut a plank to fit the space. Put the plank in place, then snap it into the end groove, as shown, using a hammer and pull bar (made by the manufacturer). Slide the assembled rows against the starting wall. Snap the long sides together with a tapping block.

3

FLOORS

Installing parquet tile

PROJECT DETAILS

SKILLS: Basic carpentry
PROJECT: Installing an 8'×10' parquet floor

TIME TO COMPLETE

EXPERIENCED: 4 hrs.
HANDY: 6 hrs.
NOVICE: 8 hrs.

STUFF YOU'LL NEED

TOOLS: Tape measure, chalk line, jigsaw, notched trowel, rubber gloves, safety glasses, pencil, floor roller
MATERIALS: Parquet tiles, flooring adhesive

3

FLOORS

▲ **Parquet comes in preassembled tiles that simplify the installation of complicated-looking patterns.**

Parquet is wooden tile made of narrow strips glued together to form a pattern. The most common pattern is a series of squares made of strips that change direction from square to square. Specialty dealers sell elaborate patterns, which cost more but are no more difficult to install than the squares.

Parquet tile can be laid in either of two ways: The first method is to lay out guidelines and start at the middle of the room. The other method is to start near a wall and lay the tile in rows. Both attempt to solve the same problem:

Because parquet tile is made of dozens of pieces of wood, the size varies from tile to tile. Nestling each tile into a corner created by two other tiles helps compensate for this, as does carefully laying out lines.

Procedures for laying out guidelines and starting at the center are shown on pages 90–93. The row method, shown opposite, is recommended by some manufacturers because it's easier to achieve a square layout and involves less cutting at the walls.

Parquet floor prep at a glance

- **Storage:** Acclimate the tiles by storing them in the room where they will be installed. The room should be between 60 and 75 degrees and 35 to 55 percent humidity for two weeks prior to installation. If the surface is a concrete slab, create a 4-inch air space between the boxes of tile and the floor.
- **Location:** On or above grade only. Not for use with full baths. Crawlspace must be at least 24 inches above ground. Ground must be covered with 6–8 mil black polyethylene sheeting. Overlap seams by 6 inches and seal with tape. Crawlspaces must have vent area equal to 1.5 percent of the crawlspace area in square feet.

- **Level/flat:** Within ⅛ inch over 6 feet.
- **Moisture:** Floor must be dry or warping will occur. Check manufacturer's specifications.
- **Acceptable subfloors:** ¾-inch CDX plywood preferred. Also acceptable: ¾-inch OSB, solid wood floor, concrete, sheet vinyl, vinyl tile, cork flooring, ¾-inch wafer board or chipboard, ceramic, terrazzo, and slate marble. Some preparation required. Follow manufacturer's specifications.
- **Trim:** Undercut door trim before installation. Remove baseboard, shoe molding, or both.

Installing parquet in a perpendicular pattern

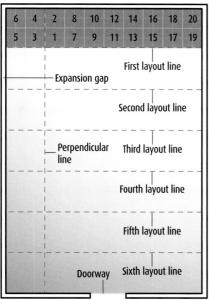

6	4	2	8	10	12	14	16	18	20
5	3	1	7	9	11	13	15	17	19

First layout line

Expansion gap

Second layout line

Perpendicular line

Third layout line

Fourth layout line

Fifth layout line

Doorway

Sixth layout line

1 SNAP LAYOUT LINES

Add the width of two tiles to the required expansion gap and snap a chalk line this distance from the wall opposite the door. Snap a second line the same distance from one of the side walls.

2 SQUARE THE LINES

Make sure the layout lines are square. Make a mark on one line 3 feet from where the lines cross. Make a mark on the second line 4 feet from where the lines cross. If the distance between the points is 5 feet, the lines are square with each other. If not, pivot one of the lines until the measurement is 5 feet.

3 SPREAD THE ADHESIVE

Spread the manufacturer's recommended adhesive between the first line you snapped and the wall. Use a notched trowel with the recommended size notches—the size and spacing of the notches controls how much adhesive is applied. Work in a well-ventilated area, opening windows and running fans as necessary.

4 LAY THE FIRST TILE

Mix tiles from several different cartons before you install any tiles. This distributes any color variations throughout the entire floor, making them less obvious. Place the first tile at the intersection of the two lines, carefully aligning it with them.

5 LAY THE REMAINING TILES

Install the second tile between the first tile and the wall. Carefully align the edge with the layout line. Push the tiles together with moderate pressure—hammers or other tools may force the tile out of position or out of square.

6 **CONTINUE TO THE WALL**

Continue until you reach the end wall. Follow the pattern shown in the illustration. Carefully align the tiles along the layout lines. If no layout line shows, nestle the tiles into the corners created by neighboring tiles.

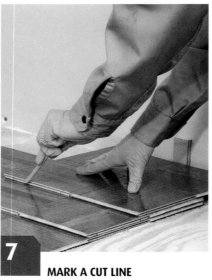

7 **MARK A CUT LINE**

When you reach the wall, trim the tile, if necessary, to leave the required expansion gap between the tile and wall. Lay out the cut by setting a tile on one of the full tiles nearest the wall. Put a spacer the size of the expansion gap against the wall, then put a full tile against it. Trace along the edge to lay out the cut.

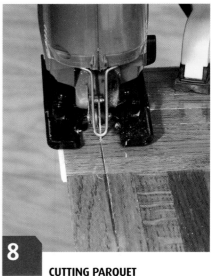

8 **CUTTING PARQUET**

Cut the tile with a jigsaw. To avoid chipping the wood, guide a knife along a straightedge to cut along the line you drew in Step 7. Cut carefully, just on the waste side of the line. In some brands of parquet, you'll find metal reinforcing bands embedded in each tile, so make the cut with a jigsaw to avoid injury.

9 **LAY OUT THE NEXT SECTION**

Snap a chalk line 24 inches away from and parallel to the first line you snapped. Lay parquet in this area, following the same pattern you used to lay tiles in the first area. Continue to lay out and install new sections of floor until you reach the wall opposite the starting wall.

10 **ROLL THE FLOOR**

You may have to roll the floor, depending on the adhesive you use. Follow the manufacturer's directions. With or without rolling, the adhesive takes time to set up, and the tiles will move if stressed too soon. Wait at least 24 hours before moving furniture into the room.

11 **INSTALL TRIM AND TRANSITIONS**

Install baseboard to cover the expansion gap between the parquet and the wall. Put the appropriate transitions between the new floor and existing flooring.

Installing parquet on a diagonal

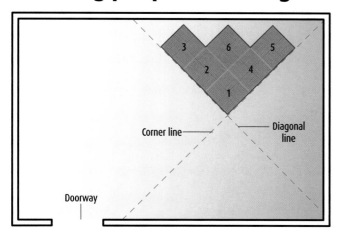

Corner line — — Diagonal line

Doorway

1 SNAP A DIAGONAL BETWEEN WALLS

Start by measuring an equal distance along two corner walls. A longer distance is better, so measure to the midpoint of the shorter wall, then measure the same distance along the longer wall. Snap a line between the two points. This will be one of the lines you follow when laying the pyramid.

2 SNAP A LINE FROM THE CORNER

To lay out the second line, find the midpoint of the first line. Snap a line from the corner, through the midpoint, to the opposite wall. Make sure the lines are square. Make a mark on one line 3 feet from where the lines cross. Make a mark on the second line 4 feet from where the lines cross. If the distance between the points is 5 feet, the lines are square with each other. If not, pivot the second line, leaving one end in the corner and sliding the other end along the wall until the measurement is 5 feet.

3 LAY THE TILES IN A STEPPED PATTERN

Spread adhesive in one of the quadrants created by the layout lines, following the manufacturer's directions. Lay the first tile at the intersection of the layout lines, aligning the edges carefully with the lines. Once the tile is in place, lay two more tiles along each of the layout lines. Lay the sixth tile between them to create a stepped pattern, as shown. Continue laying a tile along each line, then fill in the stepped pattern until you have filled the quadrant except for the tiles along the wall.

4 FINISH THE QUADRANT

Repeat, one quadrant at a time. Spread adhesive and apply tiles in the stair-step pattern. Small variations in tile size can cause the pattern to shift, and once it has, the only way to correct it is to start over. To avoid this, carefully align the tiles with the layout lines, and seat the tiles against their neighbors.

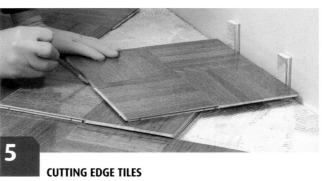

5 CUTTING EDGE TILES

Cut the edge tiles to fit. Put a full tile on top of one of the tiles in the row nearest the wall. Put $1/2$-inch spacers against the wall, and put a full tile against them as shown. Trace the edge of the second tile to mark the cut. Use a jigsaw—the metal reinforcement strips embedded in the tile make it dangerous to cut parquet with a circular saw.

Installing vinyl tile

PROJECT DETAILS

SKILLS: Measuring, cutting vinyl, and spreading adhesive
PROJECT: Installing an 8'×10' vinyl tile floor

TIME TO COMPLETE

EXPERIENCED: 2 hrs.
HANDY: 3 hrs.
NOVICE: 4 hrs.

STUFF YOU'LL NEED

TOOLS: Paint roller and tray, chalk line, tape measure, utility knife, straightedge, notched trowel (if using adhesive), floor roller
MATERIALS: Tile, adhesive

Vinyl tile is exactly like sheet vinyl, except it's smaller. Vinyl tile is made of the same materials as sheet vinyl, and you can pick a pattern that gives your room much the same look as sheet vinyl. However, with vinyl tile, you can choose different-color tiles to create borders or checkerboard patterns. You don't need a template of the room to lay tile, and you need not worry about cutting seams.

When buying tiles, you'll have to choose between self-stick tiles and tiles that you set in adhesive applied to the floor. Most ordinary tiles are self-stick, while specialty tiles are set in adhesive.

Self-stick tiles should be set on a clean subfloor that has been primed with a floor primer designed for vinyl tile. Let the primer dry thoroughly before applying tiles.

Plan the layout so tile joints fall at least 6 inches away from joints in the subfloor or underlayment.

▲ Vinyl tile is either self-stick or set in a mastic that you spread on the floor. Layout begins in the center of the room so that tiles trimmed to meet the walls will mirror those on opposite sides of the room.

Vinyl tile flooring at a glance

■ **Storage:** Remove tile from carton and store materials in the room for 48 hours before installation, keeping the room at a minimum of 65 degrees during that time, as well as during installation and for 48 hours afterward.
■ **Location:** On, above, or below grade.
■ **Level/flat:** Level is not an issue with most vinyl floors, but the floor must be flat. If installing over embossed vinyl, fill the pattern with an embossing leveler recommended by the manufacturer.
■ **Moisture:** Test for both moisture and pH to make sure the floor meets manufacturer's standards. Problems with either will prevent the floor from bonding well.
■ **Trim:** Undercut door trim before installation. Remove shoe molding.

ACCEPTABLE SUBFLOORS
■ **Wood:** Double layer of plywood with a combined thickness of at least 1 inch; or ¾-inch wood covered by ¼-inch underlayment. Leave ¹/₃₂-inch gaps between sheets of underlayment and keep the ends of the underlayment at least 6 inches from the ends of the subfloor panels. Fill all gaps, as well as the indentations left by nails, and sand smooth.
■ **Existing vinyl:** Above grade, you can apply self-stick tile over existing sheet vinyl as long as it is no more than one layer thick. Vinyl must be cleaned with the manufacturer's recommended wax-free product. Fill existing embossed vinyl with an embossing leveler.
■ **Concrete:** May be applied directly to concrete above, below, or on grade. Floor must be clean, dry, and structurally sound. Test thoroughly for moisture and pH.
■ **Ceramic tile:** May be applied over ceramic tile. Abrade the surface of the tile, fill grout lines, and level the surface by pouring a latex-modified portland cement-based underlayment over the tile.

Do not apply over chipboard, wafer board, oriented strand board, particleboard, or lauan. Floor must be absolutely smooth, as any irregularities will show through the vinyl.

3

FLOORS

Applying tiles in adhesive

🔍 CLOSER LOOK

THE SHUFFLE

Tiles come in dye lots. Colors sometimes vary from lot to lot, and frequently within the lot. To keep this from affecting the look of your floor, "shuffle" the boxes of tiles before laying them. Put the boxes near your starting point and mix their contents randomly. This way you'll spread color variations evenly throughout the floor.

THE ARROWS

Some tiles have a grain. It is virtually invisible to the naked eye, but the shade of the tile changes depending on the angle at which light hits the grain. If your tile has a grain, the arrows on the bottom of the tile tell you which way the grain runs. For a floor that has a uniform shade, lay the tiles so the arrows all point in the same direction. For a checkerboard look, turn every other tile 90 degrees. Check by making a test run before you get the glue out so that you're sure you'll like the look.

1 APPLY THE ADHESIVE

Lay out the floor in quadrants as shown on pages 90–91. Apply adhesive in one of the quadrants using the notched trowel recommended by the manufacturer. Wait about 15 minutes, and when the adhesive feels tacky but doesn't stick to your hand, set the first tile at the intersection of the chalk lines (see inset). Lay all tiles with the arrows pointing in the same direction, or turn every other tile 90 degrees, depending on the design you want to create.

2 LAY THE TILES

Put the second tile to one side of the first tile, carefully positioning it along the chalk line and tightly against the first tile. Set it exactly where you want it to go—sliding will cause adhesive to roll over the top of the tile. Install the third tile the same way along the other chalk line. Work diagonally from line to line to set tiles in the remaining adhesive, as shown above.

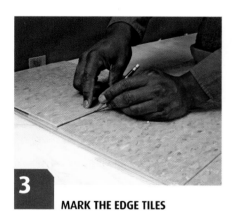

3 MARK THE EDGE TILES

You will probably need to cut the tiles against the wall to fit. To allow for expansion of the subfloor, cut the tiles to leave a ¼-inch gap at the walls. Lay out the cut by putting a ¼-inch spacer upright against the wall. Place the tile you'll cut directly over the last full tile. Place a scribing tile against the spacer and over the tile you'll cut. Mark the tile as shown and cut it with a flooring or utility knife. Lay out corner tiles the same way, putting the spacer tile against each wall in turn.

4 MARK CORNER CUTOUTS

Lay out cuts for tiles that have to fit around an outside corner with two tiles—the one you'll cut and a spacer tile. Start as if you were cutting a border tile: Put the tile you'll cut on top of the last full tile in the row. Put a scribing tile on top of that and slide it against a ¼-inch spacer at the wall. Draw a line on the tile you'll cut by tracing along the edge of the scribing tile. Lay out the other half with a straightedge. Put ¼-inch spacers against the corner wall and put a straightedge along the spacers. Draw a line along the straightedge to lay out the cut on the tile. (See inset.)

Make the cut by guiding a utility knife along the straightedge. Start the cut at what will be the corner of the cutout and work toward the edge.

5 ROLL THE FLOOR

Clean off the adhesive as soon as you have installed the tiles. Latex-base adhesive usually cleans up with soap and water, but read and follow the directions on the can. Don't soak the floor—it will ruin the glue bond. Set the tiles firmly in the adhesive by rolling the floor in both directions with a floor roller. Install baseboard, quarter-round molding, or both to cover the gap at the edge of the floor.

3

FLOORS

Applying self-stick vinyl tile

Much of the vinyl tile sold today has a peel-and-stick backing. It's a good product that makes the job of installation a little easier, which is why homeowners love it. Installing it is much like installing other vinyl tiles, except you have no adhesive. (For information on layout, see pages 90–93.) What the manufacturer's directions often fail to tell you, however, is that you need to prime the floor with a latex floor primer first. Plywood and concrete are both porous, and unlike adhesive that you trowel, the adhesive on self-stick tiles never truly dries. This seldom presents a problem as long as the floor is properly primed. The primer creates a surface to which the adhesive clings, an especially important factor when the subfloor is porous plywood or concrete.

Like other vinyl tiles, self-stick tiles vary slightly in color from batch to batch. To camouflage any shifts in color, alternate between two boxes when applying the tile. Have an empty box handy to hold the paper backing as you peel it off the tiles.

1 PREP THE FLOOR

You can apply self-stick vinyl over concrete or a ¼-inch plywood underlayment (other than lauan). If you're applying over concrete, make sure it's smooth and clean. If you're installing over any other subfloor, cover it with a ¼-inch underlayment that's smooth and clean. Space the panels ¹⁄₃₂ inch apart and stagger the seams. Fill the gaps with the material recommended by the tile manufacturer.

2 PRIME THE FLOOR

Apply the primer that the manufacturer recommends as directed. If the manufacturer doesn't recommend a primer, ask your retailer to recommend one. It's generally not a paint product, but a thinner mixture that seals the pores of the subfloor and creates a surface that the tile will stick to easily. A typical application requires two coats—a coat diluted with water, followed by a full-strength coat. Pour the primer into a roller pan and apply it with a long-handled paint roller.

3 MARK LAYOUT LINES

Snap chalk lines across the room to find the center. Check for square with a 3-4-5 triangle and move the end of one of the lines, if necessary, to bring the lines into square. Lay a trial run of tiles to gauge the size of the tiles that will meet the wall. If they will be less than half a tile wide, move the lines as needed until the tiles at the edges are the same width on both sides of the room.

4 SET THE FIRST TILE

Before you apply the first tile, flip it over and look for arrows indicating grain direction. Arrange the tiles so that all the arrows point the same way, alternate, or face in random directions (depending on the look you want). Peel off the back and put the corner of the tile at the intersection of the layout lines and the edges of the tile along the lines. When the tile is in the right spot, press it against the subfloor and press down the edges by rolling with a wallpaper roller.

5 USING A STEPPED PATTERN

Work diagonally from one layout line to the other, applying the tiles in a stepped pattern. This helps to keep the floor square: Each tile is nestled between two others. Apply as shown, filling one quadrant of the floor before going on to the next. Press down each tile once it's in place and roll the edges as before. Roll the entire floor with a floor roller when you're done.

3

FLOORS

Transitions

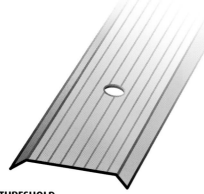

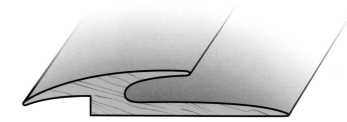

SADDLE THRESHOLD

Because vinyl is so thin, you can usually install trim made for other flooring right over it to handle any transitions. You can also install specialty moldings. A saddle threshold screws down to protect exposed edges of vinyl. Some saddle thresholds will go over concrete.

CARPET- OR WOOD-TO-VINYL MOLDING

If your vinyl floor meets a glue-down carpet, a vinyl molding like this one handles the transition. Install the molding during carpet or wood installation, then lay the tile up to it.

Vinyl cove molding

Vinyl molding is an easy-to-apply baseboard that goes up quickly in a room with no trim. It's resilient and hard to scuff, so it makes a durable molding in areas that get substantial abuse. Vinyl molding comes in strips 4 inches high and about $1/16$ inch thick. Two styles are available: one that is flat and comes in rolls, and one that has a small curve (called a cove) at the bottom. The cove molding is the better of the two because the cove sweeps out slightly from the wall to cover the expansion gap at the edge of the floor.

Installation tools are few: a utility knife, a framing square, and a caulking gun with a special tip designed for cove molding.

1 CUT TO LENGTH

Start in a corner of the room. Spread the recommended adhesive on the back of the molding using the caulking gun with a special cove-molding tip. Push the molding against the wall and press along the entire surface to attach it to the wall. If you need more than one length, butt two pieces together. If you need to cut a piece of molding, make repeated cuts across the back using a utility knife guided by a framing square.

2 CUT THE INSIDE CORNERS

Run molding into the corner on one of the walls. Carve away the cove on the other piece of molding so it nests against the first piece, then glue it in place. The technique described for outside corners in Step 3 also works on inside corners, though it may be difficult to get the molding all the way into the corner.

3 CUTTING OUTSIDE CORNERS

Put the molding in place and trace along the wall to mark where the piece will turn the corner. Bend the piece face-to-face at the mark and trim away about half the thickness of the molding along the line. Test-fit to make sure the recess is over the corner and that the piece will bend into place. Warm with a hair dryer to make it flexible. Apply adhesive and install.

Installing cork tile

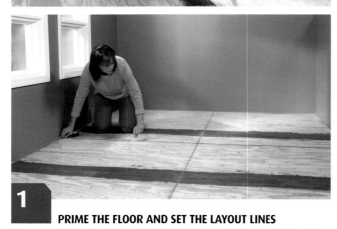

1 **PRIME THE FLOOR AND SET THE LAYOUT LINES**
Prepare and prime the floor as directed by the manufacturer, using the primer or thinned adhesive as specified. Begin the layout of the floor by finding the midpoint of each wall. Snap chalk lines between them, dividing the room into four equal sections.

Most manufacturers recommend that you offset the joints when laying a cork floor so the joints in one row don't align with the joints in neighboring rows. This helps hide the minor irregularities in size that occur in cork.

Other than that, manufacturers' directions vary widely. Some require an expansion gap between the wall and the floor; others don't. Some recommend an adhesive that rolls on; others recommend one you apply with a trowel. While the general procedures here outline the basic approach, always check the manufacturer's recommendations for specific details.

Cork floor prep at a glance

- **Storage:** Acclimate the tiles by removing them from their cartons and putting them in the room where they'll be installed 48 to 72 hours before installation. Room temperature must be between 60 and 85 degrees. (Some brands set the upper limit at 70 degrees.)
- **Concrete:** Cork can be applied on or above grade on concrete floors. Test for moisture with plastic sheeting for 72 hours (See Step 1 on page 74) to make sure the floor meets manufacturer's standards. Fill all cracks with cement patching compound. The floor must be level within $1/8$ inch over 10 feet and should be flat.
- **Wood:** Cork can be applied directly over any smooth wood floor (except oak) or over a wood or plywood subfloor. If the surface is irregular, cover the floor with $1/4$-inch underlayment. Nail every 4 inches around the edges with $1\frac{1}{4}$-inch ringshank nails and on a 6-inch grid over the face of the panel. Leave a $1/8$-inch gap between panels to allow for expansion, fill the gaps with a latex filler, and sand smooth. Above crawlspaces, floors must be at least 18 inches above ground. Cover the floor with 6-mil polyethylene.
- **Primer:** Seal the old floor with a primer or thin coat of adhesive as directed.

2   SQUARE THE LAYOUT

Make sure the lines are square with each other. Mark one layout line 3 feet from where it crosses the other line. Mark the other layout line 4 feet from the intersection. If the distance between the marks is 5 feet, the lines are perpendicular. If not, adjust one of the lines until they are. Prime over the lines if the directions call for it. The primer is clear, so you'll still be able to use your chalk lines for reference.

3   APPLY THE ADHESIVE

Apply adhesive in one quadrant with a trowel or roller, as recommended by the manufacturer. Let it dry thoroughly. Never apply cork to wet adhesive.

4   LAY THE FIRST ROW

Take tiles from three or four boxes and mix them together so any color variations will be distributed randomly. Lay the first tile in the corner formed by the intersection of the chalk lines. Work your way down the chalk line, butting the tiles together. At the wall, cut the tile to fit using a utility knife and straightedge. Leave an expansion gap if the manufacturer calls for one.

5   LAY THE SECOND ROW

Return to the middle of the room to begin the second row. Lay the first tile of this row so the middle straddles the chalk line. Work your way down the row. At the wall, cut the last tile to fit, leaving an expansion gap if one is required.

6   FINISH THE QUADRANT

Continue in this manner until you've laid tile in the entire quadrant. Repeat in the remaining quadrants, one at a time.

7   ROLL THE FLOOR

Roll the floor with a 100-pound roller several times in several directions at half-hour intervals. Let the floor sit overnight, then roll it a final time. If the manufacturer calls for a protective coat in addition to the finish that's already on the tile, apply as directed.

Installing carpet tiles

There are two advantages to carpet tiles: You don't need to master the art of stretch-in installation and the job goes much faster than a stretch-in installation. A disadvantage is that because the tiles are glued down, there's no pad underneath.

Like vinyl and ceramic tiles, you lay out carpet tiles by finding the center of the room. Once you've found the center, peel-and-stick installation starts by laying a square in it, and then working out toward the walls. Mastic installation also starts in the center, but is done one quadrant at a time because it makes glue application easier. Carpet tile is like other tiles: You can create countless patterns. Take a look at the manufacturer's brochures to see what textures and colors are available for you to work with.

1 MARK THE CENTER OF THE ROOM

Like other tiles carpet tiles are laid out and installed from the center of the room. Find the midpoints of the walls and snap a line between the midpoints on opposite walls. The lines will cross in the center of the room.

2 SQUARE THE LINES

Make sure the lines are square with each other. Check for square with a 3-4-5 triangle (see page 90). Measure 3 feet from the center point along one line and 4 feet from the center point along the other line. The lines are square if the points are 5 feet apart. Move the end of one line to make any necessary corrections.

3 DISTRIBUTE TILES FOR EQUAL EDGING

Make sure the tiles that meet the wall will be at least half a tile wide. Lay tiles along the layout lines without applying adhesive. Stop laying tiles at the last full tile before the wall. If the space between the tile and the wall is less than half a tile wide, reposition the line parallel to the wall. Move the line in either direction, keeping it parallel to the original line, to make the tiles equal widths on opposite sides of the room.

4 FIND THE PILE DIRECTION

The pile will lean in a particular direction on each tile, and an arrow on the back tells you which way. Any two tiles with pile facing in different directions will look to be slightly different colors. Depending on the carpet you will lay the arrows in the same direction, turn every other one 90 degrees, or lay the arrows randomly. Follow the manufacturer's directions. In this case, every other tile is turned 90 degrees to create a checkerboard pattern.

5 LAY THE CENTER TILES

One by one peel off the backing and put the corner of a tile in one of the corners formed by the layout lines. Put a tile in the corner of each quadrant so that the tiles form a square. The next group of tiles will be laid in a square surrounding the one you've just laid.

6 LAY THE FIRST LARGE SQUARE

Lay a square surrounding the first square. Work along the layout lines and lay a tile against each edge of the square already in place. Remove the backing one tile at a time. Pay attention to the direction of the arrows and lay the tile in the pattern recommended by the manufacturer. Always nestle a tile tightly against the corner created by neighboring tiles. Throw out the backing as you go—it's slippery, and there's no point in getting hurt.

7 LAY THE CORNERS OF THE SECOND SQUARE

Lay the corners of the second square. The tiles you have laid so far have left a void in each corner of the square. Lay tiles to fill in the corners, nestling the tile tightly against its neighbors.

8 LAY THE THIRD SQUARE

Lay a third square and work your way to the wall. Lay tiles around the square you just laid to create a stair-step pattern, as seen along the left edge of these tiles. Start at the layout lines and work along the edge of the tiles already laid. Once you've laid the stair-step pattern, fill in each of the steps with a single tile, which creates a second and larger stairway. Continue filling the steps with tiles, working your way to the wall.

3

FLOORS

9 TRIM TILES AT THE WALLS

The tiles next to the walls will probably need to be cut to fit. Measure the space between one of the tiles and the wall at the two corners of the tile nearest the wall. Draw a matching layout line on the back of a new tile. Cut along the line with a utility knife guided by a straightedge. Lay the tile and repeat the process until you've laid all the tiles.

Not peel and stick

Tiles for commercial installations don't have peel-and-stick backing and require a coat of mastic on the floor instead. Trowel adhesive onto the floor using a trowel with the notch size specified by the manufacturer. (Notch size controls the amount of adhesive you apply.) Spread the adhesive in one of the quadrants created by the layout lines. Start applying mastic at the wall and work your way back to the center of the room. Let the adhesive dry as recommended by the manufacturer: Tiles set in the adhesive too soon will be impossible to remove if you ever redo the floor. Lay the tile in a stepped pattern used for vinyl tiles. See page 126 for details.

10 ROLL THE FLOOR

Roll the floor with a 75-pound floor roller to seat the tiles in the adhesive.

Walls

Planning is the key to success for any project, especially a tile installation—undoing a mistake is not a matter of pulling nails and refastening. It can mean ripping out all your work and starting over again. Layout lines are critical when lining up a wall project. Properly established layout lines actually make the job easy by telling you exactly where each tile should go. And with a batten tacked where the bottom row goes—to get you started—you're on your way to a successful project.

A little practice can't hurt

Gravity tends to make wall tiles slide downward during installation. Mixing the mortar correctly so that it has the ability to support both itself and the weight of the tile (called "hang") helps, but its effectiveness depends some on temperature and humidity in the work site. Practice your tilesetting skills on a small wall area (or scrap plywood tacked up in the garage) before tackling an entire wall or shower stall. You'll soon gain the skill and confidence that will make the job go smoothly.

Chapter 4 highlights

Get the right tile for the job

In some ways choosing a wall tile is less complicated than choosing a floor tile. Brute strength is not required, of course, so wear ratings are not so important. Neither is the slip resistance of a tile. Pay particular attention, however, to the water absorption rating of the tile you are buying. For wet areas you should buy either vitreous or impervious tile. And although tiled walls don't require a plywood subfloor, they do require proper application of backerboard and in some cases a waterproofing membrane.

Installing backerboard

Backerboard provides a rigid surface for setting tile. There are several types of backerboards on the market—you'll find cementious, fiber-cement, plywood, gypsum, and plastic based. Which one you choose depends on the application; you can ask your retailer for advice or check with the tile manufacturer for backerboard recommendations.

Installing backerboard is similar to installing drywall. Cutting the panels requires scoring and snapping them.

And in spite of the hardness of cement backerboard, the panels are easily fastened with backerboard screws.

Getting the panels to the site, however, might prove more difficult than installing them. Cement backerboard is the heaviest, weighing in at 96 pounds for a full sheet. Others weigh considerably less. In any event this is a job that calls for a few helpers.

1 **MARK THE CUT LINE**
Using a china marker or carbide scoring tool, measure and mark the cut line at opposite edges of the panel; then snap a chalk line between the marks.

2 **SCORE THE LINE**
Using a straightedge to guide a carbide scoring tool (not a utility knife, unless you have all day to keep changing blades), score the surface of the board. Make sure to cut all the fiberglass strands.

3 **SNAP THE PANEL**
After scoring press down with one hand and knee near the scored line; lift one edge of the board to snap the panel. Use the scoring tool to cut through the back side of the board. This way you're assured you have a straight cut edge all the way through the board.

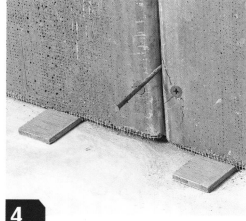

4 **SPACE THE PANEL WHEN INSTALLING**
When fastening the panels to the studs, set them on plywood spacers to keep them ¼ inch off the floor. Use a 16d common nail between each panel to keep them spaced about ⅛ inch apart.

5 FASTEN THE PANELS

Fasten the panels with 1¼-inch #8-18×⅜-inch wafer-head backerboard screws, spacing them every 8 inches over studs and around the perimeter. Keep the screws back ½ inch from the panel edges and 2 inches from corners.

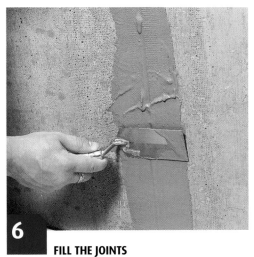

6 FILL THE JOINTS

Fill the joints with thinset mortar using the margin trowel. Press the mortar into the joint, then spread it to 3 inches.

7 BED JOINT TAPE

Bed 2-inch fiberglass tape in the wet thinset and smooth it out with the margin trowel.

8 FINISH THE JOINTS

Cover the tape after the thinset dries. Smooth with the flat edge of a square-tooth trowel, leaving no bumps to interfere with the tile. When the thinset is thoroughly dry you're ready to lay tile.

WORK SMARTER

SPEED THINGS UP BY PRESETTING THE SCREWS
Most of the time required to drive backerboard screws is taken up by fumbling in your nail apron for the screws. Although the screws pull themselves into the panel once the threads engage, they have a hard time penetrating the rocklike surface. For these reasons you will find it much faster to preset the screws by tapping them in about one quarter of the way with a hammer. You can cut the time in half again by giving the presetting operation to an assistant.

REAL WORLD

MISSED OPPORTUNITY?
The outside walls of kitchens and baths in cold parts of the country can never have too tight a vapor barrier on the warm sides. If you surface the wall with cement backerboard, a nearly perfect vapor barrier can be easily added by tacking up a continuous sheet of 4-mil poly sheeting before installing the backerboard. Don't forget!

4

WALLS

Establishing layout lines

Proper layout for wall tiles is crucial. Laying out guide lines on the wall before you start setting tiles allows you to balance the design, minimize the number of tiles you'll have to cut, and estimate the number of tiles needed.

First measure the size and shape of the area you plan to tile (here a 4×6-foot alcove). Transfer the measurements to graph paper and sketch the plan to scale (you can do this with a computer drafting program too) to make sure you have patterns, borders, and any decorative tile placed correctly.

Then snap a chalk line at the horizontal midpoint of the back wall. Measure the height of the wall and divide it by size of the tile. If the math leaves less than half a tile as a remainder, shift the horizontal line up or down to equalize the tile width of the tiles at the top and bottom. Snap a new line, making sure it's level.

Repeat the process on the other axis, snapping a vertical line at the midpoint of the wall, dividing the width of the wall by the tile width, and moving the line, if necessary, so you will have equal tiles at the edges. Using a 3-4-5 triangle, make sure the lines are square and using the lines as a reference, snap additional horizontal and vertical lines to break the wall into rectangles of 8 to 12 square feet.

Fasten a straight 1×2 batten with its top edge at the midpoint of the wall or on the first joint line above the floor. Double-check to make sure the batten is level—this will support your first row of tile.

After the upper rows have been set and the mortar cured, remove the batten (don't disturb the tile) and set the bottom row, hanging each tile from the one above with masking tape.

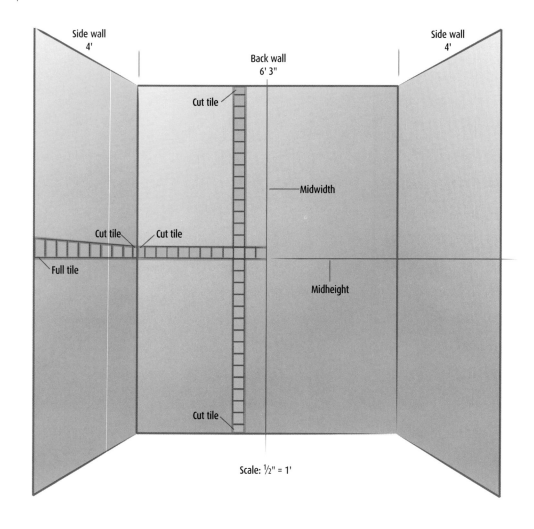

Scale: ½" = 1'

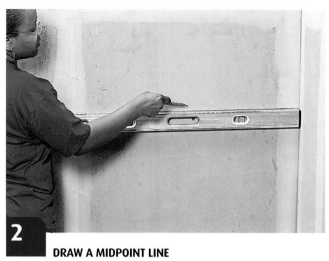

1 **MEASURE THE TILE**

Butt 10 tiles together and measure the length of the row. The length divided by 10 is the dimension to use for layout. Separate spacers are not used between these tiles which, like many wall tiles, come with spacing lugs molded into their edges.

2 **DRAW A MIDPOINT LINE**

Measure the height of wall to be tiled and draw a horizontal line through the midpoint. Extend the line to all three walls, using a 4-foot level.

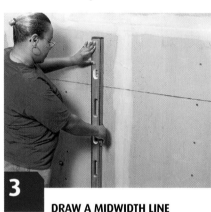

3 **DRAW A MIDWIDTH LINE**

Measure the width of the back wall and draw a vertical line through the midpoint using a 4-foot level.

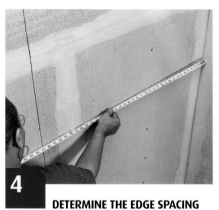

4 **DETERMINE THE EDGE SPACING**

Measure the halfwidth to find the width of the cut tiles at the ends. If less than one-half tile, shift the vertical to equalize the end tiles and snap a new line. Repeat for the halfheight reference.

5 **SNAP LAYOUT GRIDS**

Snap more lines vertically and horizontally to mark off 8- to 12-square-foot rectangles. You can use a different chalk color for clarity.

📖 WORK SMARTER

CROOKED CORNERS

Crooked walls are everywhere, whether your house is new or old. If the corner is not plumb, you'll have to cut tapered tiles to fit. If the wall is extremely out of square, you have three solutions:

- Skim-coat the corners of the out-of-plumb wall with thinset—out to a place on the wall where its condition isn't apparent.
- Use larger tiles so the variation from top to bottom on the last row is a less noticeable percentage of the width of the total tile.
- Remove the drywall or base material down to the studs and reinstall it, shimmed out to vertical. (Lots of work, but maybe the only solution!)

Corners hide cut tiles

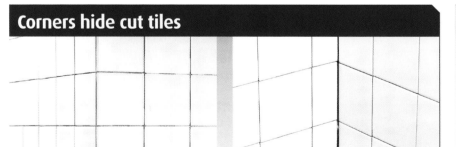

When you actually start tiling the wall, begin at an outside corner with full tiles, preferably bullnose tile or tile whose edge you have rounded with a mason's stone. Doing so will leave any cut tiles for the corners. Inside corners can better hide cut tiles whose width tapers along the wall. At the corners the cut edges are less visible.

Setting wall tile

PROJECT DETAILS

SKILLS: Mixing and spreading mortar, applying grout
PROJECT: Setting and grouting a tub/shower surround

TIME TO COMPLETE

EXPERIENCED: 4 hrs.
HANDY: 8 hrs.
NOVICE: 12 hrs.

STUFF YOU'LL NEED

TOOLS: ½-inch drill, mortar mixing paddle, ¼"×¼" square-notched trowel, 5-gallon bucket, rubber gloves, safety glasses, dust respirator
MATERIALS: Tile, thinset mortar with acrylic latex admix, 1×2 or 1×3 batten, masking tape, drop cloth

SAFETY ALERT

CAUSTIC MORTAR

Mortar is very caustic and can burn holes in skin, so wear rubber gloves. If you don't wear gloves and do get your hands into the mortar, rinse them with white vinegar, which will neutralize the alkalinity.

Gravity makes wall tiling messier than floor tiling. Properly mixed thinset will adhere in a thin layer to the surface of the wall. But when you begin combing the mortar, it's inevitable that a fair proportion of it will end up on the floor.

Don't adjust the mix to control this problem. Stick with the manufacturer's instructions, keeping the proportions of water to mix as specified.

Before setting tile on a wall, cover surfaces with drop cloths and tape the cloth in place.

When tiling a tub surround, don't use polyethylene sheeting as your drop cloth. Polyethylene is slippery and will make the sloped bottom of the tub dangerous. Use a canvas drop cloth or an old sheet or blanket instead.

1 FASTEN THE BATTEN
Fasten a level 1×2 or 1×3 batten just below the bottommost tile joint or at the midheight reference line as shown here. Wherever you locate it the batten will keep your first row of tiles straight. Then the rest of the tiles will be straight too.

2 MIX THE MORTAR
Mix latex-modified thinset mortar at slow speed with a mortar paddle and variable-speed drill. Weigh out and mix one quarter of the bag at a time. After mixing let mixture slake (rest) for 10 minutes, then mix again.

4

WALLS

3

SPREAD THE THINSET

Apply thinset to an area bounded by reference lines not more than 15 square feet at a time. Press the thinset into the backerboard with the straight edge of a square-notched trowel held at a shallow angle.

4

COMB THE MORTAR

Rake the thinset into straight lines with the notched edge of the trowel. Hold the trowel at a steep angle to the surface and press down so that the teeth contact the backerboard, ensuring a uniform thickness of mortar.

5

SET AND CHECK THE TILE

Set the tile along the batten and lift the fourth or fifth tile and check the back to make sure the thinset covers the entire surface. If the thinset on the tile is in rows, the mortar bed is not thick enough. Scrape off the first application and use a trowel with a larger notch size.

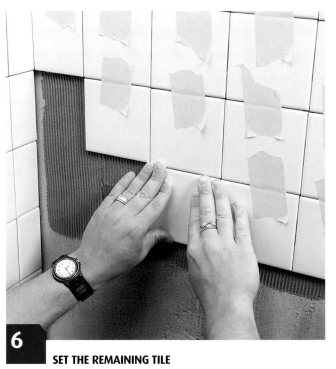

6

SET THE REMAINING TILE

After setting the tile above the batten, let the mortar cure for 12 hours; then remove the batten. Set the rows below the batten from the middle down, supporting each with a strip of masking tape attached to the tile above.

Marking and cutting wall tiles

PROJECT DETAILS

SKILLS: Marking, cutting tile
PROJECT: Cutting tiles

TIME TO COMPLETE

EXPERIENCED: 1 hr.
HANDY: 2 hrs.
NOVICE: 3 hrs.

STUFF YOU'LL NEED

TOOLS: China marker, snap cutter
or wet saw, tile nippers, carbide
hole saw or rotary cutter, safety
glasses, dust respirator
MATERIALS: Tile

 nap cutter or wet saw? The question is one of utility and ease of use rather than price. The snap cutter makes only straight cuts, but those are the cuts you'll make most often. Once you set the snap cutter fence, you can cut about 10 tiles per minute. The snap cutter also is silent and clean.

One of the disadvantages is that snap cutters can't make L-shape, notch, or irregular cuts. Snap cuts also have sharp edges that require smoothing if exposed.

A wet saw cuts about as quickly as the snap cutter, and it can make the more intricate L-shape, notch, irregular, and square cuts. It also produces a clean cut with slightly rounded edges. The wet saw is messy, however, spewing a mist of water and tile dust.

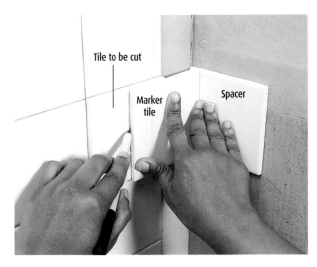

LINE UP STRAIGHT CUTS by placing tile to be cut over the tile last set, butting the marker tile against a ¼-inch spacer and tracing the edge of the marker tile.

TIMESAVER

UNUSUAL SHAPES
If you have many irregular cuts, consider purchasing a carpenter's contour gauge—a set of small pins that slide in and out to record any shape. The gauge is then placed on the tile and the shape transferred with a marker.

Ask to demo a snap cutter and a wet saw before renting either one.

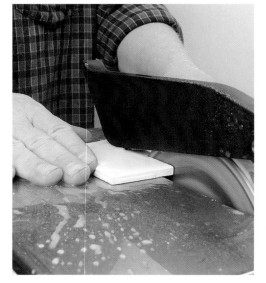

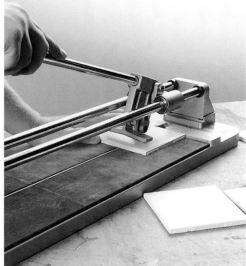

CUT STRAIGHT CUTS ON A WET SAW OR SNAP CUTTER

The wet saw is the most versatile of the cutting tools. It will cut through the hardest tile with ease. With practice you can use it to make straight, L-shape, notched, square, and even intricate cuts. See pages 105–106 for making the various cuts. Unless you're doing a lot of tiling, this is a rental.

The snap cutter is the quickest, easiest tool for making straight cuts. While it leaves little mess, it does leave sharp cut edges that, if exposed, must be smoothed. For details on its use, see page 104.

Cutting edge holes for pipes

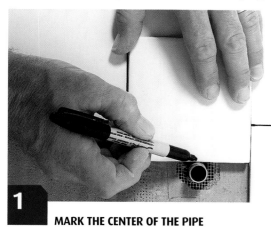

1 MARK THE CENTER OF THE PIPE

Mark a hole by holding the tile over the last tile set and sliding forward to butt against the pipe. Mark the pipe center on the tile edge. Slide the tile up to the pipe from the side to mark the adjacent edge in a similar fashion.

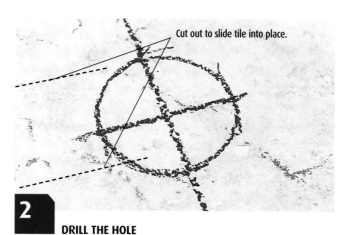

Cut out to slide tile into place.

2 DRILL THE HOLE

Extend lines from the edge marks across the tile. Where the lines cross, drill a hole ½ inch larger than the pipe diameter. This leaves room for the pipe to expand. Make the cutout on a wet saw and fill in the gap behind the pipe with a piece cut from scrap tile.

Cutting interior holes for pipes

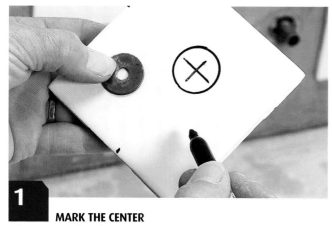

1 MARK THE CENTER

Where you can place the tile over the pipe, mark the center of the pipe on two edges of the tile and extend the marks until they intersect. Trace the hole on the tile face using a washer the size of the pipe.

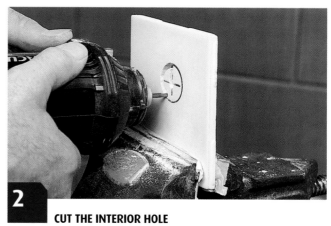

2 CUT THE INTERIOR HOLE

Use a rotary cutter, an adjustable carbide hole drill, or a carbide hole saw to cut holes in the interior of a tile. See pages 106–107.

Making corner cutouts

Use tile nippers to make irregular cuts at the edges of the tiles. See page 107.

GOOD IDEA

CUTTING TILE

You are ready to set tile and your helper hasn't yet arrived with the snap cutter? Or the rental store is about to close and you have to return the snap cutter? No problem—just score the tile with an ordinary glass cutter and straightedge. Snap the scored tile over a dowel.

Grouting wall tile

1

MIX THE GROUT

Mix the powdered grout with the recommended liquid using a margin trowel. Follow the manufacturer's directions. After mixing let the grout rest for 10 minutes, then remix. Add liquid only if the grout is too stiff to spread.

2

SPREAD THE GROUT WITH A FLOAT

Spread the grout with a rubber grout float. Pick up about a cup of grout with the float and smear it on the tile. Hold the float at a shallow angle to the tile and press the grout into the joints with several sweeps.

3

REMOVE THE EXCESS

Remove excess grout with diagonal sweeps of the rubber float held at a steep angle to the tile. Hold the float diagonal to the tiles so the edge of the float doesn't cut into the joints and remove grout.

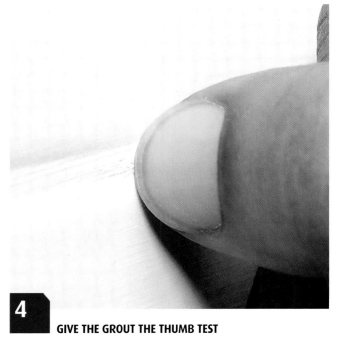

4

GIVE THE GROUT THE THUMB TEST

The grout will require 5 to 15 minutes to set up. It is hard enough to start the final cleanup when your thumbnail leaves no impression.

5 **CLEAN THE TILE**

Wipe the tiles diagonally with a damp—not dripping wet—sponge, rinsing it often in the clean water. If the grout is too resistant to sponge, use a plastic scrub pad, but avoid scrubbing the grout in the joints.

6 **REMOVE THE HAZE**

Remove the haze left after sponging, first with a damp rag, then with a clean dry rag. Continue damp and dry wiping until the tile is reflective as glass. Check by holding a lamp to the surface.

7 **WET CURE THE GROUT**

Cure the grout by misting it with water several times a day for three days. Damp curing maximizes the strength and minimizes the water absorbability of the grout. Do not mist tinted grout. Misting can dissolve the tint and leave an inconsistent color.

8 **SEAL THE SURFACE**

Apply penetrating sealer to grout with a sponge. Wipe off excess before it dries. If the tile is not glazed, seal the tile as well.

Do not damp cure tinted grout. Damp curing can dissolve the tint and leave an inconsistent color.

Tiling a tub or shower surround

 PROJECT DETAILS

SKILLS: Design, installing backerboard, basic tilesetting
PROJECT: Tiling a tub or shower surround

TIME TO COMPLETE

EXPERIENCED: 10 hrs.
HANDY: 14 hrs.
NOVICE: 18 hrs.

 STUFF YOU'LL NEED

TOOLS: Carbide scorer (or utility knife with plenty of blades), ½-inch drill, mixing paddle, ¼"×¼" square-edged trowel, 4-foot level, 5-gallon bucket, stapler, caulking gun, grout float, spray bottle, snap cutter or wet saw, sponge or plastic scrub pad, safety glasses, dust respirator
MATERIALS: ½-inch cement backerboard, thinset mortar with acrylic latex admix, backerboard screws, fiberglass tape, 4-mil poly or 15-lb. felt, bath and tub caulk, asphalt roofing cement, tile, dry-mix grout with acrylic latex admix, masking tape, penetrating sealer, marker, soap tray

Whether you build a new bathroom or remodel an old one, a tub and shower surround can enhance its appearance and convenience. The job averages 80 square feet and involves all of the basic tilesetting skills: designing, measuring, laying out, installing backerboard, setting tile on a vertical surface, and cutting holes as well as making straight cuts. Once you have everything on hand, the job can be finished in a weekend.

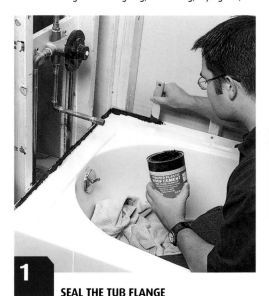

1 SEAL THE TUB FLANGE
Apply asphalt roofing cement to the flange of the tub edge. The cement will seal the tub to the 15-lb. felt (or 4-mil poly if an outside wall) shown in the next step.

2 INSTALL THE WATERPROOFING FELT
Staple 15-pound felt to the studs. Bed the first layer in the asphalt cement and overlap succeeding sheets by at least 2 inches. Use only enough staples to hold in place.

3   INSTALL CEMENT BACKERBOARD

Fasten backerboard to the studs with backerboard screws setting the sheets on ¼-inch shims on the tub. This way water on the rim won't wick up behind the panels.

4   MUD AND TAPE THE SEAMS

Reinforce the corners and joints with fiberglass tape and skim and level the joints with thinset.

5   SEAL THE TUB JOINT

Caulk the gap where the backerboard meets the tub with clear or white silicone, which is flexible enough to allow minor tub expansion and contraction.

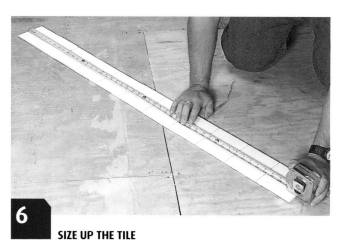

6   SIZE UP THE TILE

Determine the actual tile size by butting 10 tiles, measuring the total length, and dividing by 10.

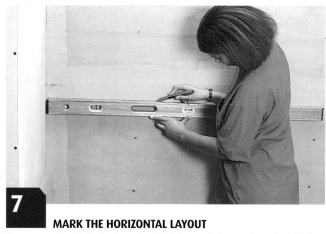

7   MARK THE HORIZONTAL LAYOUT

Measure and mark the horizontal midheight on all three walls. Adjust the line so you have even tiles at the top and bottom of the walls.

8   MARK THE LAYOUT

Use a 4-foot level to draw a vertical line midwidth on the back wall. Shift the line as needed to equalize the end tiles.

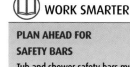 WORK SMARTER

PLAN AHEAD FOR SAFETY BARS

Tub and shower safety bars must be securely fastened to framing. Avoid the expense of ripping out and retiling down the road by installing 2×6 or 2×8 blocking between the studs of the back wall and the wall opposite the shower controls. The bars and blocking should be centered 33 inches to 36 inches above the floor.

4

WALLS

TIMESAVER

MARKING CUTS FOR AN INSET

To mark the cuts for an inset, lay out a close-fitted array of field tile. Place the inset on top. Align the inset with the field below. Trace the inset edges onto the field tiles with a china marker. Sketch the layout on paper and number the back of each tile and its location in the sketch.

9 BATTEN THE BOTTOM ROW

Set the bottom row on a ¼-inch batten high enough from the rim to leave at least a half tile at the bottom. First check to see if the rim of the tub is level. If it is not, shim the strip itself until it is level.

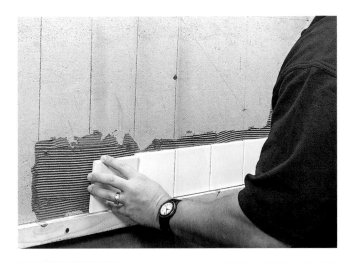

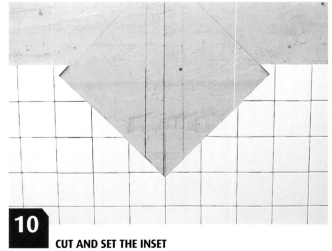

10 CUT AND SET THE INSET

Set precut tile around an inset design. The surrounding field tiles have been marked and precut as described in Timesaver above.

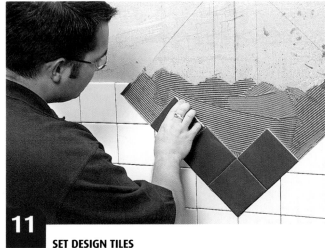

11 SET DESIGN TILES

Although the design has been carefully traced, the notched field tiles at the corners may have to be recut and reset at this point.

12 SET TILE AROUND FIXTURES

Mark, cut, and set tile around the shower arm. See the instructions for marking and cutting an interior hole on page 141.

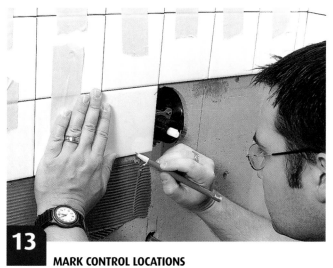

13 MARK CONTROL LOCATIONS

Remove the batten and hang the rows below it, using masking tape to keep the tiles from sliding down. Mark the interior holes for the shower controls.

14 SET ACCESSORIES

Set accessories, such as a soap tray, after the tile has set, supporting its weight with masking tape. Do NOT install a tray with a towel bar that may be mistaken for a handhold.

15 GROUT THE TILES

Mix the grout with a margin trowel. Let the grout rest for 10 minutes, then remix. Add liquid only if the grout is too stiff to spread. Wear rubber gloves for this and the next four steps. Spread the grout with a grout float. Hold the float at a shallow angle to the tile and press the grout into the joints.

16 REMOVE THE EXCESS

Remove the excess with the rubber float held at a steep angle to the tile. Make sure the direction is diagonal to the tiles. Allow the grout to set 10 to 15 minutes, then clean.

17 CLEAN THE HAZE

Remove the haze left after sponging, first with a damp cloth then with a dry cloth. Alternate damp and dry wiping until the tile is as reflective as glass. Apply penetrating sealer to the grout joints with a sponge. Wipe off the excess within 10 minutes so the sealer doesn't dry on the tile.

18 RINSE, RINSE, RINSE

Use clean water. The more you rinse the sponge, the less haze you will have to remove later. Wring every drop of water from the sponge so it is barely damp.

19 CAULK THE TUB/TILE JOINT

Caulk the tub and tile joint with bath and tub caulk that matches either the tile or the tub. Smooth the bead by wetting your finger and drawing it across the grout, using slight pressure.

Building a custom shower pan

 PROJECT DETAILS

SKILLS: Carpentry, mixing and spreading mortar, setting tile, applying grout
PROJECT: Installing a shower pan, grouting and sealing tile (per 100 sq. ft.)

 TIME TO COMPLETE

EXPERIENCED: 4 hrs.
HANDY: 8 hrs.
NOVICE: 12 hrs.

 STUFF YOU'LL NEED

TOOLS: Hammer, framing square, tape measure, level, carbide scorer, utility knife, adjustable wrench, scissors, stapler, ½-inch drill, mixing paddle, finishing trowel, notched trowel, grout float, jigsaw, marker, wood screed
MATERIALS: ¾-inch exterior plywood, 2×4 studs, pressure-treated 2×4s, pressure-treated 2×6s, backerboard screws, ½-inch cement backerboard, sand mix, mortar, 4-mil poly sheeting (walls), 40-mil CPE shower pan liner, masking tape, CPE adhesive, shower drain, thinset, wall tiles, floor tiles, grout, silicon caulk

I f your shower will be a standard size or shape you can install a prefab liner (available at your home center). But if your shower must fit a special space, you'll need a custom unit. A custom shower floor requires a thick, carefully flattened mortar bed to support the tiles and to prevent them from cracking. A bed consists of three layers. The first is sand mix, a mixture of portland cement and sand that forms a strong substructure. The second layer is a plastic liner. The third layer is regular mortar that goes on top of the liner. Together the three layers provide a dense, watertight surface that won't flex. The bed is covered by a layer of thinset and, finally, the tile.

The liner—a flexible 40-mil sheet of CPE plastic—keeps the water from soaking through the tile and mortar into the subfloor. When you buy the drain fitting for the shower stall, make sure you get one called a tile shower drain that is designed to make the whole system watertight.

🌐 **REAL WORLD**

TILE THE WALLS BEFORE YOU TILE THE FLOOR
One do-it-yourselfer laid a perfect mortar bed for the floor tiles, put the tiles in thinset, and then started to tile the walls. Big mistake. Mortar falling off the trowel quickly covered the floor tiles, and when he accidentally dropped the trowel, it chipped a floor tile. Once you get your mortar bed laid, tile the walls before you tile the floor. Things dropping on the mortar bed will do far less damage to it than they would to a tile.

1

PREPARE THE FLOOR

If the subfloor is not ¾-inch plywood in good repair, replace it with ¾-inch exterior plywood.

2

FRAME THE UNIT

Frame the shower stall with 2×4 studs. Install pressure-treated 2×6 blocking on edge between the bases of the studs.

3

BUILD THE THRESHOLD

Build a threshold by facenailing three pressure-treated 2×4s into the shower door opening.

4

CUT THE DRAIN HOLE

Cut a hole in the floor and install and connect the lower piece of the drain, called the drain base. Temporarily tape the opening shut.

5

PREPARE FOR THE FIRST MORTAR BASE

Use a level to transfer the level position of the floor at the drain to the walls and curb to account for any irregularities on the surface of the floor.

6

MAKE GUIDE MARKS AROUND THE SHOWER BASE

Measure ¼ inch above the original mark for every foot between the drain and the wall, and make marks around the walls and curb to act as guides for the mortar base.

7 **PREPARE THE MUD MIX**

Mix mortar mix with enough water to make a crumbly cement mixture that just holds together.

8 **SPREAD THE MUD FLOOR**

Lay a mortar bed between the drain and the marks on the wall to create the slope of the shower.

CLOSER LOOK

TO SEAM CPE SHOWER MEMBRANE

1 Remove dust, dirt, oil, and water from a 2-inch-wide strip along surfaces to be joined.

2 Coat a 2-inch-wide strip on the mating surfaces of both pieces with the recommended adhesive.

3 Immediately join the two surfaces. The adhesive must be wet when you do.

4 Press the surfaces together for 2 to 3 minutes by rolling the seam with a rolling pin.

5 Place a heavy object along the entire seam for 2 to 4 hours.

6 Install the liner. Allow it to cure overnight before conducting the water test described in Step 17.

9 **SCREED THE FLOOR**

Screed the mortar base with a piece of wood so the bed slopes from the line on the wall to the floor at the drain base but not over it.

10 **TROWEL THE FLOOR SMOOTH**

Finish with a steel trowel to create a smooth surface. Let the bed cure per manufacturer's instructions before applying the plastic liner.

11

CUT THE LINER

Cut the liner to size, seaming it if necessary. On the side walls, the liner should extend 2 inches above finished height of curb. At the curb it should be long enough to go over the curb and about halfway back down to the floor.

12

CAULK THE DRAIN BASE

Apply a bead of 100 percent silicon caulk around the face of the drain base. Screw the drain bolts part way in. (See inset.)

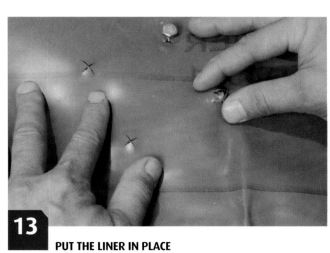

13

PUT THE LINER IN PLACE

Cut a small X over each bolt head so the liner will slip over it. Push the liner into the caulk. Flatten the liner with your hands, working from the drain toward the walls to smooth out the air bubbles.

TO MAKE A HOSPITAL CORNER

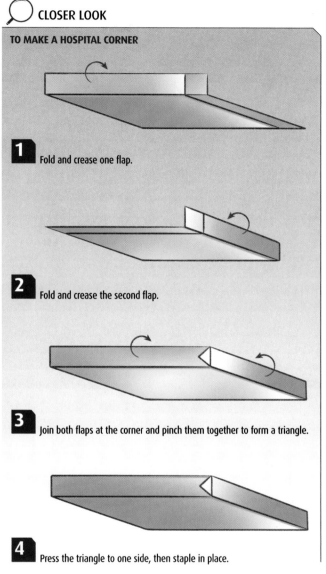

1 Fold and crease one flap.

2 Fold and crease the second flap.

3 Join both flaps at the corner and pinch them together to form a triangle.

4 Press the triangle to one side, then staple in place.

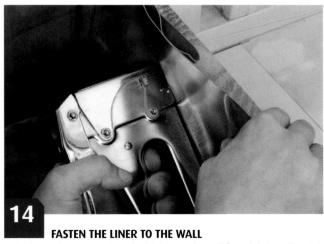

14

FASTEN THE LINER TO THE WALL

Make hospital corners and staple the liner to the wall ½ inch below the edge of the liner.

15 LINE THE THRESHOLD

On outside corners or curbs, cut along the corner to allow the material to make the bend. Cut out the excess. Glue on a patch made by the manufacturer that's shaped to fit corners and curbs using the same adhesive you use to make a seam.

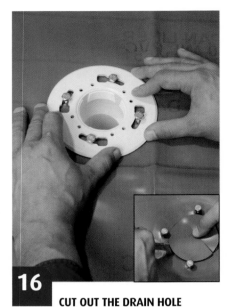

16 CUT OUT THE DRAIN HOLE

(See inset.) Put the clamping ring (the second part of the drain) over the bolts and tighten. The clamping ring has weep holes to drain away any water that might gather underneath the finished surface. Allow the liner to cure overnight before applying the mortar bed.

17 TEST FOR LEAKS

Plug the drain with a test plug, available in the plumbing department, and fill the pan to the top of the curb. The plug goes far enough into the drain to keep the water from draining out through the weep holes. Check for leaks after 4 hours. Patch as needed.

18 INSTALL POLY WATERPROOFING

Staple 4-mil poly to the walls, letting it overlap the liner by 2 inches. Staple it to the studs just above the top of the liner, but don't staple through the liner.

19 INSTALL THE BACKERBOARD

Install $\frac{1}{2}$-inch backerboard on the walls and curb. Leave 1 inch between the bottom edge of the wall and the liner. Don't drive any screws through the shower pan liner. Install backerboard on both sides of the curb before you install the top of the curb. The curb panels need to be screwed in, but use no more than three screws on each.

20 SET IN THE DRAIN BODY

Put the drain barrel in and set the top at finished height—$1\frac{1}{2}$ inches above the liner, plus the combined thickness of the tile and thinset.

WALLS

4

21 **MARK THE HEIGHT OF THE FLOOR**

Mark the walls, curb, and drain barrel 1½ inches above the liner. Cover the area around the drain with pea gravel to keep the mortar from sealing the weep holes. You will cover the gravel with the final mortar bed.

22 **MUD THE SECOND LAYER**

Fill the pan with mortar to the level of the marks you made. Use a cement product designed for mortar beds. Cover the pea gravel, being careful not to plug the weep holes.

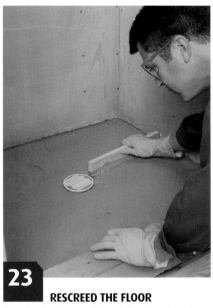

23 **RESCREED THE FLOOR**

Screed as before, creating a flat surface that slopes toward the drain and is even with the marks on the wall and drain.

24 **FINISH THE FLOOR**

Finish with a steel trowel, creating a smooth plane between the marks on the wall and those on the drain. Let the mortar cure for 24 hours.

25 **TILE THE WALLS**

Although you can tile the floor before you tile the walls, most professionals tile the walls first to avoid damaging the floor tile in case a tool is dropped. It will also be easier to clean up mortar spills. Protect the shower floor with cardboard. Use a notched trowel to apply latex modified thinset and set the wall tiles. (See page 138.)

26 **TILE THE FLOOR**

Set the floor tile in thinset, cutting the tile to fit around the drain. Let the mortar cure as directed on the bag, and then apply grout first to the wall and then to the floor.

4

WALLS

Countertops

Tile is often chosen as a surface for countertops in kitchens, baths, and wet bars. It holds up to almost any level of wear and tear, cleans up easily, requires little or no maintenance, and lasts—stylishly—forever.

All these characteristics to some extent assume the proper tile selection and proper installation techniques and materials—a ³/₄-inch exterior plywood base, waterproofing membrane, backerboard, and the proper grout.

In most cases a new countertop does not mean you have to install new cabinets. You should be able to take the old countertop off and build a new one on your existing cabinets. And even though it is possible to install tile on an existing laminate surface, it's best to remove the old one and build the new one—correctly. The best choice for tile is a material rated either impervious or vitreous, and grout must contain latex additive. (Epoxy grout is suitable as well but can be difficult to work with until you've had some tiling experience.)

Scratch resistance is important

Floor tiles usually have a high enough wear rating to resist scratching, but wall tiles generally do not. If you choose wall tile

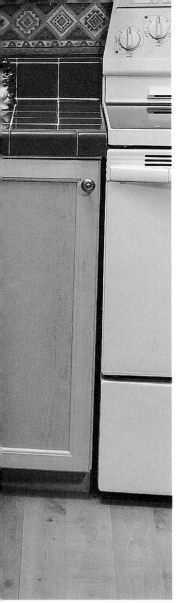

Chapter 5 highlights

for your countertop, provide wood or plastic surfaces for chopping.
These can be traditional chopping blocks or cutting boards stored
in cabinets or resting against the backsplash. Or you can design
them right into the countertop and set them into the tiled surface.

You can mix materials for style too. Incorporate 12×12-inch
squares of polished granite into your layout; they accent almost
any tile nicely.

If you're setting a tiled backsplash, lay the backsplash tiles
before you set the countertop trim. That way you won't have to
worry about disturbing the trim tiles as you lean over them to
work on the backsplash.

Preparing the base

The minimum requirement for a tiled countertop is a 3/4-inch exterior plywood base.

If no countertop exists, rip a 4×8-foot sheet in half and fasten a strip of the same plywood to the back edge as a backsplash. A countertop over 8 feet long or an L-shape countertop may be formed by gluing and screwing a 3/4-inch plywood splice plate from below.

In almost all cases, it's best to remove the old countertop surface and start afresh, with a new base and backerboard. Old laminate may not be properly or consistently adhered. And it must be cleaned, degreased, and sanded. By the time you get done with these activities, you could have removed the old base and installed a new one. The steps below demonstrate how to install a new 3/4-inch base. Make sure you build it from 3/4-inch exterior-grade plywood.

1 **DON'T FORGET THE OVERHANG**
Fasten the base to the cabinet with the front edge projecting 1 inch beyond the face of the cabinet.

2 **SPLICING LONG UNITS**
Extend a countertop that is longer than 8 feet or around a corner by attaching a 3/4-inch plywood splice plate at the butt.

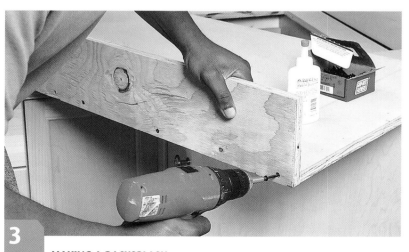

3 **MAKING A BACKSPLASH**
Form a backsplash by gluing and screwing a strip of 3/4-inch plywood to the rear of the countertop.

Laying backerboard

 PROJECT DETAILS

SKILLS: Measuring, scoring, sawing, fastening, troweling
PROJECT: Laying backerboard for countertop

 TIME TO COMPLETE

EXPERIENCED: 2 hrs.
HANDY: 3 hrs.
NOVICE: 4 hrs.

 STUFF YOU'LL NEED

TOOLS: Tape measure, marker, carbide scorer, dry-cutting diamond saw, jigsaw, 3/4-inch variable-speed drill, mortar mixing paddle, square-notch trowel, 5-gallon bucket, safety glasses, dust respirator
MATERIALS: 1/2-inch cement or fiber-cement backerboard, thinset mortar with acrylic latex admix, backerboard screws, 2-inch fiberglass tape

The purpose of backerboard is to provide a rigid surface for setting tiles. The 3/4-inch plywood subsurface establishes stability for the surface. You can make the sink cutout in the plywood before installing the backerboard or make it once the backerboard is installed.

If you make the cutout in the plywood first, cut and dry-fit sections of backerboard on top of the plywood, covering the entire surface. Make sure there are no joints that cross the sink hole. Then trace the perimeter of the sink hole on the underside of the backerboard, using the cutout in the plywood as your guide.

Spread thinset on the plywood subbase, then lay on the backerboard pieces, fastening them with backerboard screws and spacing them with 16d spacer nails. Install the fasteners 4 inches on-center, 1/2 inch in from the panel edges and every 6 inches in both directions in the interior. Don't fasten within 2 inches of a panel corner to avoid breaking off a corner.

Cover the base cabinets and appliances with plastic for protection from thinset splatters.

Mix another small batch of thinset to bed the fiberglass reinforcing tape. With the margin trowel, spread a 3-inch-wide layer of thinset over a joint between two panels. Apply a strip of 2-inch-wide self-adhesive fiberglass reinforcing tape to the thinset and bed it into the mortar. Apply more thinset over the tape and smooth and feather the thinset to just cover the tape. Repeat this process over all joints.

1

MEASURE AND MARK BACKERBOARD
Measure and mark the backerboard to fit the counter dimensions. Cut the marked pieces with a carbide scoring tool (see page 95).

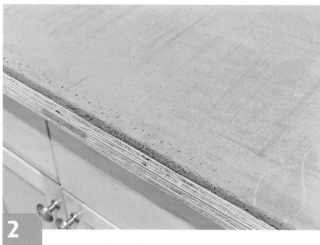

2

LINE UP THE EDGES
The edges of the backerboard and plywood countertop base must be perfectly flush on all sides.

3

CUT THE SINK HOLE
If you have cut the sink hole in the plywood base, use it to trace the outline of the sink on the underside of the backerboard. Cut out the sink hole in the backerboard with a dry-cutting diamond blade, finishing the corners with a jigsaw.

COUNTERTOPS

5

4 **CUT BACKERBOARD FOR THE BACKSPLASH**

Cut the backerboard for the backsplash so it clears the counter backerboard by $^1/_8$ inch and allows for the radius bullnose trim at top.

5 **MIX THE THINSET**

Add the dry thinset mix to the acrylic latex admix in a 5-gallon bucket. Pour in half of the liquid, then weigh and add half of the bag contents. Mix the thinset with a mortar mixing paddle and a $^1/_2$-inch variable-speed drill. Use slow speed (150–200 rpm) to avoid incorporating air and bubbling the mortar.

 TIMESAVER

ELIMINATE MEASUREMENTS

Don't transfer measurements from a sink cutout in a plywood countertop to the backerboard that will form the base for the tile. Instead place the uncut backerboard (you may need a helper to steady it) over the plywood. Line up the back edge and one of the ends. Then trace the cutout from underneath into the bottom face of the backerboard with a black felt-tip pen.

FRAGILE CUTOUT

When the sink cutout is made, the backerboard will be fragile. To avoid breaking the narrow strips at the front and back of the cutout, slide the cut backerboard onto a 2-foot-wide strip of $^3/_4$-inch plywood. Then, using the plywood as a stretcher, slide the backerboard into place on the countertop. Another way is to remove the narrow strips from the front and back of the sink cutout before they break and install them separately. The installed strips will be strong, provided they are well fastened and bedded in thinset to the plywood.

6 **SPREAD AND COMB THE THINSET**

Apply the thinset to the plywood base. Comb it with a $^1/_8 \times ^1/_8$-inch square-notched trowel.

7 **MORTAR THE BACKSPLASH BACKERBOARD**

Spread thinset onto the back of the backsplash backerboard strip. This will allow you to position the strip $^1/_8$ inch above the countertop backerboard.

8 **GAP THE BACK OF THE COUNTERTOP**

Leave a ⅛-inch gap at the back of the countertop backerboard for expansion. The vertical strip for the backsplash and horizontal surface of the countertop backerboard must not touch.

9 **GAP THE JOINTS**

Leave ⅛-inch joints between sections of backerboard. A 16d common nail provides perfect spacing. Don't drive the nails into the plywood, however.

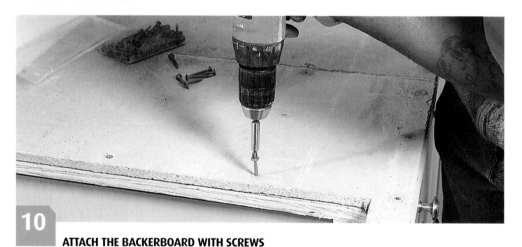

10 **ATTACH THE BACKERBOARD WITH SCREWS**

Drive in special backerboard screws 4 inches on center, ½ inch from the edge, all around the panel. Tap the screw lightly with a hammer to start it, then drive it in until the top of the head is flush with the surface.

11 **BE CAREFUL AT CORNERS**

Keep the screws 2 inches from the corners of the board to avoid breaking off a corner. If you do break a corner, you'll have to install a new sheet.

12 **DRIVE INTERIOR FASTENERS**

Drive in screws every 6 inches in both directions in the field of the board. Some tilesetters use 1¼-inch galvanized roofing nails as field fasteners.

5

COUNTERTOPS

13 **MUD THE JOINTS**

Fill the joints between sections of backerboard with thinset. Using a margin trowel held at a shallow angle, force the thinset into the joint, then spread a layer 3 inches wide.

14 **TAPE THE JOINTS**

Reinforce backerboard with 2-inch-wide, alkali-resistant fiberglass tape at any joint with a square-edge panel. Apply a skim coat over the tape with a trowel.

15 **TAPE THE EDGES**

Wrap the edges of the countertop with fiberglass tape. Apply a coat of thinset, tape, then a top skim coat to bury the tape in mortar.

 **TIMESAVER**

NO TAPING NECESSARY

Cement backerboard with rounded panel edges that have exposed fiberglass reinforcing doesn't require the application of fiberglass tape and will make for speedier installation.

WORK SMARTER

FOR A STAINLESS SINK

Many kitchen sinks are made of stainless steel. To reinforce the thin steel, the sinks have vertical stiffening bars welded under the rim on all four sides.

For a more rigid installation, make the sink cutout in both the plywood and the backerboard just large enough (except for the back of the rim where the faucets are mounted) to fit the sink bowl.

To accommodate the stiffeners, place (don't attach yet) the backerboard on the plywood and line up the edges

and openings. Then center the sink in the cutout. With a felt-tip pen, trace the locations of the sink stiffeners on the backerboard. Remove the sink, place the backerboard where you can work on all sides, and cut a groove along the stiffener lines. Use a dry-cutting masonry blade on a 4-inch grinder to make the cut, and make sure the groove is just deep enough to take the stiffener.

Now the sink will sit flush on the backerboard, and the tile will lip over the sink rim perfectly.

Marking layout lines

The more accurate your layout, the better the end result will be. The key to success is preparation.

The first principle in laying out a countertop is simple: No cut tiles on the front edge. The second principle is applied when there is a sink: Adjust the sink location, if possible, so that cut tiles are of equal size on the left and right.

To tile an existing countertop that has a sink size and location that will remain the same, determine whether to have full tiles at the corner or equal size tiles at the sink. Sinks and their mountings are so variable this book cannot address all of the ways to edge them. Your best option

is to take an accurate sketch of the sink's rim or, better yet, the actual sink, to your tile supplier to work out the installation details.

Another layout requirement may be that of an inset chopping block. Rather than cutting tiles, design the opening so that it is an integral number of tiles in both width and depth. Then cut the chopping block to leave a $\frac{1}{4}$-inch gap all around. The gap will be caulked with silicone to allow for the block's expansion.

1 MARK THE V-CAP ENDS
Hold the V-cap against the front edge of the counter and mark the location of the joint. Repeat for other end.

2 SNAP CHALK LINES
Snap a chalk line between marks to indicate the first joint line. Repeat for the other leg if the counter is L-shape.

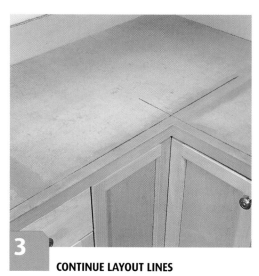

3 CONTINUE LAYOUT LINES
The intersection of the first chalk lines indicates the starting point for the tile, assuring full tiles on both front edges. Continue to snap chalk lines that will divide the surface into grids.

4 ADJUST THE SINK TEMPLATE
If you haven't cut the sink hole already, center the sink template on features such as cabinet doors or a window. If possible, make the side tiles equal widths.

5

COUNTERTOPS

Setting the tile

PROJECT DETAILS

SKILLS: Mixing and spreading mortar, setting tile
PROJECT: Setting tile on a 12-foot L-shape countertop

TIME TO COMPLETE

EXPERIENCED: 3 hrs.
HANDY: 6 hrs.
NOVICE: 8 hrs.

STUFF YOU'LL NEED

TOOLS: ½-inch variable-speed drill, mortar mixing paddle, trowel
MATERIALS: Field tile, V-cap trim tile, bullnose tile, thinset mortar with acrylic latex admix, ⅛-inch shims

You can install the trim tile before the field tile or vice versa. In either case back-butter the trim tile before applying it. You can also tack a batten under the front edge of the counter to temporarily support the V-cap tile until the mortar sets.

Set the field tiles in small sections. Mix only the amount of thinset needed for each section. Install the field tiles starting from the intersection of the layout lines at the inside corner of the sink. Continue setting the field tiles, expanding outward to the end of the counter and around the sink.

Treatment of the sink edges depends on the way the sink is hung or set on the countertop. This calls for the installation of the sink after the tiles are set.

1   **MORTAR THE V-CAP**
To set the V-cap apply mortar to both the countertop inside the layout line and the vertical back of the V-cap.

2   **MORTAR THE FIELD IN SECTIONS**
To set the field tiles, spread and comb thinset onto the countertop, then place the tile and twist into place.

3   **RAISE THE BACKSPLASH TILES**
To set the backsplash spread and comb thinset onto the backerboard, then set the vertical tiles onto ⅛-inch shims.

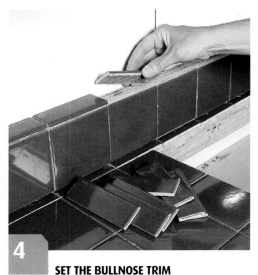

4   **SET THE BULLNOSE TRIM**
To set the bullnose trim, back-butter the trim pieces; press in place. Clean up excess mortar immediately.

5

COUNTERTOPS

Marking and cutting tile

PROJECT DETAILS

SKILLS: Marking, cutting tile
PROJECT: Marking and cutting tile
for a 12-foot L-shape countertop

TIME TO COMPLETE

EXPERIENCED: 1 hr.
HANDY: 2 hrs.
NOVICE: 3 hrs.

STUFF YOU'LL NEED

TOOLS: China marker or felt-tip
pen, wet saw or snap cutter,
safety glasses
MATERIALS: Field tile

I t would be great if countertops were built based on tile size and grout spacing. No awkward corners. No cutting tiles. Well, they aren't, and that is why there are snap cutters and wet saws.

When laying tile it is best to use a wet saw rather than a snap cutter. There are likely to be several difficult cuts. A snap cutter will make the job difficult and time-consuming.

Get used to making cuts by first cutting a series of tile strips at the back of the counter or along the sides. Next lay out and cut the more difficult and awkward cuts around the sink.

When marking and cutting the back row of countertop tiles, allow a ¼-inch horizontal gap between the countertop and the backsplash. A ⅛-inch vertical gap will be needed between the countertop tile and the bottom of the backsplash tile. This is allows slight movement of the joint once it is filled with silicone sealant.

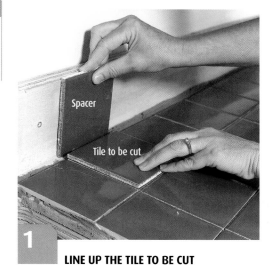

1 LINE UP THE TILE TO BE CUT
Align tile to be cut with the last tile set, then hold a spacer tile against the backerboard of the backsplash.

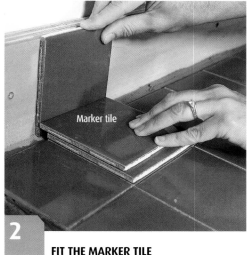

2 FIT THE MARKER TILE
Slide a marker tile over the tile to be cut and against the spacer tile at the back.

3 MARK THE CUT LINE
Use a china marker or felt-tip pen to trace the edge of the marker tile onto the tile to be cut.

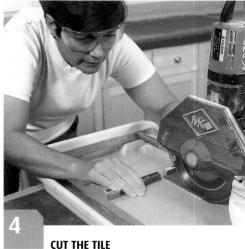

4 CUT THE TILE
Cut the tile with a wet saw (see Cutting Tile on a Wet Saw, page 105) or a snap cutter (see Using a Snap Cutter, page 104).

Grouting the joints

PROJECT DETAILS

SKILLS: Grouting tile joints, sealing tile
PROJECT: Grouting and sealing tile countertop

TIME TO COMPLETE

EXPERIENCED: 2 hrs.
HANDY: 3 hrs.
NOVICE: 4 hrs.

STUFF YOU'LL NEED

TOOLS: Margin trowel, rubber grout float, round-cornered sponge, nonabrasive pad, clean cloth, rubber gloves, bucket for mixing, bucket for rinse water
MATERIALS: Powdered grout with acrylic latex admix, tile and grout sealer, tile and grout cleaner, tile and grout penetrating sealer

Choosing a grout color requires some forethought. White grout will emphasize a darker tile but requires frequent cleaning and sealing to prevent staining. White grout also may emphasize joint-line swelling and shrinkage. Grout that closely matches the tile color masks stains and deemphasizes joint-line changes.

High-glaze tile scratches easily, so it's not a good choice for countertops. If you do use it, however, use a polymer-modified, nonsanded grout to avoid scratches while grouting.

The face of unglazed tile should be sealed before grouting because the grout will be impossible to remove otherwise. If you have a lot of tile to seal, butt it all together on the floor and apply the sealer with a foam roller.

When the front lip of V-cap extends below the bottom of the plywood, there is nothing behind the V-cap to grout against. Hold a short length of wood corner molding against the back and bottom of the V-cap as you force the grout into the joint from the front with the grout float.

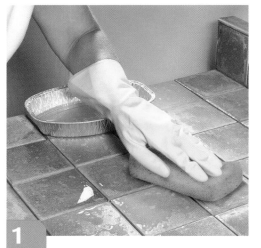

1

SEAL BEFORE GROUTING (UNGLAZED TILE)
Seal unglazed tile before grouting them. Apply penetrating sealer with a sponge; don't let it run into the joint.

2

GROUT THE TILE
Mix the grout with an acrylic latex additive, using a margin trowel. Let the grout slake 10–15 minutes, then remix. Force the grout into the joints with a grout float held at a shallow angle.

3

REMOVE THE EXCESS
Remove excess grout with the float held nearly vertical. Sweep diagonally to avoid dipping into the joints.

4 **TEST THE GROUT**

When your thumbnail leaves no impression (10 to 15 minutes or per manufacturer's instructions) clean the tiles.

5 **CLEAN THE TILES**

Use short strokes with a clean, damp—not wet—sponge. Try to keep the sponge away from the grout.

6 **REMOVE THE HAZE**

Remove the residual haze with a clean, dry cotton cloth. If the haze resists remove with an acid tile cleaner.

7 **SEAL THE TILE**

Apply a food-safe sealer with a sponge. Follow the instructions and reapply several times a year.

 WORK SMARTER

SEAL AGAINST STAINS

I used my kitchen countertop before sealing the grout. Big mistake! The grout was stained a deep red in a few places. I solved the problem! First I tried equal parts white vinegar and water, but that did little. So I tried a heavy-duty commercial tile and grout cleaner. I applied and scrubbed it in with a scrubby pad, let it set for 10 minutes, then scrubbed with a stiff bristle brush. Voilà! White as snow. I rinsed off the cleaner, let the grout dry, and finally applied the grout sealer.

 GOOD IDEA

TEST GROUT ON TILE

Before grouting test the hardness of the tile surface by scrubbing the face of a spare tile with wet grout and a plastic scrub pad. If the grout dulls the finish, you will have to be very quick and very gentle in removing the excess grout and grout haze. Rinse the sponge often and use plenty of soft clean rags.

5

COUNTERTOPS

Patios

Patio is the Spanish word for an interior courtyard in a home that is open to the outdoors. Today it usually refers to a paved area adjacent to the home intended for outdoor living. Whether it's actually a courtyard or just near your home, a patio is an outdoor space for the family to enjoy.

Easy isn't always the way to go

It's possible to put in a patio simply by laying bricks, flagstones, or other pavers on the ground. While simple to install this method will lose its charm quickly as grass and weeds begin to appear between the pavers. The surface will shift due to movement of the soil beneath, and it will soon become impossible to find a level spot to set your furniture, which creates a potentially hazardous situation.

It's a good idea to build a patio as you would any other room in your home—with a proper foundation and using tile with the proper qualities for resisting weather-related damage. A concrete

Chapter 6 highlights

slab offers the perfect base for setting tiles, provided it meets three conditions:

■ It is flat.

■ It is stable.

■ It is clean.

Getting good results

The right tile, set in water-resistant, latex-modified thinset mortar and sealed with a penetrating sealer, will create an attractive and comfortable outdoor room, increasing your living space and enhancing the value of your home.

Tiling a concrete patio is no more difficult than tiling any other floor. This chapter will lead you every step of the way, from pouring the slab to grouting the tile.

Pouring a concrete slab

Pouring a slab for an outdoor patio requires patience and common sense. Even if you've never poured concrete before, you'll be successful if you proceed one step at a time. Pouring a patio slab is also a good way to learn the basic techniques required for larger projects, such as pouring a slab for a garage or even pouring a slab to finish a basement in preparation for a ceramic tile installation.

Concrete is a mixture of sand, gravel, water, and portland cement. A chemical reaction between the water and the mix causes concrete to harden, and you must keep the slab moist while it cures.

You can buy cement and mix your own, buy concrete premix in bags, or buy it ready-mixed from a truck.

Because concrete is heavy and mixing is hard work, you're probably better off ordering ready-mix if your job requires more than a cubic yard (27 cubic feet), which is the equivalent of 40 to 50 bags of concrete premix.

The process is straightforward. You lay out the area for the slab using batterboards, stakes, and mason's line. Then you remove dirt and organic matter to a specified depth, pack the hole with gravel, and build 2× forms to hold the concrete while it cures. The final step is mixing, pouring, and finishing the slab.

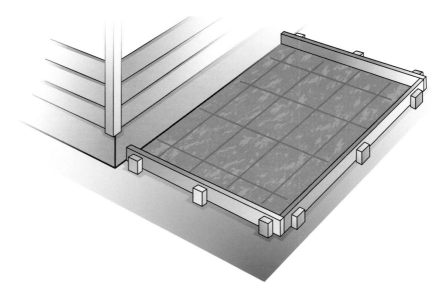

1 LAY OUT THE EXCAVATION

Lay out the excavation area with 1×3 batterboards and mason's line tied to the crosspieces. Make the area at least 1½ inches wider on each side than the finished slab size to allow for the 2× forms. Check for square and adjust the lines as necessary by sliding them along the crosspiece. Mark the outline with flour and remove the mason's line.

2 EXCAVATE

Following the outline remove 10 inches of soil (6 inches for gravel and 4 inches for the slab) so the finished height will be approximately level with the surface. (Adjust thicknesses to meet local code specifications as necessary.) Level the bottom of the excavation as much as possible.

3 SET THE FORMS

Position a 2×4 form and drive stakes on the outside of the form. Make the 2×4 length equal to the length of the slab plus 3 inches (so it overlaps the adjacent form pieces). Make 1-foot-long stakes from 1×3 lumber. Drive them about 6 inches from the ends of the form. Retie the mason's line to help position the 2×4 if necessary.

4 LEVEL THE FORMS

Level the form board at the correct height. Attach it to the stakes by driving screws through them into the 2×4.

5 SET THE OPPOSITE SIDE FORM

Install the opposite 2×4 form board so it is level with the first. This second piece will be the same length as the first. Attach it to stakes parallel to the first form piece. If the distance between form pieces is greater than the length of the level, place the level on a flat piece of lumber.

6 FASTEN THE FORMS

Drive screws through the first two form pieces into the ends of the remaining 2×4 form pieces. The length of these pieces is equal to the width of the pad. Square the form by measuring the diagonals and adjusting as necessary until they are equal. Make sure the form is level. Attach the last two form pieces to stakes driven near the ends. Use a reciprocating saw to remove the top of a stake that is higher than the top edge of the form.

A long level is more accurate than a short one.

6

PATIOS

7 INSTALL EXPANSION STRIP

Apply an expansion strip to the side of the house with masonry nails or construction adhesive. The expansion strip prevents the concrete from bonding to the structure and cracking as natural shifts occur. If you are pouring a freestanding slab, a 2×4 form will replace the expansion strip.

8 TAMP THE GRAVEL BED

Tamp a 6-inch layer of compactible ¾-inch gravel. Make it as level as possible so the correct thickness of concrete can be poured. Coat the inside of the form with vegetable oil or a commercial release agent for easy form removal. You can make a tamper, buy a hand tamper, or rent a power tamper, depending on the size of your job.

Reinforce the concrete with rebar.

BUYER'S GUIDE

REINFORCING CONCRETE

Concrete expands and contracts with changes in temperature, and it sometimes cracks as a result. Reinforcing the concrete with wire mesh or metal rods, called rebar, helps control the cracks. Rebar minimizes the size of the crack and it holds the concrete together when cracks occur.

On a well-tamped surface, rebar is optional. If you use it, it should be in the middle of the slab. Rebar is laid in a grid and the corners are tied together with wire. Rest it on wire supports made especially for the job. You can pour once the rebar is in place. It should be covered with at least 1½ inches of concrete.

9 MIX THE CONCRETE

Mix the concrete. Mix small batches of concrete in a wheelbarrow. Wear eye protection, a particulate mask, and gloves. Fill the wheelbarrow approximately three-quarters full with premixed concrete or dry ingredients. Dig a crater in the center. Pour water slowly into the crater and mix well with a shovel or hoe. The concrete is the right consistency when it clings to the side of the tool. For larger batches, rent a power mixer.

10 TEST CONSISTENCY

Test the consistency. Slice the mixed concrete with a shovel. The edges should hold straight without crumbling. If the edges crumble the mix is too dry and needs more water. If the edges fall the mix is too wet and needs more dry ingredients.

11 POUR CONCRETE INTO FORMS

Make a ramp for the wheelbarrow with a 2×8 and a concrete block. The ramp makes pouring easier and prevents the wheelbarrow from damaging the form. Fill the form in sequence, pouring loads next to the previous one to get a seamless mix. When you have filled the form, work the concrete with a shovel or hoe to break up air pockets. Tap the edges of the form with a hammer to help release trapped air.

6

PATIOS

Finishing a concrete slab

1 SETTLE THE CONCRETE
Plunge a scrap piece of lumber into the concrete in various spots to settle it and to remove air pockets. Don't disturb the reinforcement. Add more concrete until the form is slightly overfilled.

2 SCREED THE SLAB
With a helper draw a straight 2×4 in a zigzag motion to fill in depressions and remove mounds. Repeat to level the slab. Add concrete as needed.

3 SMOOTH THE SLAB
Sweep the surface with a darby, pressing down slightly to remove mounds and fill in depressions. Sweep in arcs until water begins to rise to the surface. Let the concrete rest until the water evaporates. When the water is gone, slide a small pointing trowel along the forms to separate them from the slab. Then shape the edges using an edging tool with a 1/2-inch radius. You want the edges of the slab to be smooth and rounded to prevent chipping when the forms are removed.

4 CUT CONTROL JOINTS
Control joints help prevent the slab from cracking. Cut a control joint in the center of the slab (3 feet in this case) using a jointer with a blade that is one-quarter the thickness of the slab (1 inch in this case). Draw the jointer across the slab using a straight 2×4 as a guide. As soon as the water sheen is gone, smooth and compact the surface with a wood or magnesium float.

5 BROOM THE SURFACE
To create a nonskid surface, drag a concrete broom at right angles to the flow of traffic. The longer you wait to broom, the smoother the surface will be. For best results buy a mason's concrete finishing brush.

DESIGN TIP

ROCK SOLID

For a different look sow stones the size of large gravel. Use clean, damp stones, and spread them the way you would sow seeds. Press the gravel into the concrete with a screed or darby. Brush any excess concrete off the top of the stones by sweeping with a push broom. Clean the surface by spraying with a fine mist of water until you've washed the concrete film off the stones. Let the concrete cure as you would with a broomed finish.

6 CURE THE CONCRETE
Concrete needs to cure slowly and retain moisture for about 5 days to prevent cracking. With a sprinkler or hose, run water onto the surface every few hours. Cover the slab with water whenever it appears dry. You also can cover the slab with plastic or burlap, which you can dampen with a hose or sprinkler. Don't let the plastic touch the surface, however, because it can create a mottled appearance. Also try to prevent water from puddling on the cover. Remove the forms when the concrete has fully cured.

Establishing layout lines

PROJECT DETAILS

SKILLS: Measuring, marking, snapping chalklines
PROJECT: Establishing layout lines for a small patio

TIME TO COMPLETE

EXPERIENCED: 1 hr.
HANDY: 2 hrs.
NOVICE: 3 hrs.

STUFF YOU'LL NEED

TOOLS: Tape measure, chalkline, mason's line
MATERIALS: None

Slab without expansion joints

 areful planning at the design stage will ensure a patio that lasts. For the most attractive layout, keep these three principles in mind: Locate full tiles where they will be most visible, place full tiles at doorways, and use cut tiles larger than half tiles.

You can't always satisfy all three criteria. In the following example full tiles are placed along the most visible planter border and front patio edge.

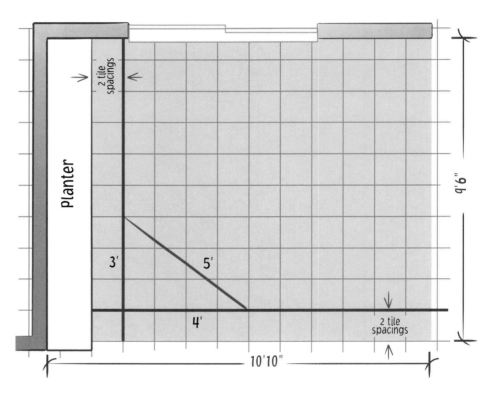

1
SNAP THE FIRST REFERENCE LINE
Snap the first reference line several grid spaces from a row with full tiles. In this project full tiles are located at the outside.

2
SNAP THE SECOND LINE
Snap a second reference line several grid spaces from the edge of the adjacent slab edge. The design has full tiles at the slab edges.

3
CHECK FOR SQUARE
Measure 3 feet and 4 feet from the intersection to check for square. If the diagonal line opposite the corner does not measure 5 feet from the marks, readjust them. When everything is square, snap layout grids.

6

PATIOS

Slab with expansion joints

When laying out tile on a slab with expansion joints, the joints take precedence over tile layout because the slab can move at the joints. If you tile over the joints, the tile will probably crack. Match the tile joints to the slab joints and caulk, rather than grout, the joints.

If you cut crack control joints in the slab, make the cuts where you want tile joints. The joints will serve as the reference lines for your layout.

Check the lines using a 3-4-5 triangle. If an adjustment is required, make it to the shorter line.

WORK SMARTER

WHERE DID THAT LINE GO?

Sometimes in a tiling project you will encounter the unforeseen event that brings you to a crisis—that is, you either have to figure out how to correct a mistake or start all over. For example, if you wait several days after you've snapped the layout lines on your patio slab, the lines might be obscured by rain or foot traffic.

If a misplaced line causes your tile to span an expansion joint, lay a 4-inch strip of 15-pound felt over the joint. The mortar won't stick to the concrete there and the concrete can move beneath the tile.

6

PATIOS

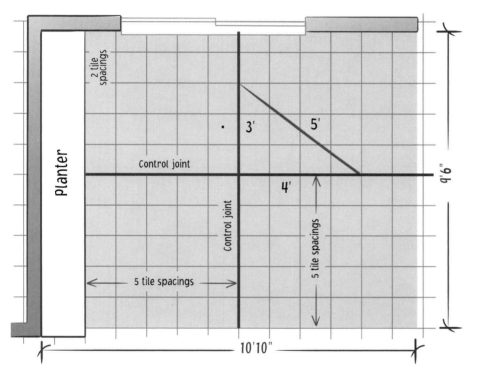

Planter

2 tile spacings

Control joint

Control joint

3' 5'

4'

5 tile spacings

5 tile spacings

9'6"

10'10"

1

SET UP THE FIRST LINE

Stretch mason's line (strong, 3-strand nylon line) over the center of the longest control joint in the slab.

2

SET UP THE SECOND LINE

Stretch a second line over the other control joint. Make sure the lines are square, then snap chalklines.

3

CHECK FOR SQUARE

Mark points 3 feet and 4 feet from the intersection of the lines. Measure between points. If not 5 feet, adjust one of the lines, then snap the chalklines in layout grids.

Setting the tile

 PROJECT DETAILS

SKILLS: Spreading mortar, setting tile
PROJECT: Setting tile for a 100-square-foot patio

 TIME TO COMPLETE

EXPERIENCED: 3 hrs.
HANDY: 6 hrs.
NOVICE: 8 hrs.

STUFF YOU'LL NEED

TOOLS: Trowel, 5-gallon bucket, tile spacers, wet saw or snap cutter
MATERIALS: Tile, thinset mortar

Before settling on your final patio tile pattern, check out patterns shown in a variety of exterior decorating books and magazines. Many of them don't require any more tile than would a simple basketweave. Some patterns do require more attention while you lay them or more cutting.

Lay the first tile at the intersection of the lines. Twist the tile back and forth slightly to make sure it is embedded in the mortar. From time to time remove a tile and inspect its back. If you find only parallel ridges, the bed is not thick enough. Once you are satisfied with the mortar bed, set the tile with spacers placed on end so that you can remove them easily.

After setting all of the tiles in an area, lay a short 2×4 on top of the tiles and lightly tap with a rubber mallet to level the tiles.

 WORK SMARTER

SAVE YOUR KNEES
You may need your knees later in life. Short of playing in the NFL, there is nothing harder on knees than working on rough concrete. Get a set of knee pads from a home center or gardening center.

1

SPREAD THE FIRST SECTION OF MORTAR
Start at the intersection of the layout lines and spread mortar over an 8- to 10-square-foot area. Press the mortar into the slab with the trowel held at a shallow angle.

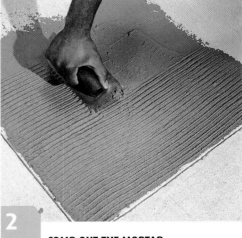

2

COMB OUT THE MORTAR
Comb the mortar in straight lines, holding the trowel at a 45-degree angle to the slab, forcing the teeth of the trowel against the concrete.

3

LAY THE TILES
Lay the first tile at the intersection of the lines. Twist the tile to make sure it's embedded in the mortar. After about the fifth tile, inspect the back for proper mortar coverage.

4

PLACING SPACERS
Place spacers on end so they will be easy to remove. Use two in the long joints, one in the short joints. Spacers can be removed and reused after 30 minutes.

5

RECHECK THE MORTAR COVERAGE

Pull up a tile occasionally to make sure the mortar is wetting the tile as well as the slab. If it isn't pull up the last batch of set tiles and start over with fresh mortar. After setting all of the tiles in an area, lay a short 2×4 on top of the tiles and lightly tap with a rubber mallet to level the tiles.

6

CLEAN JOINTS WITH A SPACER

Use a spacer to remove excess mortar before it hardens. Mortar remaining in the joint will show through the grout—particularly if the grout is light color.

7

CUTTING TILE

When you reach a place that requires a cut tile, place the tile to be cut on the last set tile. Place a marker tile on top, against a spacer tile at the wall. Trace the cut line at the edge of the marker tile onto the tile to be cut.

6

WORK SMARTER

PREPARING TO GROUT

Before grouting, let the thinset mortar cure for at least 24 hours.

1 Remove the spacers and clean any mortar out of the joints with a spacer or a bristle brush before applying the grout.

2 If the tile is rough or porous, such as brick, the grout is likely to get into pores and crevices and be difficult to remove after it has set. Seal the face of porous tile before grouting. Don't let the sealer run into the joints, however, because the sealer will prevent the grout from adhering to the joint.

3 Seal the control joints and the joints between the patio and the building foundation.

4 Stuff foam backer rod into the joint (it comes in a wide range of sizes); then caulk over it with colored silicone caulk.

1

2

3

4

Grouting the joints

PROJECT DETAILS

SKILLS: Mixing and spreading grout, cleaning tile face, applying sealer

PROJECT: Grouting tile for a 100-square-foot patio

TIME TO COMPLETE

EXPERIENCED: 3 hrs.
HANDY: 6 hrs.
NOVICE: 8 hrs.

STUFF YOU'LL NEED

TOOLS: 5-gallon bucket, ½-inch drill, mixing paddle, rubber gloves, rubber grout float, water supply, sponge, rags, small bucket, sponge mop

MATERIALS: Unmixed dry grout, sealer

Grout is as important for an outdoor patio as for a kitchen or bathroom floor. Water penetrating the joints between tiles may creep under the tile and, if it freezes, break the bond between tile and slab. Grout also keeps dirt from building up in the joints so grass and weeds won't grow there.

Tile for a patio should be nonporous. It can, however, be very rough textured. If it is you will find cleaning up the grout residue nearly impossible. Presealing the tile before setting will make cleanup a lot easier.

The simplest way to preseal tile is to lay it out, tightly fitted with no gaps, and then apply sealer with a roller. Don't do this on the slab, however, as sealer that runs between the cracks will seal the slab, preventing a bond between the setting bed and the slab.

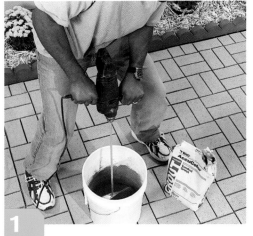

1

MIX THE GROUT

Mix the grout at slow speed in a 5-gallon bucket with a mortar paddle and ½-inch drill. Let the grout rest for 10 to 15 minutes to let the dyes develop; then remix.

2

SPREAD THE GROUT

Spread the grout with a rubber grout float held at a shallow angle. Press the grout into the joints to fill them. For joints wider than ⅜ inch, use a grout bag (opposite page).

Grout estimator

(Sq. ft. per pound of sanded grout)

Tile size, inches	Joint width, inches			
	⅛	¼	⅜	½
1×1×¼	2.5	1		
2×2×¼	3.5	2		
4¼×4¼×⁵/₁₆		3		
6×6×½		2.5	1.75	1.25
4×8×½		2.25	1.5	1
8×8×⅜		4.5	3	2
12×12×⅜	14	7		
16×16×⅜		9	5.75	3.75
24×24×⅜		13	9	6

3

REMOVE THE EXCESS

Remove excess grout with the grout float held at a steep angle. Sweep the float across the tiles diagonally so that the float doesn't dip into the joints.

4 CLEAN GROUT RESIDUE

Remove grout residue with a damp—not wet—sponge. If the mortar has set up too much, use a plastic or stainless-steel scrub pad, staying out of the joints.

5 DAMP-CURE THE GROUT

Damp-cure the grout by misting (not drenching) several times a day for three days. If the patio receives direct sunlight, cover it with plastic sheeting between mistings.

6 SEAL THE TILE

Apply penetrating sealer with a sponge mop. Wipe up the excess before it dries. Follow the manufacturer's directions for number of applications.

CLOSER LOOK

FOR WIDER GROUT JOINTS

Use a grout bag to fill joints wider than $\frac{3}{8}$ inch or with rounded or irregular edges. Apply just enough grout to fill the joints so you won't have to remove excess.

Smooth the joint with the end of a PVC pipe or the rounded end of a wooden trowel handle. Any cylindrical object with a diameter 2–3 times the joint width will work.

Tiling a stone patio

F or a truly rustic, indigenous look, surface your patio with local natural stone. Many regions of the United States are known for certain types of stone. New Hampshire is the "granite state," for example, and Vermont is known for its slate and marble.

One reason to choose local material is to minimize shipping costs. One cubic foot of most rock weighs about 170 pounds. Even if the stone were free at the source, it could cost thousands of dollars to have an average patio's worth shipped interstate. Instead, if you are lucky, you may find an excavation contractor who will let you pick through the rubble from a blasting operation.

Cleft stone has random shape and thickness, which is its charm and its weakness. Unless the stone is slate, the surface will be uneven. Patio furniture will have to be shimmed in order not to rock and wobble.

The solution to fitting the randomly shaped stones together is to treat them as pieces of a jigsaw puzzle. Arrange the largest pieces first, fill in the spaces with smaller stones, then cut even smaller pieces to fit the remaining gaps.

The problem of variable thickness is easily solved by creating a mortar bed that varies in depth.

Whether you need to apply penetrating sealer depends on the nature of the stone and the climate. In areas subject to freezing and thawing, use mortar with latex additive and a nonporous variety of stone, such as granite, and apply sealer several times a year. If there is only occasional frost where you live, water penetrating the stone and mortar is unlikely to cause a problem.

1 ARRANGE A PATTERN OF LARGER STONES
Start by spreading the largest stones randomly over the surface of the slab. This is the quickest way to fit the stones together.

2 CONTINUE FITTING LARGE STONES
Fit the remaining large stones like pieces of a puzzle between the first set of larger stones. Don't worry about the inevitable empty spots.

3 MARK THE STONES FOR SHAPE

To fill the voids, place large stones over the empty spaces and sketch the required cut lines on the stone surfaces with a felt-tip marker.

4 CUT THE STONES TO SHAPE

Shape the stones to the marked cut lines with a mason's hammer. Use the pointed end of the hammer to chip away outside the line.

5 MAKE A HEIGHT GAUGE

Make a height gauge that just clears the thickest stone. Use it to set the height of each stone as it is laid. Make it just long enough to span the widest stone.

6 MORTAR THE SLAB

Drop a thick bed of mortar on the slab where a stone will be placed. Turn the stone over and apply mortar to its underside to wet the stone and make a thick bed.

7 REPLACE THE STONE

Place the back-buttered stone back in place. If the stone surface is below that of the other stones, pick it up and add mortar to the bed.

8 BED THE STONES

Using the height gauge tamp the stone down to the proper height. After all of the stones have been set, grout the voids between the stones with the same mortar.

Creative tiling projects

Tile isn't just for walls, floors, and countertops. It's a versatile tool rich with potential for creating special decorative accessories that will enhance the inside and outside of your home. Whether you are looking for an easy project to involve the entire family, an elegant touch to add beauty to your home, or a craft you might turn into extra money, you will find it here.

The projects on the following pages range in complexity from using small pieces to enhance an outdoor birdbath to facing a fireplace. Many of them rely on a simple method for making your own mosaics—drop pieces of tile into a burlap bag or fold them in a towel and break them with a hammer. Use different colors and textures to add that special "genius" to your project.

Use the same thinset you would use in any other tiling project. Thinset mortar comes in dry form and is mixed with water or liquid-latex additive. Small amounts can be mixed by hand with a margin trowel. To mix large amounts use a 1/2-inch drill and a mortar mixing paddle in a 5-gallon plastic bucket.

Chapter 7 highlights

A range of tiling skills

Many of these projects require minimal skills and an inexpensive materials budget. Some can be completed in an hour; none require more than a weekend.

Start with something simple, even if it does seem slightly intimidating, and as your skill and confidence levels grow, you'll be tackling a kitchen floor, countertop, or patio before you know it.

Tiling a tabletop

A tiled tabletop can serve as the focal point of a room and as a work of art. Create a dramatic tabletop or an elegantly simple surface.

If you have particular tiles in mind, make your tile design first; then look for the table. If you already have the table, subtract 3 inches from its width and length and sketch a tile layout to fill that space.

You will cover up the original tabletop, so you can salvage a tag sale or discarded table. You need a solid base and legs to which you will fasten a new top of 3/4-inch AC plywood, as shown in the drawing below.

Match the 15/16-inch corner guard trim to the structure or design of the table. Determine the type of wood and have a custom millwork shop mill stock of that species.

If you don't like the looks of full-scale tile and want to try a mosaic pattern, break up some tiles in a towel and use them to create your own specialized design.

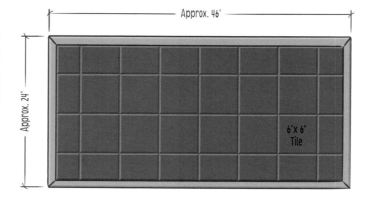

Approx. 46"
Approx. 24"
6"x 6" Tile

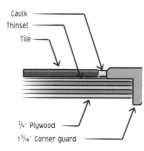

Caulk
Thinset
Tile
3/4" Plywood
1 5/16" Corner guard

1 **CUT THE TRIM**

Use a framing square to measure the four trim pieces; then cut them with a backsaw and miter box or mitersaw. With the tabletop upside down, measure and cut identical pairs of pieces so that the frame is 1/8 inch larger.

2 **GLUE AND CLAMP THE TRIM**

Apply glue to the perimeter of the table and fit the trim pieces. Clamp the pieces loosely with C-clamps; make the final adjustments, then tighten the clamps securely.

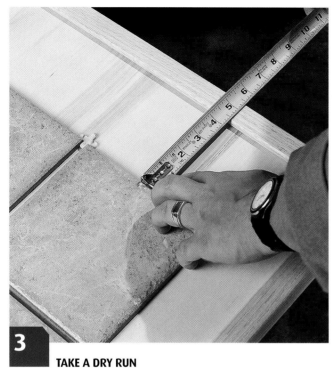

3 TAKE A DRY RUN

Dry-fit the field (center) tiles; then adjust so the perimeter gaps are symmetrical. Measure the gaps to determine the width (allowing for joints) to cut the border tiles.

4 NUMBER YOUR LAYOUT ORDER

Mark cut lines using a combination square. Number cut tiles on the paper design and on the back of the tile to eliminate mistakes when setting tiles in the planned order.

5 MORTAR AND SET TILES

Comb thinset onto the tabletop inside the trim; then set tile from one corner inward. Use tile spacers instead of layout lines.

6 GROUT THE TILES

Grout the joints after 24 hours. Protect the wood trim from the grout with masking tape. Remove excess grout, allow to cure 10 to 15 minutes, then clean up the grout haze and apply a penetrating tile and grout sealer.

Tiling a wall mural

 PROJECT DETAILS

SKILLS: Measuring, drawing to scale, calculating dimensions
PROJECT: Setting a mural backsplash behind a range

 TIME TO COMPLETE

EXPERIENCED: 4 hrs.
HANDY: 6 hrs.
NOVICE: 8 hrs.

 STUFF YOU'LL NEED

TOOLS: Carbide scorer, chalkline, drill/driver with bit, framing square, felt-tip pen, wet saw, notched trowel, grout float, safety glasses
MATERIALS: Cement backerboard, field tile, mural tiles, listellos (optional), thinset mortar, grout, backerboard screws, fiberglass reinforcing tape, sealant

7

CREATIVE TILING PROJECTS

The alcove above a kitchen range or stovetop begs for a window, or at least something different than an expanse of plain wall. A window may be out of the question because of the grease that gets splattered there. In fact, the prime requirements are that the surface be heat resistant, unaffected by grease, and easy to wipe down.

What could be better than a mural in tile? A tile mural can depict a scene one might see out a window, a cooking theme, or something dear to the heart of the cook.

Most tile stores display murals in a variety of motifs; catalogs picture hundreds more. If you don't find exactly what you want, take a sketch or photograph to a tile artisan to make one for you.

Mural techniques are the same as for tiling a wall (see page 138). Lay the mural out on a table, cut listellos to frame and set it off (optional), and measure the total width. Determine the center of the space between the wall cabinets and draw a pair of vertical lines equidistant from the center to mark left and right mural edges. After setting the bottom row of field tiles, set the mural between the vertical reference lines. After the mural is in place, cut and fit the rest of the field tile around it. Seal the grout and tile against cooking splashes.

1 **INSTALL BACKERBOARD**

Apply cement backerboard as a base for the backsplash to protect it from steam and cooking, which can soften drywall.

2 **SET THE FIELD TILES AND FRAME**

Set the mural frame after the bottom row of field tile is in place. Use the bottom tiles as the straightedge for setting the listellos (optional) of the frame.

3 **SET THE MURAL TILES**

Set the mural tiles tightly together and centered between the vertical lines. (It is more important that the mural be centered on the frame than on the lines.)

4 **FINISH THE FIELD TILES**

Set the remaining field tiles. Most of the cuts will be straight; use a wet saw to make the L-shape cuts in the top corners.

Door casing rosettes

PROJECT DETAILS

SKILLS: Simple carpentry, tiling
PROJECT: Install a pair of
tile rosettes

TIME TO COMPLETE

EXPERIENCED: 1 hr.
HANDY: 2 hrs.
NOVICE: 3 hrs.

STUFF YOU'LL NEED

TOOLS: Tape measure, pencil,
combination square, backsaw and
miter box or mitersaw, hammer,
drill/driver with bit, safety
glasses
MATERIALS: Lauan plywood,
3/4-inch square cove molding,
finish nails, drywall screws,
silicone sealant, two 3-inch-
square decorative tiles

Install tile rosettes to decorate your door or window casings. This design uses 3-inch-square tiles; use the size and design that fits your casings.

Prefinish the plywood edges so you won't have to cut in later when painting or staining.

Saw off the ends of the top door casing with a backsaw, using the inside edges of the side casings as a guide. If the remaining top casing is loose after removing the ends, drive 6d or 8d finish nails into the framing header.

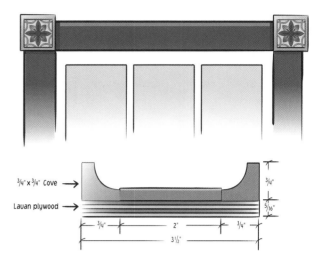

3/4" x 3/4" Cove →

Lauan plywood →

3/4"

3/4"

2"

3/4"

3 1/2"

3/4"

5/16"

1

MARK CASING FOR CORNER

Mark and remove the ends of the top casing with a backsaw, using the side casings as a guide.

2

BUILD FRAME

Fasten cove molding to squares of lauan plywood to fashion frames; prefinish the frames.

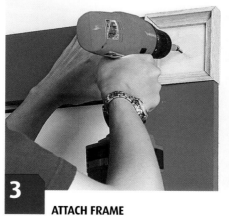

3

ATTACH FRAME

Attach the frames to the framing beneath the drywall or plaster with several 1 5/8-inch drywall screws.

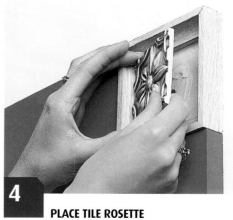

4

PLACE TILE ROSETTE

Affix the tile to the plywood with clear silicone, spread sparingly on the back of the tile.

Chair rail

PROJECT DETAILS

SKILLS: Measuring, leveling, cutting and setting tile
PROJECT: Applying a tile chair rail to drywall, per 10 feet

TIME TO COMPLETE

EXPERIENCED: 1 hr.
HANDY: 2 hrs.
NOVICE: 3 hrs.

STUFF YOU'LL NEED

TOOLS: Tape measure, 4-foot level, pencil, wet saw, notched trowel, margin trowel, tablesaw, safety glasses
MATERIALS: 220-grit sandpaper, listellos, ceramic tile mastic, masking tape

Pencil a line around the room at a height of 36 inches. Lightly sand the wall surface with 220-grit sandpaper. Starting at an inside corner, miter the corner pieces and affix them to the wall with ceramic tile mastic. Support each tile with masking tape for at least an hour.

If the wall is new, you can add blocking between the studs to give added support behind the chair rail, as shown below.

REMODEL   NEW

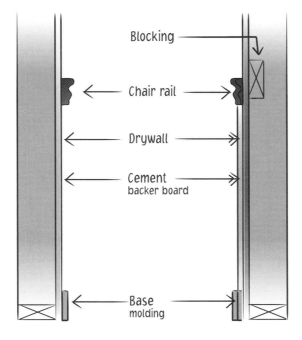

Blocking

Chair rail

Drywall

Cement backer board

Base molding

1

LAY OUT LEVEL LINE
Use a 4-foot level (or a laser level) to lightly pencil a horizontal line around the wall 36 inches above the floor.

2

ROUGH UP TILE AREA
Lightly sand the strip of wall above the pencil line with 220-grit sandpaper. Be careful not to raise the nap of the paper or to break through paint.

3

MITER ENDS FOR CORNER
Miter the ends of two inside-corner pieces of tile with a wet saw. Bevel a piece of wood at 45 degrees on a tablesaw for a tile-cutting jig.

4

APPLY TILE
Apply ceramic tile mastic to the backs of the tiles and set them along the pencil line. Support the tile with strips of masking tape.

5

BUILD-IN BLOCKING
In new construction back the chair rail with blocking and install backerboard under both drywall and tile, as shown.

7

CREATIVE TILING PROJECTS

Window treatment

PROJECT DETAILS

SKILLS: Simple carpentry, tiling
PROJECT: Replace window casings with tile

TIME TO COMPLETE

EXPERIENCED: 2 hrs.
HANDY: 4 hrs.
NOVICE: 6 hrs.

STUFF YOU'LL NEED

TOOLS: Hammer, pin driver or thin nailset, drill/driver with bit, backsaw and miter box, tape measure, safety glasses
MATERIALS: Lauan plywood, 3/4"×3/4" cove molding, 1 5/8-inch drywall screws, 6d finish nails, 2-inch-square tile, silicone sealant

7

CREATIVE TILING PROJECTS

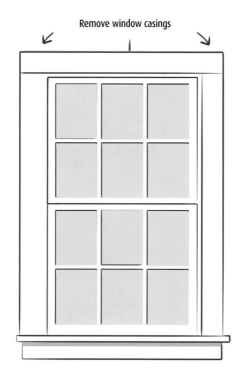

Remove window casings

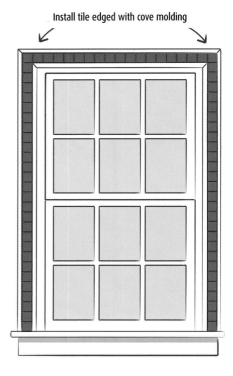

Install tile edged with cove molding

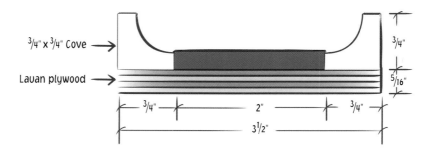

3/4" x 3/4" Cove →
Lauan plywood →
3/4" | 2" | 3/4"
3 1/2"
3/4"
5/16"

Tile window casings enhance and complement kitchen or bathroom tile. Wall paint or wallpaper touch-up is not required when a new casing is at least as wide as the one it replaces. New casing should not project beyond the existing windowsill that it abuts.

Remove the old casing, using a pin driver if you wish to salvage the wood. Replace the casing with strips of 5/16-inch lauan plywood. It's thin but strong enough as a stable base for the tile and a nailer for the trim.

To hide the plywood edges and to avoid having to cut in the casing or wall joint, prime and paint the edges of the strips first.

Install the outside lengths of molding; use tiles as spacers to fit the inside molding.

Paint or stain the molding before installing the tile. Install vertical columns first, placing the tiles that need to be cut to fit at the bottom as shown above. Center the row of tiles across the top so tiles needing to be cut to fit fall at both ends of the row.

1 **DRIVE NAILS FOR REMOVAL**

Use a pin driver or thin nailset to drive the finish nails most of the way through the window casing to allow salvage of the casings without damage.

2 **REMOVE THE CASINGS**

Cut through the paint with a utility knife where the casing and wall meet to avoid lifting the face of the drywall or wallpaper.

3 **REPLACE CASINGS WITH LAUAN PLYWOOD**

Fasten strips of $5/16$-inch lauan plywood in place of the wood casing with $1 5/8$-inch drywall screws driven into the framing around the window.

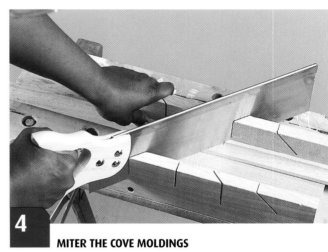

4 **MITER THE COVE MOLDINGS**

Purchase long lengths of molding. Cut, measure, and cut—each cut produces both an inside and an outside corner.

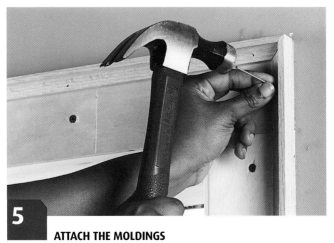

5 **ATTACH THE MOLDINGS**

Fasten the molding with 6d finish nails. Install the outside molding first. Use tiles as spacers to position the inside molding. Paint or stain the trim before installing the tiles.

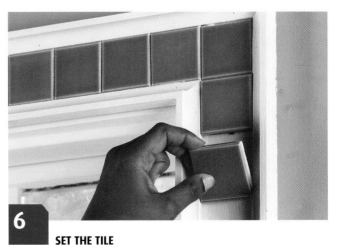

6 **SET THE TILE**

Set the tile with clear silicone sealant. Smear the silicone on the back of the tile, using only enough to achieve the bond so excess sealant won't squeeze out.

Tiling a window recess

 PROJECT DETAILS

SKILLS: Prying, troweling, sanding, setting tile
PROJECT: Installing tile in a window recess

TIME TO COMPLETE

EXPERIENCED: 4 hrs.
HANDY: 5 hrs.
NOVICE: 6 hrs.

 STUFF YOU'LL NEED

TOOLS: Pry bar, hammer, handsaw, trowels, float, putty knife, caulk gun
MATERIALS: Joint tape, joint compound, mortar, tile, caulk, spacers, grout, rags, water, nails, insulation

iling a window recess adds a new level of interest to the design of a room—for a small amount of effort and expense, you can achieve the effects of a complete makeover. Tile adds color, texture, and shape to a plain window. Plus the tile won't rot or stain, so there's less chance of moisture damage from condensation, potted plants, or rain entry.

Choose the color of the tile first, then the texture. It's the color that has to work with the rest of the room before any of the other attributes of the tile. If you've got the wrong color on the windows, they can either end up dull and lifeless or make you want to tear them out and start all over again.

A neutral color will make the window seem to recede or blend in with the wall. This is a place where terra-cotta tiles are a good choice. If you want to call attention to the architecture of the window, use decorative tiles but design judiciously.

1

REMOVE THE WINDOW CASING
Using a flat pry bar, remove the casing by inserting scrap wood under the bar to avoid damaging the surfaces. Take off the stop molding if the tile will extend to the sash. Remove the sill, cutting it with a handsaw if necessary.

2

INSULATE THE GAP
Stuff fiberglass insulation into the gap between the jamb and the wall. If you're tiling the wall, apply fiberglass drywall tape and compound. Feather the compound level with the wall. Let it dry and sand smooth.

3

PLACE THE TILES
Spread thinset and install the face tiles. Then spread thinset on the sill plate and lay these tiles before the sides. Then mortar the jambs and set the side tiles, holding them in place with painter's tape if necessary.

4 SET THE TOP TILE

Set the top tile in mortar and support it with a batten. To avoid pushing the end tiles too deeply into the mortar, don't force the supports. Let the mortar dry, then grout the tile.

5 CAULK THE JOINT

Caulk the joint between the tiles and the window. Choose a caulk that's the same color as the grout and smooth it with a caulking tool or a wet finger.

Tiling a ceiling

Brace backerboard while driving screws

1 INSTALL BACKERBOARD

Measure the dimensions of the ceiling and cut backerboard sections to fit the area. If the adjoining walls are covered, subtract ¼ inch from this measurement. Mortar the ceiling and then brace the backerboard and fasten it to the ceiling with backerboard screws.

2 MORTAR THE BACKERBOARD

Comb thinset on a section of backerboard—only over an area you can tile before the mortar begins to set. For heavy tiles use a piece of ⅜-inch plywood supported with 2×4s to keep the tiles in place until the mortar dries.

3 SET THE TILES

Back-butter each tile and set it in the mortar with a slight twist. After the mortar has cured, grout the tiles, applying grout only to an area you can finish and clean before the grout begins to set. Clean off excess grout and remove the haze.

Staircase risers

 PROJECT DETAILS

SKILLS: Measuring, cutting, setting tile

PROJECT: Tiling a stair riser (time per riser)

 TIME TO COMPLETE

EXPERIENCED: 30 min.
HANDY: 1 hr.
NOVICE: 1.5 hrs.

 STUFF YOU'LL NEED

TOOLS: Tape measure, felt-tip pen, combination square, wet saw, safety glasses, caulk gun
MATERIALS: 8-inch square tiles, silicone adhesive

Tiling stair risers originating at a tiled floor ties the tiled floor to the rest of the room. Choose tiles and colors for the stair treads to complement the floor tile.

You may need to trim the height of the tile and the widths of the two end pieces (make the two end cuts symmetrical). Since the height cut will be narrow, the cuts will have to be made with a wet saw (see page 105 for a description of its use).

You could also tile the surfaces of the treads. If you do so, however, the specifications will be more demanding:

- The tread tile must be rated as a floor tile.
- The tile's coefficient of friction must be 0.6 or greater.
- The base should consist of at least $^3/_4$-inch underlayment plywood.
- The tile should be set in epoxy with no caulked joints.

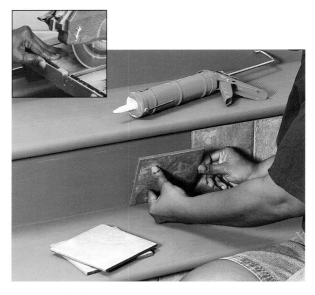

CUT AND APPLY THE TILE
Measure the stair riser and cut the tile if necessary. Apply silicone caulk to the back of each tile and press it into place. Apply sparingly to avoid squeezing out caulk. Use a damp rag to clean up any caulk immediately. Use the caulk gun carefully to avoid excess.

Tile name sign

 PROJECT DETAILS

SKILLS: Measuring, basic carpentry
PROJECT: Making a tile name sign

 TIME TO COMPLETE

EXPERIENCED: 2 hrs.
HANDY: 3 hrs.
NOVICE: 4 hrs.

 STUFF YOU'LL NEED

TOOLS: Tape measure, table saw, paintbrush, C-clamps or nails, pencil, safety glasses, dust respirator, earplugs
MATERIALS: Animal alphabet tiles, lauan plywood, $^3/_4$-inch quarter-round molding, carpenter's glue, silicone sealant, wood stain, polyurethane finish

The family name on a mailbox, a child's name on a bedroom door, or a piece of hanging art—all are made simple with animal alphabet tile. The project becomes a family affair when, under the family banner, you hang each child's name. Make each sign as shown and string them together with pairs of screw eyes.

Start by laying out the name in animal characters. Fit the tiles tightly, using a straightedge to keep them aligned, and measure the total length and width.

Make a frame, as shown opposite, of $^3/_4$-inch quarter-round molding glued to a backing of lauan plywood. Adjust the 4-inch dimension of the drawing below to fit the actual tile.

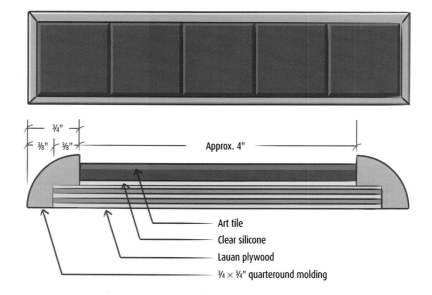

Art tile

Clear silicone

Lauan plywood

$^3/_4 \times ^3/_4$" quarterround molding

1 LINE UP THE TILES

Line up the tile on a piece of lauan plywood with the tile flush with two panel edges; then hold a trim piece against the tile and draw the cut lines.

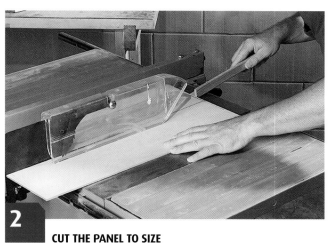

2 CUT THE PANEL TO SIZE

Cut the lauan panel on a table saw. Make the panel ⅛ inch larger than the first marks. You can always trim it, but you can never make it larger.

3 RABBET THE MOLDING

Cut the ⅛×⅛-inch rabbet in the ¾-inch quarter-round molding stock. Then miter the four corners to make the four sides of the frame.

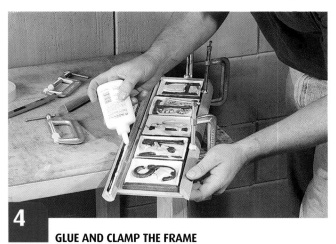

4 GLUE AND CLAMP THE FRAME

Glue and clamp the frame to the lauan backing. Use carpenter's glue and C-clamps. If you don't have clamps, nail the trim from the back of the panel.

5 PREFINISH THE FRAME

Finish the frame before setting the tile so you don't have to mask or clean up. For interior use just stain; for exterior use apply stain and polyurethane.

6 SET THE TILE

Set the tile by applying clear silicone to the backs of the tiles and pressing into place. You can change the name later if you use contact cement instead.

Fireplace surround

PROJECT DETAILS

SKILLS: Drawing to scale, cutting and setting tile and backerboard
PROJECT: Installing a tile fireplace surround

TIME TO COMPLETE

EXPERIENCED: 1 day
HANDY: 1.5 days
NOVICE: 2 days

STUFF YOU'LL NEED

TOOLS: Tape measure, framing square, carbide scorer, wet saw, notched trowel, grout float, chalkline, felt-tip pen
MATERIALS: Tile, cement backerboard, thinset mortar, unsanded grout, masking tape, 6d finish nails

T ile dresses up a plain fireplace and can be substituted for brick in new construction at little or no additional cost.

After you form an idea of what you want to do, check local codes. Codes specify approved materials and the proximity of the fireplace opening to the mantel, trim, and other projections.

Make structural changes to the fireplace before you plan your tile design. You may wish to install a fireplace insert to increase heating efficiency. New tile can cover gaps between the insert and the old fireplace. Visit tile suppliers for inspiration. Ask them to show you what other customers have done.

Once you have the design on paper, lay the tiles out on the floor in front of the fireplace to determine how they will look and what cuts you will need to make. When you are ready follow the steps in the photos.

1

INSTALL BACKERBOARD
Apply backerboard to the face of the fireplace as a flat base for the tile. Use thinset mortar rated for heat-producing installations.

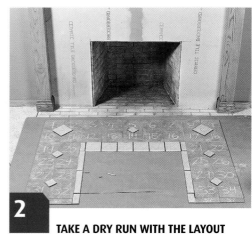

2

TAKE A DRY RUN WITH THE LAYOUT
Lay out tile pieces on the floor to make sure the design will fit. When you are satisfied, number the back of each tile and note its position on the sketch.

3
MARK THE INSET CUTS
Use the inset tiles as templates to mark the cut lines on the field tiles to fit the tile insets exactly.

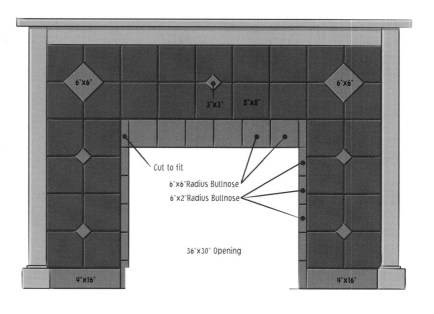

6"x6"   6"x6"

3"x3"   8"x8"

6"x6"

Cut to fit

6"x6" Radius Bullnose
6"x2" Radius Bullnose

36"x30" Opening

4"x16"   4"x16"

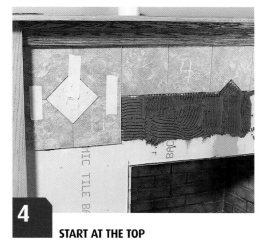

4
START AT THE TOP
Set the top tiles in thinset, supporting the tiles with 6d finish nails driven into the backerboard. Support tiles below with strips of masking tape.

5
FINISH WITH BULLNOSE TILE
Use bullnose trim tiles to finish the edges of the fireplace opening. The alternative is to bevel the exposed edges of the opening tiles.

Fireplace inspiration

Fireplace hearth

 PROJECT DETAILS

SKILLS: Measuring, cutting, and setting tile and backerboard
PROJECT: Installing a tile fireplace hearth

 TIME TO COMPLETE

EXPERIENCED: 4 hrs.
HANDY: 6 hrs.
NOVICE: 8 hrs.

 STUFF YOU'LL NEED

TOOLS: Tape measure, framing square, carbide scorer, wet saw or circular saw with a masonry blade, $1/2"\times 1/2"$ square-notched trowel, $1/4"\times 1/4"$ trowel, grout float, chalkline, felt-tip pen, safety glasses, dust respirator
MATERIALS: Tile, cement backerboard, thinset mortar, unsanded grout, sanded-texture polyblend ceramic tile caulk, hardwood, 8d finish nails, sealer

Once you've tiled the surround, you may want to redo the hearth in the same or, perhaps, a complementary tile.

Consult with your local codes official for fire code regulations. Two areas of concern are the required dimensions of the hearth to the front and sides of the fireplace opening and the required thickness of the noncombustible hearth and its base. The Safety Alert on page 197 lists the most common requirements, but check locally to make sure.

As with the fireplace surround, the hearth shown illustrates the principles involved. Check with local authorities for building code requirements.

The design uses a double layer of $1/2$-inch backerboard base. The double layer, mortared to the bricks beneath and to each other, adds fire resistance and stiffness to the base.

Before applying the first mortar bed, scrub the hearth to remove all traces of soot and ash. Apply and comb a thick layer of heat-resistant thinset mortar to the hearth with a $1/2\times 1/2$-inch squared-notch trowel. Let the first layer of backerboard set for several hours before setting the second layer in a thinner mortar bed.

Frame the backerboard with prefinished hardwood strips. If you have trouble finding hardwood strips to match the existing flooring, look in the Yellow Pages for a hardwood flooring installer and see if the installer has any scrap tongue-and-groove strips of the same species. Rip the $3/4$-inch scrap into the desired dimensions and prefinish it to match your floor.

To prevent staining by soot, select floor tile with a smooth, nonporous finish. Set the tile in plain thinset with no spaces. Wait 24 hours; apply plain, unsanded grout. Use penetrating sealer to make cleaning the hearth easier.

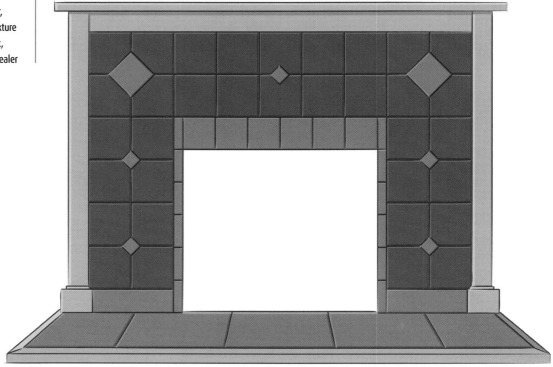

1

CUT BACKERBOARD TO FIT

Cut two strips of backerboard with a carbide scoring tool. The corner notches will have to be cut with a wet saw or a circular saw with a masonry blade.

2

SET BOTH LAYERS OF BACKERBOARD

Use mortar without additive. Apply the first layer with a $1/2 \times 1/2$-inch square-notched trowel; the second with a $1/4 \times 1/4$-inch trowel.

3

FRAME THE HEARTH

Cut and miter strips of hardwood. Match the species and finish if the surrounding floor is wood. Fasten the strips to the floor with 8d finish nails.

4

SET THE TILE

Set the tile in a bed of thinset without additive. Fit the tile tightly to eliminate gaps and caulk the joint between tile and wood strips with sanded-texture caulk.

5

GROUT THE TILE JOINTS

Apply unsanded grout without additive to prevent sparks from falling between the cracks. Remove excess grout, allow to cure 10 to 15 minutes, and clean away haze. Apply penetrating sealer liberally to keep the hearth clean.

Stove base

Tile is a popular material for stove bases because it is noncombustible, attractive, and easy to keep clean. Consult your local codes official before proceeding, however. If the official considers a stove base to be the same as a fireplace hearth, then the noncombustible base must be at least 4 inches thick. The exception would be for a stove with a heat shield attached to the bottom. Many stove manufacturers offer a shield as an option.

Cast-iron wood and coal stoves commonly weigh between 200 and 500 pounds. Because the immense weight is concentrated on four small feet, it is imperative that the selected tile be tough and that it be fully supported beneath with mortar and a stiff base.

The combination of 3/4-inch plywood and 1/2-inch backerboard, mortared together with thinset, provides the support and stiffness. Setting the base on strips of strapping lends the base the appearance of thickness while creating a dead-air layer to retard downward heat flow. (The dead-air effect can be enhanced by stapling aluminum foil to the plywood.)

Don't let our choice of neutral gray tile intimidate you. This is your canvas! See what you can find at the tile store.

Although we used spacers between the quarry tile to emphasize the pattern, you may choose to eliminate the spaces, as is common in tiled hearths.

Finally seal the tile and grout with a penetrating sealer so that they won't pick up soot and ash.

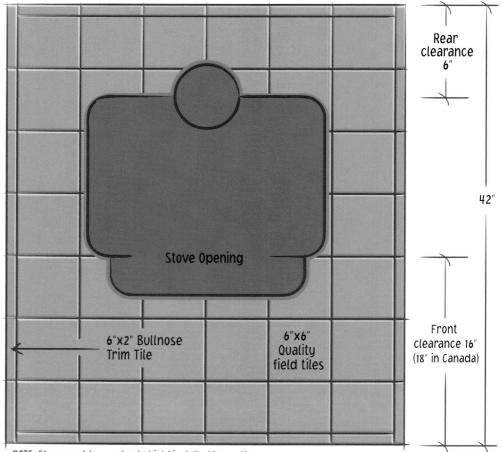

Rear clearance 6"

42"

Stove Opening

Front clearance 16" (18" in Canada)

6"x2" Bullnose Trim Tile

6"x6" Quality field tiles

NOTE: Stove must have a heat shield installed beneath

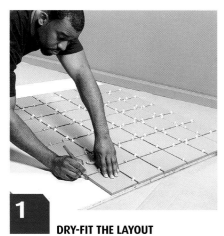

1
DRY-FIT THE LAYOUT

Dry-fit tiles and spacers on a sheet of ¾-inch plywood. Make the edges of tile and plywood flush; trace the other edges on the panel.

2
REINFORCE THE BASE

Fasten strips of strapping to the underside of the plywood with drywall screws. Space the strips 16 inches on-center and around the perimeter.

WORK SMARTER

GET A GRIP
After finishing the stove base, one homeowner discovered there was no way to get fingers under the edge to pick it up. To avoid the problem leave off the bullnose trim tiles on the back and drill several ¾-inch finger holes through the back edge.

3
CUT AND MARK BACKERBOARD

Cut a matching panel of ½-inch backerboard, place it over the plywood, and snap chalklines on its face along the wood strip centers.

4
MORTAR THE BACKERBOARD

Remove the backerboard. Apply thinset mortar without latex additive to the plywood using a ¼×¼-inch square-notched trowel.

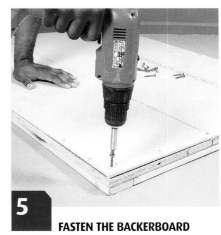

5
FASTEN THE BACKERBOARD

Place the backerboard on the mortared plywood. Fasten with backerboard screws every 6 inches along the chalklines.

6
ATTACH THE EDGE GUIDES

Nail strapping strips around the edges of the base as a temporary guide for setting the tile flush with the edges.

7
SET THE TILE

Set the tile in a layer of unmodified thinset. Work from one corner outward, with the tiles flush against the wood strips.

8
FINISH AND GROUT THE TILE

Remove the strips after 24 hours and set back-buttered bullnose trim to the edges. Grout the joints and seal both tile and grout.

7

CREATIVE TILING PROJECTS

Stove heat shield

A heat shield can reduce the required clearance of a radiant stove from the wall. All wood and gas stoves have designated clearances—with and without heat shields. Consult a stove dealer and local codes before designing a heat shield.

Key heat shield requirements are:

- noncombustible shield materials
- noncombustible shield supports
- specified free air space between the shield and the wall
- clearance at top and bottom of the shield to allow free air circulation

Begin your project by cutting a ½-inch panel of backerboard to the required size of the heat shield. Lay out tiles and spacers on the floor and lay the shield over them to mark the tile cut lines. Also cut three lengths of metal hat channel to the height of the panel.

Next find and mark the centers of the studs in the wall behind the shield. Place a 2×4 shim at the base of the wall and fasten the shimmed hat channel to the studs. Fasten the backerboard to the hat channel with wafer-head self-tapping screws.

Set the tile to the panel using heat-resistant (no latex) thinset. Remove the shim and grout the joints.

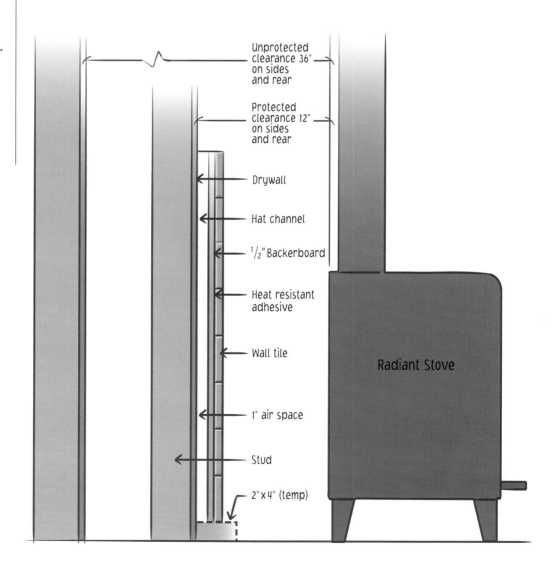

1
MARK THE FLOOR FOR CUT TILES
Place the sized ½-inch backerboard over a field of tiles and spacers on the floor. Trace the edges of the panel onto the tiles for cut lines.

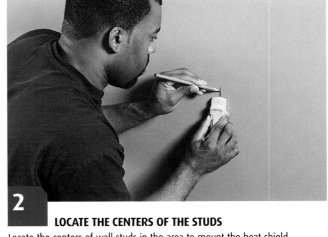

2
LOCATE THE CENTERS OF THE STUDS
Locate the centers of wall studs in the area to mount the heat shield. Use a 4-foot level to draw a pencil line along the stud centers.

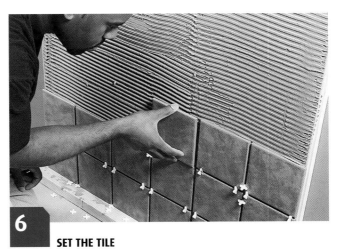

3
CUT HAT CHANNEL TO LENGTH
Cut three lengths of metal hat channel with a hacksaw; stand on end on a 2×4 shim and fasten to the studs with 2-inch drywall screws. Wear safety glasses when drilling.

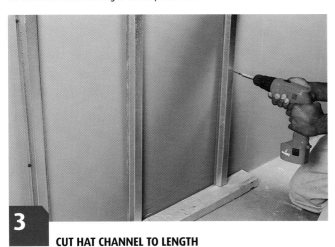

4
SET BACKERBOARD AND LAY OUT LINES
Set the backerboard on the 2×4 shim and use the 4-foot level to draw the centerlines of the hat channels on the face of the panel.

5
ATTACH BACKERBOARD TO HAT CHANNEL
Fasten the backerboard to the hat channel with wafer-head, self-tapping screws spaced every 4 inches. Drive the screw heads flush with the surface.

6
SET THE TILE
Set the tile in heat-resistant adhesive (unmodified thinset mortar). After 24 hours remove the 2×4 shim and spacers and grout the joints with unmodified sanded grout.

Birdbath

PROJECT DETAILS

SKILLS: Measuring, calculating, mixing mortar and grout, setting tile
PROJECT: Mosaic tiling a concrete birdbath

TIME TO COMPLETE

EXPERIENCED: 4 hrs.
HANDY: 6 hrs.
NOVICE: 8 hrs.

STUFF YOU'LL NEED

TOOLS: Tape measure, rubber mallet, tile nippers, putty knife, notched spreader, margin trowel or rubber spatula, towel or burlap bag, scrub pad, soft cloth, safety glasses
MATERIALS: Assorted glazed tile, 1-inch-square bead tile, one art tile, latex-modified thinset mortar, latex-modified grout, sealer

7

CREATIVE TILING PROJECTS

Birds will love this mosaic-tiled birdbath. Purchase a plain cast-concrete birdbath at a home center or garden supply store. Search local tile stores for decorative tiles to set in the bottom of the bath. After you have found the centerpiece, look for plain glazed wall tiles and 1-inch-square bead trim tiles to complement the decorative tile.

Calculate the area to be covered with mosaic pieces using the formula below right. Making mosaics results in about 50 percent waste, so purchase three times the area in plain tile. Make the mosaic pieces by wrapping tiles in a towel or burlap bag and breaking them with a rubber maller. Set the rim first. Back-butter 1-inch-square bead tiles with a putty knife and set them around the inside circumference.

Next back-butter the center tile heavily and press it into the bottom of the bowl.

Spread thinset over half of the remaining area at a time with a plastic notched spreader and set the mosaics. After 24 hours grout the spaces using a rubber spatula. After the grout hardens remove it from the tile with a scrub pad and seal the bowl.

Area=$(.78539 \times C \times C) - (A \times B)$

1

MARK THE RIM

Measure the 1×1-inch bead and the circumference of the rim. Mark the rim to take evenly spaced pieces. Back-butter each piece with thinset and set between marks.

2

PLACE THE CENTERPIECE (OPTIONAL)

Select an art tile as a centerpiece—such as this entertaining frog. Back-butter the tile heavily and set it into the bottom. Remove excess mortar.

3

MAKE THE MOSAIC

Make a batch of mosaic pieces by smashing glazed tile in a towel or burlap bag. Round the sharp points with tile nippers.

4

MORTAR THE BOWL

Apply and comb out latex-modified thinset with a plastic notched spreader. Cut down the spreader if necessary to conform to the curve of the bowl.

5

SET THE MOSAICS

Set the mosaic pieces as tightly as you can while maintaining a random color pattern. Work quickly so the mortar doesn't stiffen before you finish.

6

GROUT THE PATTERN

Spread latex-modified grout in the joints with a margin trowel or a rubber kitchen spatula. Remove excess, allow the grout to cure 10 to 15 minutes, then clean the haze away with a plastic scrub pad and soft cloth. Seal the bowl.

Garden bench

Garden benches are widely available in cast concrete, and the flat surfaces are ideal for a personal touch.

The key to keeping the job manageable is the availability of surface bullnose and surface bullnose down-angle trim tiles, which save smoothing edges.

Dry-fit perimeter tiles to determine which straight cuts you have to make to one or more interior rows. Once all the tiles fit, draw layout lines for the center field of tiles.

Set the center field within the layout lines first, using latex-modified thinset mortar. Then set the perimeter tiles, aligning them with the previously set tile.

Back-buttering the perimeter tiles saves cleaning excess mortar from the edges of the bench.

After 24 hours fill the joints with latex-modified grout using a grout float. After the grout stiffens clean the tile with a scrub pad and clean, damp rags. Apply a penetrating sealer to tile and grout.

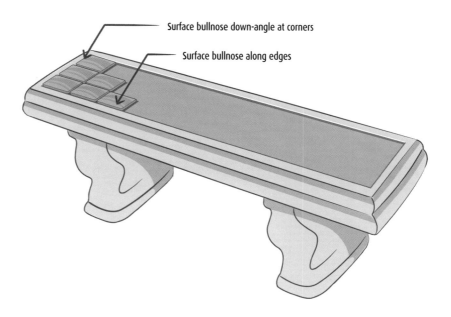

Surface bullnose down-angle at corners

Surface bullnose along edges

1

DRY-FIT THE TILE TO THE BENCH TOP

Use surface bullnose tile along the edges and surface bullnose down-angle tile at the four corners. Cut interior tiles as needed.

2

MARK THE TILE LOCATIONS

Mark the locations of the dry-fit tiles with a pencil or pen. The only tiles you have to mark fully are the tiles along the center row.

3

SPREAD THE MORTAR

Spread latex-modified thinset mortar for the center row of tile using a notched spreader.

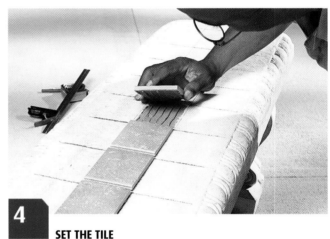

4

SET THE TILE

Place it straight down, twist it back and forth slightly, and align it with the marks. Place a short 2×4 board over the tiles and tap with a mallet to level the row.

5

BACK-BUTTER THE TILES

Back-butter the remaining tile and set them with joints aligned with the center row joints. As you set tap tiles level with the center row.

6

GROUT THE BENCH

Spread latex-modified grout with a rubber grout float. When the grout is thumbnail hard (10 to 15 minutes), clean the tile with a plastic scrub pad and soft cloth, then apply sealer.

Maintenance and repair

All the tile covered in this book, from laminates to vinyls, ceramics to stones, are relatively—but not automatically—permanent as building materials go. Some will last forever, others will need replacement. All will benefit from a regular maintenance schedule. After all, it's not too unusual to think that to keep a heavily used floor and walls in kitchens and baths looking like new you will have to periodically clean and seal them. This may, however, come as a surprise if you are a first-time user of ceramic tile. Even that is not immune from this requirement. Unless you have chosen a particular tile because it was natural and maintenance free and expect it to develop its own patina as it ages, you will need to do some periodic maintenance to keep your floor looking its best.

Chapter 8 highlights

Tile needs TLC too

Grout is typically more porous than tile and so has an even greater need for sealing. Even if you don't seal your tile, do seal your grout as soon as it has cured. Being of uniform color, and usually light in color, it will immediately show stains and appear mottled.

With sealers you get what you pay for. Don't waste your money and time on surface coatings; go for a penetrating sealer that will soak into the pores of the tile and grout and give deep protection against stains.

Even a penetrating sealer will eventually evaporate, but the best (and most expensive) will require resealing once a year at most; the least expensive will require resealing every few months, depending on traffic.

Keep your leftovers

If you have set your tile on a proper base, it will be fully supported. In all likelihood, however, someone will eventually drop a 400-pound cast-iron stove and crack a tile, or roughhouse a hole in a tiled wall, or make skid marks on the vinyl. Here's the answer to what you do with the leftovers. You save them for when such repairs become necessary. Make sure you have a few leftover full tiles stored away because there's no guarantee you will be able to match the tile a few years down the line. Equally important, save a little of the original dry grout in an empty paint can or a sealed glass jar so that you can match the grout when you repair or replace it.

Replacing a ceramic tile

You dropped your bowling ball on the kitchen floor and cracked a tile. Now what do you do? If you saved a few full tiles when you set the floor, you can replace the broken tile. Remove all of the grout with a grout saw. Then score the tile from corner to corner with a carbide scoring tool. Break up the tile with a hammer and cold chisel and remove the adhesive. Then it's just a matter of buttering up a replacement, setting it in place, and regrouting.

 TOOL TIP

CHISELS WITH SAFETY GRIPS
You can buy cold chisels that come with plastic safety handles. It's not a bad idea. They will protect your hand from misplaced hammer blows.

1 REMOVE THE GROUT
Remove the grout from around the tile using a grout saw or rotary tool. Score the tile diagonally with a carbide scoring tool and a straightedge. Repeat passes until the score is at least 1/16 inch deep.

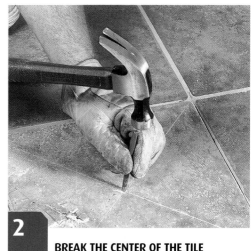

2 BREAK THE CENTER OF THE TILE
Strike the center of the tile at the intersection of the score lines with a point punch. Wear protective goggles.

3 BREAK UP THE TILE
Break up the tile with a cold chisel and hammer. Strike all along the scored lines, which are zones of weakness.

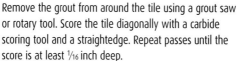

4 REMOVE THE ADHESIVE
Remove the adhesive with a bricklayer's chisel. You don't have to remove all adhesive, but enough to make room for the new thinset.

5 SPREAD NEW MORTAR
Spread and comb thinset on the floor. Use the minimum amount required to wet the floor and comb with a 1/4×1/4-inch square-notch trowel.

6 **BACK-BUTTER THE REPLACEMENT**
Back-butter the tile with the minimum amount of mortar required to wet the surface. Too much mortar will prevent the tile from lying flat.

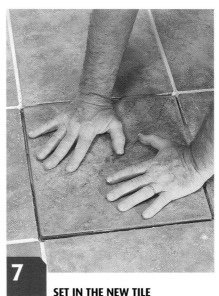

7 **SET IN THE NEW TILE**
Set the tile in place and twist it back and forth. Tap it down with a flat board and mallet. Remove the excess mortar that squeezes into the joints.

8 **GROUT THE JOINTS**
After 15 minutes clean the tile with a scrub pad. Mist the grout for three days. Apply penetrating sealer to the tile and grout.

Maintaining ceramic and stone

A lthough regular cleaning will keep ceramic and stone tile in good condition, sometimes you're going to need to remove stains from these seemingly impenetrable materials.

When stain removal becomes necessary, start with the procedures outlined in the chart at right. If these don't work ask a tile supplier for a commercial stain-removal agent made for your tile.

Stubborn stains often come out with a stain-removing poultice, a cleaning agent mixed with baking soda, plaster of paris, or refined clay. Deodorant-free cat litter works well too. Mix the ingredients into a wet paste and apply it to the stain. Tape a plastic bag over the paste and let it sit for a couple of days. Then brush off the paste.

Unglazed tile requires a sealer, and even presealed tile may need periodic stripping and resealing. There are two main kinds of sealers. Penetrating sealers soak into the tile bisque and preserve the natural color of the tile. Topical sealers lie on the surface of the tile and may lighten or darken the tile colors or change its sheen. Topical sealers wear off and sometimes require yearly reapplication. When tiles look dull it is probably time to strip and reseal them.

Removing stains from tile

Stain	Cleaner and method
Ink, coffee, blood	Start with a 3 percent hydrogen peroxide solution; if that doesn't work try a nonbleach cleaner.
Oil-base products	Use a mild solvent, such as charcoal lighter fluid or mineral spirits, then household cleaner in a poultice. For dried paint scrape with a plastic (not metal) scraper.
Grease, fats	Clean with a commercial spot lifter.
Rust	Use commercial rust removers, then try household cleaner.
Nail polish	Remove with nail polish remover.

Always rinse the stained area with clear water to remove residue.

Replacing grout

1 f grout begins to fall out, it means that it was improperly mixed or applied. Even worse it could be that the wall behind the tile is moving, necessitating the removal of the tile and fixing the problem. In the former case follow these steps.

1 REMOVE THE GROUT
A diamond wheel on a rotary grinding tool makes fast work of removing large amounts of grout.

If there is just a little grout to remove, use a utility knife or a grout saw, which is designed for the purpose.

If you have a whole wall of grout to remove, see if you can get a rotary grinder with a diamond wheel. Do not use a screwdriver blade—the wedge-shape blade might dislodge a tile.

Clean out the debris with a toothbrush and wash down the surface to remove all dust. Let the wall dry completely before regrouting.

If the grout was colored, save some of the old chips and dust to try to match them to the colored grout samples at the tile dealer.

Mix dry grout with latex additive to make it stick better and be more water-resistant. Mix it with a margin trowel in a plastic container.

Apply the grout with a rubber grout float, forcing the grout into the joints. Remove the excess grout immediately by sweeping the edge of the float diagonally across the joints. When the grout resists denting with your thumbnail, scrub the grout from the tile with a damp sponge. Wipe the remaining haze from the tile with clean, damp cotton rags. Mist the grout several times a day for three days, then seal the tile and grout with a penetrating sealer.

2 MIX NEW GROUT
Wash out joints with water, let dry a minimum of 24 hours, then mix the grout in a plastic container using a margin trowel.

3 APPLY GROUT TO THE JOINTS
Use a rubber grout float. Hold the float at a 45-degree angle to the surface of the tile and press the grout into the joints.

4 REMOVE EXCESS GROUT
Using the same grout float, hold the float at a 90-degree angle to the surface of the tile and sweep it diagonally to the joints.

5 CLEAN THE TILE

Use short strokes with a damp sponge. Avoid a wet sponge; too much water may change the color and strength of the grout.

6 REMOVE THE HAZE

Use clean, soft rags. When the tile is clean, cure the grout by misting several times a day for three days. Seal the grout per the manufacturer's directions.

Isolating a crack

f the substrate beneath a tile floor shifts and cracks, the tile above will crack as well. Unless you know the crack is stable (see Evaluating Cracked Concrete, page 76), tiling over it is not a good idea. You should find and repair what's causing the substrate to shift before you do any repairs or install a new floor. If the crack is reasonably stable, you can often isolate it with some form of bridging material that will relieve the stress on the tile.

Materials are sold specifically as isolation membranes, although 15-pound roofing felt (common tar paper) serves as well. Cut strips of felt about the same width as the tile and center the strips over the crack. Use as many strips as necessary to follow the course of the crack.

Tile over the slab and felt strips. Spread and comb thinset over but not under the felt. Set the tile as usual. When you grout the tile joints, however, fill the joints on both sides of the crack with silicone caulk. This way the tile over the crack is free to float, attached elastically to the tiles on both sides, but not to the slab beneath.

AN INEXPENSIVE ISOLATION MEMBRANE

Fifteen-pound roofing felt (tar paper) is often used to isolate tile from active cracks in a concrete slab. Strips are centered over the length of the crack to prevent the thinset from bonding the tile to the concrete and will prevent the tile from cracking.

8

MAINTENANCE AND REPAIR

Replacing damaged parquet

Parquet is the "fine furniture" of wood floors. If you treat it as such, it will give you years of service. If you mistreat it, it soon can look deteriorated and shabby. One of the best things you can do for this floor is to clean it with a product either made by or recommended by the manufacturer. Never clean a parquet floor (or any wood floor, for that matter) with water or water-base products.

The same general rules for maintenance of wood floors apply to parquet. Wipe up spills immediately with a damp cloth and dry the area with a dry cloth. Old T-shirts are excellent for this purpose. Do not use cleaners that contain abrasives, caustic chemicals, bleach, or ammonia. For routine cleaning, it is best to use a solvent-base cleaner or a one-step cleaner/polish combination.

Most prefinished parquet tile comes with a durable acrylic or polyurethane finish. Some finishes are no-wax, others benefit from waxing. Check the manufacturer's directions before you purchase cleaning products. Acrylic waxes are not generally recommended for wood floors, and some polyurethane finishes must never be waxed.

Almost all wood finishes change color over time. You can slow this process somewhat by keeping the drapes closed. Areas covered with rugs won't be subject to color changes, and the color difference will be revealed if you decide to move the rugs later.

Preventive maintenance for parquet

Regular vacuuming is the best thing you can do for a wood floor. Aside from water nothing ruins a wood floor more quickly than the abrasiveness of tracked in dirt and dust. Vacuuming removes these offending particles and keeps them from residing in the joints (which brooming or dust mopping won't do).

To help keep the grit from getting on the floor in the first place, set slip-resistant mats (with nonstaining backs) at your doorways, use casters or felt pads under furniture legs, and avoid walking with any kind of spiked shoes (athletic or heels).

Floor mats in front of stoves, refrigerators, and sinks help prevent stains. Use them in the bathroom too.

Always use the cleaner that the manufacturer recommends. Generally these are solvent-base solutions, but several new environmentally friendly cleaners are showing up on the market.

1

SCORE THE DAMAGED TILE
Put a fine-toothed blade on your circular saw and set it so it just cuts through the parquet and not the subfloor. Make a series of plunge cuts in the damaged tile—about 2 inches apart.

Refinishing parquet

Parquet tile, especially a quality product with a thick veneer, is an excellent candidate for refinishing. Refinishing methods, however, differ substantially. First, use a pad sander. A drum sander is too aggressive and may strip the veneer from the tile. Secondly begin sanding on the diagonal. Work the sander from one side of the room to the other. Then shift directions and sand along the other diagonal of the room. Make a final pass parallel to and along the longest wall of the room. Repeat this three-pass process with successively finer grits of sandpaper.

Stain and varnish the floor with the product of your choice, either a penetrating or surface finish. Penetrants sink into the wood pores; they won't wear out unless the wood does. Surface finishes don't soak into the pores of the wood; they stay on top and generally are less durable.

2

CHISEL OUT THE DAMAGED TILE

Starting at one of the plumbed cuts you made, chisel out the damaged sections. Clean the recess completely and scrape out any leftover adhesive.

3

CUT AND FIT A REPLACEMENT TILE

Cut a replacement tile to fit the recess (you may have to cut the tongues and the bottom off the grooved sides). Apply the same adhesive you used to lay the floor in the recess and set the tile in carefully.

4

WEIGHT—TILL THE GLUE DRIES

Clean off any excess adhesive that seeps out (press down on all parts of the tile to make sure it will seat properly). Make sure the tile is dry. Lay some waxed paper over the tile (in case more adhesive seeps through, the waxed paper will keep it from sticking to the books) and weight the tile with books or other heavy objects till the glue dries.

8

MAINTENANCE AND REPAIR

Maintaining and cleaning laminate flooring

Regular vacuuming with a floor attachment will keep your laminate floor looking as beautiful as the day it was installed. Grit and debris left on the surface can damage the floor.

Preventive maintenance

If you care about keeping your floor shiny and clean, do a little preventive maintenance. Start by putting a mat or rug at each entrance to the room to collect dirt. Put a rug over the floor in high-traffic areas too, such as the area in front of the kitchen sink. Any rug laid on a laminate floor should have a rubber backing to keep it from slipping. If the rubber causes discoloration, remove it by wiping the area with ammonia.

Vacuum the floor immediately after installation to remove any construction debris that might scratch it. Put felt pads on the feet of chairs, tables, and other furniture to avoid scratching the floor. Replace plastic casters with rubber casters.

 **REAL WORLD**

THE ICEMAN COMETH

The kitchen was looking pretty good as one do-it-yourselfer started putting everything back together. The painting was done, the cabinets were in, and now, at last, so was the floor. There were protective felt pads on the table and chair legs. The last appliances to place were the refrigerator and stove. The homeowner and a helper heaved the refrigerator onto a blanket and slid it across the floor—no problem until they got to the wall and had to slide the fridge off the blanket. In that last few blanketless inches, they scratched that new floor. At least the scratch was small, but once you've run a refrigerator through the finish on laminate, you can't do much to repair it.

The homeowner did some checking before moving the stove and found the solution: rent an air sled. An air sled is a rubber mat that slips under the appliance. When you attach the air sled to the blower that comes with it, air shoots out of the bottom of the mat and lifts the appliance a fraction of an inch off the floor. You can push the hovering appliance into place with little effort and without marring the floor. Then turn off the blower and slide out the deflated mat.

Keep the shine

Vacuum or dry-mop instead of sweeping. If you dry-mop shake the mop out thoroughly to avoid rubbing dirt across the floor the next time you mop. If you vacuum use an attachment designed for wood floors. Running a vacuum with a beater across the floor damages the floor.

When the floor needs to be washed, mop it using the no-wax cleaner recommended by the manufacturer. Regular detergents and soap products build up on the floor, making it look dull.

Clean up stains caused by chocolate, grease, juice, or wine with the no-wax cleaner. To remove tar, crayon, lipstick, shoe polish, or nail polish, use mineral spirits, nail polish remover, or denatured alcohol. Do not rub with steel wool.

Laminate floors don't require wax and won't benefit from applying it. Wax leaves a film on the floor that actually deadens the shine.

Repairing minor damage

1 **SQUARE THE DAMAGED AREA**

Square off the damage. You can patch damaged areas 1/4 inch in diameter or smaller with finishing putty sold by the manufacturer. Make sure you get the putty that matches your floor. Cut along the edges of the damage with a utility knife to create a spot that has four straight edges. Vacuum up the debris.

2 **APPLY FINISHING PUTTY**

Apply finishing putty. Put tape around the hole, as shown, to make cleanup easier. Squeeze some putty onto the damaged area and level it off with a plastic putty knife.

3 **REMOVE THE PROTECTIVE TAPE**

Remove the tape. The putty shrinks as it dries and should now be flush with the floor. Wipe up the putty on the floor, if any, with a damp cloth.

Repairing major damage

Repairing major damage in a laminate plank requires replacing the plank. All major manufacturers of laminate advise you to leave the job to a pro. Here's what's involved.

First the repair person will lay out lines that are about an inch from each edge of the damaged plank. The repair person also will draw lines connecting the corners of these lines with the corners of the plank. Each of these lines represents a cut that will be made; a few pieces of tape will show exactly where to stop the cut.

Once the lines are drawn, the repair person will cut out the rectangle formed by the first four lines, then remove the cutout with a suction cup. Careful cuts along the diagonal lines break the rest of the plank free.

To replace the plank the repair person will cut off the tongue and the underside of the groove from a matching plank. After the plank is glued in place, sandbags hold it down until the glue dries.

Maintaining vinyl and cork

Replacing a vinyl tile

1 WARM THE TILE

The key to removing a damaged vinyl tile is heat. Set a hair dryer on high heat and concentrate the heat for a minute or so on one edge of the tile. Insert the blade of your putty knife and work it back and forth, pushing forward to break the adhesive bond.

2 SCRAPE OUT THE PIECES

Even warmed up tile will tear and leave small pieces stuck in the adhesive. Warm and scrape each piece until you have removed all of them.

3 APPLY THE ADHESIVE

Notch the end of a plastic scraper and use it to comb adhesive in the recess of the damaged tile. Make sure the adhesive covers the entire area of the recess.

4 INSTALL THE NEW TILE

Eyeball the pattern of the tile so you can match its grain with the rest of the floor. Otherwise it will stick out noticeably. Set the tile at an angle with one edge tight against the other and lower the tile into place.

5 ROLL THE REPAIR

Make sure the new tile adheres tightly to the adhesive by rolling it with a rolling pin. Warm the surface slightly before you roll it. The heat will soften the adhesive and help bond the tile.

Preventing dents and scratches

Resilient flooring is softer than other flooring materials and will dent, scuff, and scratch more easily. With resilients you can't remove the damage. The best care for a resilient floor is therefore preventive maintenance. Here are some ways to prevent dents:

- Protect the floor when moving appliances. Lay plywood panels on the floor and "walk" the appliance across the panels.
- Use floor protectors to keep furniture legs from denting the floors; the heavier the furniture, the wider the protector should be.
- Avoid furniture with rolling casters. If you must have casters, use double rollers.
- Keep dust and dirt outside the house—use mats or rugs at entrances but avoid rubber-backed rugs. They can discolor resilient flooring.
- Keep the floor clean with regular sweeping or vacuuming but don't use vacuums with beater bars.

The iron-off alternative

You can do little to repair a damaged tile, and most of it isn't worth doing. But you can replace a vinyl tile with a few low-tech tools. The first is an iron—you may want to buy one at a thrift store solely for this purpose. Set the iron on medium to high and put a rag over the tile you're replacing. Iron the rag for 10 or 15 seconds to warm the tile and the adhesive that holds it in place. Keep the iron away from the neighboring good tiles to avoid ruining the glue beneath them. Once the tile is warm, slip a wide putty knife under it and try to pry it up. If it won't budge iron a bit more and try again. If you damage a neighboring tile, remove it after you remove the first tile. Scrape away any adhesive with a putty knife. Clean the area thoroughly and spread glue in the opening with the recommended trowel. Let the adhesive cure for about 15 minutes or as recommended on the can. Just before you put the new tile in place, put the rag over it and warm it with the iron to make it more pliable. Then set—don't slide—the tile in place.

Cleaning cork tiles

1

VACUUM THE FLOOR

Vacuum the floor with a canister vacuum, not an upright vacuum or canister attachment with beater bars—doing so can tear up the surface of the tile.

2

DAMP-MOP

Damp-mop the floor. Don't overwet the surface—you'll warp the tile and weaken the adhesive bond. Because it is a wood product, don't use commercial cleaners. Purchase a cleaner made by the manufacturer.

Refinishing cork tiles

Even though modern cork flooring products come with a wear-resistant varnish, it is one you must periodically renew. Clean the floor as described at left and let it dry. Then use a sponge or lamb's wool applicator to reapply the varnish. Never use a generic product—always use the solution made especially for cork.

RESOURCES

T=Top, C=Center, B=Bottom,
L=Left, R=Right

Armstrong World Industries
2500 Columbia Avenue
Lancaster, PA 17603
www.armstrong.com
37TL, 37B, 88-89

Daltile
800-933-8453
www.daltileproducts.com
8B, 26BR, 30TR, 31T, 31BR, 32TR, 32BR,
42T, 43BR, 45BR, 49T, Back Cover L

Pergo, Inc.
800-33PERGO
www.pergo.com
38T

INDEX

iINDEX

INDEX

Billy Jones
Hiram, GA

David L. Weller
Geneva, IL

Marcus M. Muldez
Albuquerque, NM

Mark Whitmore
Canton, GA

John Carter
Albuquerque, NM

Donald Andert
Roswell, GA

Anne Reissing
Atlanta, GA

Eric H. Hunger
Atlanta, GA

Eaton Adams, III
Atlanta, GA

Carlos Hernandez
Westmont, IL

Many thanks to
the employees of
The Home Depot® whose
"wisdom of the aisles"
has made *Tiling 1-2-3*™
the most useful
book of its kind.

John A. Vrbovsky
Matteson, IL

Patt Kox
Grand Chute, WI

Marya Towson
Atlanta, GA

Al Pacheco
Tampa, FL

Tom Sattler
Atlanta, GA

Juan C. Albizures
Chicago, IL

Tom Ignoffo
Schaumburg, IL

Paul A. Shea
Marietta, GA

Chris Potis
Santa Fe, NM

Joyce Scarborough
Griffin, GA

Rick Whitfill
Atlanta, GA

Nathan D. Ehrlich
Atlanta, GA

Jim Robinson
South Plainfield, NJ

Toolbox essentials: nuts-and-bolts books for do-it-yourself success.

Save money, get great results, and take the guesswork out of home improvement projects with a growing library of step-by-step books from the experts at The Home Depot®.

Packed with lots of projects and practical tips, these books help you design, remodel, decorate, and repair your home or garden. Easy-to-follow, step-by-step instructions and colorful photographs ensure success. Projects even estimate time, skills, materials needed, and tools required.

**You can do it.
We can help.**℠

**Look for the books that help you say "I can do that!"
at The Home Depot® www.meredithbooks.com,
or wherever quality books are sold.**

DPT0141_0406